D1592799

Books by Gladys Hasty Carroll

Novels

AS THE EARTH TURNS

A FEW FOOLISH ONES

NEIGHBOR TO THE SKY

WEST OF THE HILL

WHILE THE ANGELS SING

CHRISTMAS WITHOUT JOHNNY

ONE WHITE STAR

SING OUT THE GLORY

COME WITH ME HOME

THE ROAD GROWS STRANGE

THE LIGHT HERE KINDLED

MAN ON THE MOUNTAIN

Collected Short Stories

HEAD OF THE LINE

CHRISTMAS THROUGH THE YEARS

Nonfiction

DUNNYBROOK

ONLY FIFTY YEARS AGO

TO REMEMBER FOREVER

YEARS AWAY FROM HOME

YEARS AWAY FROM HOME

Gladys Hasty Carroll

LITTLE, BROWN AND COMPANY – BOSTON – TORONTO

FIRST EDITION

T 10/72

Library of Congress Cataloging in Publication Data

Carroll, Gladys (Hasty) 1904-
Years away from home.

Autobiographical.
I. Title.
PS3505.A77533Z522 813'.5'2 [B] 72-5328
ISBN 0-316-13004-4

Portions of this book first appeared in slightly different form in *The New-England Galaxy*.

Published simultaneously in Canada
by Little, Brown & Company (Canada) Limited

PRINTED IN THE UNITED STATES OF AMERICA

To my husband,
Herbert A. Carroll

Works of imagination are of significance to the extent that what is imagined by the creator and imagined later by those who respond to his product has the pure, resounding ring of basic human or artistic truth. Enduring works of imagination have both.

The value of a true story or a true account lies primarily in its not being imagined but actually, in itself, true to ascertainable facts and to at least one person's experience and impression. This is no mean value in a time like ours when change is everywhere. The links between yesterday and today are difficult to find and few feel justified in digging deeply for them, most of us being urgently engaged in looking for links between today and tomorrow which, to our considerable alarm, remain totally obscured, thus leading to some doubt that they have yet been forged. If, as has been said, we can never know where we are — much less lay out our future course — until we know where we have been, then we must have many true records of past events, if possible combined with the personal experiences, feelings, attitudes, and reactions of one or more of those involved in those events, who were the cause of some of them and to some degree shaped by all of them. Such records may provide at least clues to the composition and even perhaps to the location of links in the sequence of human history which we desperately need for the untangling of the knotted chain by which we are now surrounded.

In the earnest desire to uncover even one small clue and make it recognizable, I tell my true story of the first third of the twentieth century.

Contents

I

My Home

IN THE BEGINNING was The House. Everything started there and ended there. Everyone went out from it to where he had to go and returned to it when the mission had been accomplished. I was not visible in it until 1904, but from my early years it seemed to me, nevertheless, that I had been there when my grandfather built it in Civil War time, for his bride, on land which had been given to him on his twenty-first birthday by his father. Yet so ever-was-and-ever-shall-be was The House that what I carried over from the time-track of the mid–eighteen hundreds was the memory not of its original construction but of its becoming tangible and occupied.

Surely it must have been there when the first James Warren fought in the Battle of Dunbar, became one of the Scots taken prisoner by the forces of Cromwell, was shipped to the New World and bound over to the Saugus Iron Works, near Boston, Massachusetts, to pay the cost of his passage. Surely he and his son James must have seen The House, some twenty years later, when they left the Warren farm in the Parish of Unity, paddled up the Newichewannock, and tramped through the Maine wilderness, with their broadaxes putting the mark of a crow's-foot on virgin pines tall enough and straight enough to become masts for the sailing vessels of the King's navy.

The House, painted glistening white with dark green — almost black — blinds, together with the attached, clapboarded Shed, also white, which was in turn attached to the Barn, larger than House and Shed combined, and stained red with a mixture of skim milk and bloodroot, all must have smiled out at the James Warrens, father and son, from a sunny clearing in the forest primeval and enchanted them. It must have been the reason why, when the king offered the Warrens, as a reward for rendered services, their choice of the lands they had explored, they asked for the tract extending from the Newichewannock River on the north to a certain pond (ever after to be known as Warren's Pond) on the south, and lying between two brooks which flowed from pond to river to form eastern and western boundaries. I could see our Jameses clearly, in their high, hard leather woodsman's boots and soft fringed leather woodsman's jackets, sprawled on the steps of the Back Porch, drawing their careful surveyor's chart on a paper spread on the porch floor; N at the top and S at the bottom, so many poles, more or less, along a brook flowing between pond and river on the right (E) and so many more or less through a marsh on the left (W). They kept glancing at each other and at House and Barn and Shed, and their eyes twinkled mischievously as Warren eyes always have. How could the king, who had never been here, know what jewel was set in this special tract?

And of course he didn't. In due time the Jameses received their King's Grant and James the Younger came to live on it.

It would have puzzled me that it was not he who first laid hands upon The House, drove nails into it to pin it down, and moved into it, if I had not always known excellent reasons why he did not. First of all, Warrens believed in wee folk and would have suspected such a house was their domain. Also, The House had upstairs rooms and quite certainly neither of the Jameses had ever occupied an upstairs. Surely their house in Scotland had been broad and low and black like the house our first James had built on the riverbank in the Parish of Unity. Thus James the Younger naturally preferred a broad, low, black house for his family. More than that, James the

Younger, moving into Indian country, needed to live on the highest point of his grant, in a house surrounded by a stockade for protection. So the Warren Garrison was built on a hilltop where it stood for two centuries until, long after, a chink by a kitchen window was large enough for a gourd vine to creep in, hang over the back of a basket-bottom chair, bloom, and produce a smooth brown gourd which sat in the chair until later hollowed out and used for tying to a saddle and transporting New Orleans molasses. I knew that gourd well. It was in a way a member of the family.

So the seventeen hundreds came in, and James the Younger's sons and grandsons grew and took wives and built houses and had sons until there was Gilbert who joined the Continental Army, and his son Joseph, and Joseph's daughter Lydia who, when she married John Brown went south from the Warren Grant to live with him two miles beyond the Pond Field. John and Lydia Warren Brown had, among their children, a daughter named Sarah Jane.

Meanwhile, a mile or two east of the Warren Grant, across the boundary line of another township, one John Hasty, born of Scottish parents in County Antrim, Ireland, had built a sawmill run by the power of a wilderness brook they christened Hasty's Brook and thus procured the timbers and boards with which to build a broad, low, black house. John Hasty's grandson Nathan, was born in that house in 1788, married Olive Hamilton, and their son Joseph, who married Joanna Shaw, had eleven children of whom the youngest was George.

This George at the age of fourteen was walking crosslots eight miles to the Kittery Navy Yard each morning and eight back each night, six days a week for six months of each year, to earn the cost of his boots, of the cloth he paid his mother to make into shirts, pants, and jackets for him to wear, of his board for the year, and of his schooling. For the alternate six months, under a neighbor, Sylvester Chadbourne, brother of President Paul Chadbourne of Williams College, he studied trigonometry, calculus, surveying, and architecture. Farming and lumbering he learned from his father.

At twenty he concluded his education, worked at the navy yard the year round, and married Sarah Jane Brown.

At twenty-one, expecting his first child, he received the patrimony of the field and pasture his father had bought of the widow Sally Warren Blaisdell, ceased to work for wages, and began instead to pull over with a fall a great stand of giant oak trees in the lower part of his field, hew each down to the size of its largest root and haul them to the navy yard to sell as boatribs. He saw The House and, with no qualms whatever, laid hands upon it as suitable for Sarah Jane, upon its Shed to hold tools and firewood, and upon its Barn to shelter the stock which would provide his family with food and his field with fertilizer. Laid hands upon them, pinned them down, and settled in with Sarah Jane and the baby Vinnie. Another daughter and a son Warren were born there.

I understood how it would seem to George and others that he had built it. It was he who had dared to make it part of the real world, fastened it to the earth he knew and loved, and brought human life into it.

By the year I was born to Warren and his wife Frances, Sarah Jane had been gone from The House some time. Even my brother, eight years older than I, could not remember our grandmother, though I was told she had seen him. I wished she had seen me. There was a green earth-bed for Sarah Jane inside a fence of granite posts and iron railings on the pasture hill, and when we went there in May to leave bunches of white and purple lilacs and pick the graveyard pinks, I remembered her and knew why my grandfather never spoke of her. I put the pinks in a cup of water and set it by his place at the table. I was sure he would understand that Sarah Jane had sent them, and he did.

As I have said, everyone went out from The House to where he had to go — to Shed or Barn or Yard or Field or Pasture or Berry Woods or Church or School or a Neighbor's — and returned to it when the mission had been accomplished. I assumed that one day my Grandmother Hasty would come back.

In the meantime George, her husband, lived there without her, but with Vinnie, their daughter, who was a schoolteacher and had not married, with Warren, their son, who was a carriage and sign painter and every day rode to his shop in the village seated in a scarlet gig with gold striping behind a half-broken little racing horse born on the place, and with his son's family, my mother, Frances Dow Hasty (always called Frankie), my brother Harold, and me.

The House had three doors for the going out and coming in. The one most used was the porch door. Going out through it we crossed the porch which ran the length of the ell, went down three shallow steps, and were in the Yard from which one could go to Shed or Barn or Icehouse or Carriage House or Mailbox or Field or Pasture. Coming in we passed through the back entry where there were rows of high and low hooks for caps, jackets, shawls, and mufflers. A black chest of drawers in the corner of the entry held tablecloths, dish towels cut from sugar bags, dishcloths cut from salt bags, work aprons of calico and sewing aprons of sheer white cotton trimmed with handmade lace, and sheets or the thin cotton blankets which in winter replaced sheets on our feather beds and my grandfather's cornhusk mattress. The top of the chest was for the mending basket.

The back entry led into the ell-kitchen. Here one could hear the family heartbeat. Here was the black cookstove and the woodbox behind it. Above the woodbox ran the lamp shelf and a row of hooks for wet mittens. The bare floor was of pine, scrubbed every Friday morning as soon as my grandfather left for market with eggs, butter, vegetables, and dressed fowl for his customers. The oval drop-leaf table where we ate all our meals was between the sitting room door and the back stairs door. Unless the minister was there it always had a red tablecloth on it, and our biggest unshaded lamp (the one with the cloudy pink glass font), the spoonholder which had been my great-great-grandmother Warren's spillholder, the flashed-red sugar bowl, the dark green pepper sauce bottle, the opalescent syrup pitcher filled with molasses except in sugaring time, and the ironstone cider pitcher which my grandfather drained of water at each meal, doubtless thinking of the well from which it had come and which he had dug and stoned and put a chain pump into. The latter five items on the table were always covered with a length of cheesecloth except at mealtime. The chairs around the table were black with cane seats. On the kitchen wall beyond the door into the sitting room there was a couch my grandfather had made to fit the space; above it hung a bookshelf, and on the floor under its raised head the big County Atlas rested on its spine. From a hook on the bookshelf Leavitt's Family Almanac was suspended. The flowered cretonne throw covering the couch was washed each Monday. The kitchen had four windows, two facing north and two south. Between the south windows which overlooked the porch was my blackboard, and the chairs in which my brother and I sat at the table when its leaf was raised. I had to move the chairs to use the blackboard. Between the north windows a rectangular pine drop-leaf table served as a cutting and sewing table, with Auntie's rocker at one end of it and my mother's at the other. A wall rack held newspapers and magazines. Across all four sides of the room there was a chair rail on which to stand paper dolls cut from mail order catalogs.

If a woman had to leave the kitchen, but was not going Out, and was not going to bed, she might open the cellar door and go down the cellar stairs to where potatoes and other vegetables, apples, home-canned fruit, jellies and raspberry shrub were stored in winter, butter and pans of milk and homemade root beer were kept in summer in the white-washed dairy, and there was salt pork in tubs, eggs in baskets, and vinegar in barrels year round. But most often she went through an opening into the sinkroom where the water pails set on a shelf beside the iron sink, her bread-board rested on top of the flour barrel, her saleratus and cream of tartar and nutmegs and extracts and raisins were in one cupboard, her everyday dishes in another, and in cold weather curtained shelves held in shallow open pans the milk she had strained through cheesecloth and from which she would skim the cream as soon as it rose. Thursday was churning day. Hot water for washing up came from the tank of the stove, for cooking from the teakettle, both filled from the pails which had been filled at the chain pump my grandfather had put into the well he had dug.

The House was heated by wood stoves. We had four besides the kitchen cookstove. Three of these were set up each fall and taken down each spring at housecleaning time. One was a large chunk stove which stood on the brick hearth of the sitting room fireplace, and its funnel went through a metal fireboard into the chimney. Every winter afternoon about five o'clock a fire was started in this stove so that by bedtime the biting edge of the cold was off not only that room but also my grandfather's bedroom which opened from it, the chamber above it (there was a register in the ceiling over the stove) where Aunt Vinnie slept, and perhaps even the parlor guest-room, if there was need, since a door opened into that from my grandfather's room. But there was a smaller chunk stove in the parlor, and another in the chamber above it where my parents slept, and I in a crib until I was five years old. Here fires could be built on bitter cold nights or in times of sickness. But there was never heat in the long front entry between the sitting room and the parlor, nor up its steep front stairs with the black walnut banister which led to our chamber on the northeast corner. As a child, whenever there were frost pictures on the front entry windows, I always rode past them on my father's shoulder, wrapped in a shawl or small comforter, having undressed or being on my way to dress in front of the open oven door in the kitchen. The windowless alcove in which my brother slept at the head of the back stairs was warmed by opening the kitchen door at the foot; what daylight and fresh air he had came from the single window in Aunt Vinnie's chamber. When the door between her room and the alcove was closed, he still got some light and air because two openings the size of window panes had been cut in the door's panels, near the top.

But our best warmth on winter nights came from big smooth beach rocks and from cushions filled with beach sand heated in the oven until they scorched their ticking covers, and taken to bed with us. As my father carried me upstairs I hugged my sand cushion which had a smiling face embroidered on it in red Tambo; my mother went ahead of us with a lamp in one hand and a beach rock cradled in her other arm.

The House's fifth stove was another cookstove and not exactly in The House, but in the old store, by my time more often called the shedroom. It opened from the sinkroom and was the end of the shed which my grandfather had finished off for Sarah Jane's father, John Brown, to keep store in. After John Brown came back from the Civil War, to which he had gone as a volunteer in his mid-forties, he was never well, and by the age of sixty he was an old man, too feeble to make his little farm feed his wife Lydia and himself, so they had come to live with Sarah Jane. But John wanted to be doing something which would at least pay for their medicines, so my grandfather had taken down the little Brown house beyond Warren's Pond and with the salvaged timbers and boards built a small store for him across the road from the Warren house where he had courted Lydia and where her brother Columbia still lived and attracted children and older people as the honeysuckle draws bees. It was a likely site for a store selling tea, crackers, cheese, sugar, and stick candy, and John did well there until his legs could no longer carry him across the Warren field. Then my grandfather took down the building and used the beams and boards to finish off the end of the Hasty shed. John Brown could shuffle to this new store through Sarah Jane's sinkroom. It had pine cupboards to hold his stock, a stove to keep him warm, and a counter just inside a door which opened onto the porch. He was there seven days a week until he died. After that Sarah Jane and Lydia — and later Vinnie and Frankie — used this room as a summer kitchen, for Thanksgiving and Christmas extra baking, and for trying out lard after the butchering in the fall. In addition to the door from the sinkroom and the one off the porch, it had another leading up into the shedchamber where my grandfather hung his corn and his herbs to dry, and the women their strings of peeled and quartered apples, and where the hickory, hazel, and beechnuts were kept in wooden tubs. A fourth door out of the shedroom led down a long flight of stairs into the shed.

In the shed there was wood of all needed kinds and sizes; edgings and chips for kindling (with the help of a few drops of kerosene from the whiskey bottle with the quill in the cork), dry pine for quick, high heat, hardwood for steady heat, chunks which would burn all night. There were also the sawhorses, and the chopping block with the axe driven in too deep for a child to be able to pull it out. The walls were hung with chains, ropes, tubs, pails, shovels, hoes, diggers, saws, hand scythes, and sickles. At one end a great door opened into the cider cellar which had, too, a huge iron kettle set into a brick block under which my grandfather built fires to cook a mixture of potatoes and meal to feed to his pigs in cold weather, when whole and cracked corn was heated in the kitchen oven for the hens. Past the barrels and hogsheads of the cider cellar the vegetables were carried to The House cellar in the fall, the sprouting potatoes brought out to be cut for planting in the spring, and the milk taken to the dairy in summer. At the opposite end of the shed there was the grain chest with five deep compartments; the workbench; the toilet with three seats, two large and one small, each with its own hinged cover; a thick mail order catalog, a box of corncobs, and walls papered in old calendars and magazine covers; a stairway down into the barn cellar where the hens had nests for laying and poles for roosting; and a door into the barn.

The barn was big. It had a sheep pen, stanchions for eight cows, stalls for two horses, space for the forge, anvil, and other equipment with which my father shod the horses, a sawdust heap for bedding and for banking The House, many mows of hay, low mows, upper mows, and top mows, a hay cart suspended between seasons from the rafters, the mowing machine, the horse rake, the hand rakes, the harnesses, and the sleighs in winter, the wagons and gig in summer. Out-of-season vehicles were kept in the carriage house beside the icehouse. The plow and the dumpcart when not in use were in the barn cellar, waiting for the time to open the earth and fertilize it.

Every spring the sawdust banking was taken away from the foundation of The House. Every fall it was put up again. I often rode on the dumpcart with my father when he went into the woods to where a sawmill had been, and while he loaded the cart with sawdust for the winter I climbed the rosy peak to jump from it into the pit he was making. There is no other fragrance like that of fresh sawdust and new-sawed lumber.

Every spring the parlor furniture was set in the front yard while the ingrain carpet was strewn with wet shredded newspaper and swept. The parlor sofa and chairs were upholstered in red plush. On the grass they looked like thrones. Every spring all the comforters were washed before being packed away, and all the hooked and braided rugs were hung on the clothesline and beaten.

Every Fourth of July the three big barn doors were opened and the barn was swept from the ridgepole down, mow after mow, and spare floor, to be ready to receive the new crop of hay.

The ticking which held the feathers of our beds and the cornhusks of my grandfather's mattress had openings which were unbuttoned every morning for a woman to reach in and fluff the feathers or rearrange the husks. Each fall the husks were replaced by new ones when the tick had been washed and dried in the sun; feathers were taken out, to be washed or replaced.

Every morning the breakfast fire to be built, the wood to be sawed, the stock to be fed, the milking to be done, the lamps to be cleaned, trimmed, and filled, the chamber work. Then the day could begin; the farmer to his field or the chopper to the woods, the painter to his shop, the teacher to her school, the housekeeper to her washing if it was Monday, ironing on Tuesday, baking on Wednesday, churning, making out butter, and dressing out fowl on Thursday, cleaning on Friday, baking on Saturday. The housekeeper sought to complete the special day's work before starting noon dinner, after which she would put on her sewing apron and be busy with her needles until lamplighting and supper-getting time.

After supper my grandfather snored softly on the kitchen

couch, and my father read his newspaper or the Town Report by the big table where my brother was doing his schoolwork. When the dishes were finished the women did rough mending, holding the work close to the hand lamps on either end of the small table. A little girl played with her paper dolls or made letters of the alphabet on the blackboard or with toothpicks or wooden matches on the windowsill. Finally, Strawberry Baldwins were peeled and quarters passed around on the point of my father's jackknife, and last drinks of water were dipped from the pails in the pantry. If by then a thin skim of ice had formed there, all the house plants had to be brought from the windows and left near the middle of the kitchen for the night. Bedtime came early and ended with sunrise or before.

Beyond House, Shed, and Barn was the Yard, and by the age of three a child of the family would have had no difficulty finding his way about the yard if suddenly blinded. I know because one of my earliest memories is of realizing that I should prepare myself for this possible catastrophe and promptly beginning by closing my eyes very tight and marching down the porch steps, dropping on my knees to "look" with my hands at the flower bed into which my mother poured a big panful of dishwater every warm, dry morning, then going down the incline to the driveway and across it to one after another of the three maples and the ash tree my father had set out when he was twelve years old. East of the maples was the entrance to The Lane, with a Porter apple tree on each corner. South of the maples were the Duchess, Striped Porter, and black cherry trees, beyond them the shingled icehouse, the clapboarded carriage house, and the smokehouse. As I moved west from these buildings I circled the woodpile, leaned briefly against the chopping block, stroked the curve of the grindstone, turned the handle of the pump and heard the water drip back from the empty chain. I touched the wooden trough and knew that if I had had a pail to bring up full I could have emptied it neatly into the trough and heard it run down through the barnyard fence and rush into the wooden tub where the cattle and horses drank. I walked blind beside the trough to the barnyard fence, pulled at the iron ring in each hitching post, smelled the barn through an open door (one of three doors large enough for a load of hay to be drawn through), turned east again and walked steadily down the hill beside the shed and up the steep incline to the porch steps where I sat down and opened my eyes.

Such detailed knowledge of the grounds at the east end of The House, between The House and the lane which led to the Main Road, and of the area immediately north of The House was a slightly more advanced course, partly because no house door opened to the north side and the one to the east was the front door, hardly ever opened except in housecleaning time since in cold weather it let in only air off North Atlantic icebergs and in warm weather only morning sunshine to fade the front hall carpet. Another and longer-lasting reason to keep small children from going by themselves to the nor'-nor'-east was that there was little there one was allowed to touch without express permission. The remnants of Sarah Jane's garden were between The House and the lane, — her Hundredleaf and Seven Sister rosebushes, her syringas, fire and snowball bushes, flowering almond, and yucca, her daffodils, narcissus, and lilies of the valley. Where Sarah Jane had planted was hallowed ground. On the north there was, near The House, only my mother's garden, fertilized by the sink drain, and carefully laid out in beds and walks, all inside a picket fence (as once Sarah Jane's had been) to protect it from the cattle who were turned into the field after the mowing, when the pasture feed grew poor. As one grew older one learned that my mother's garden was full of exotic things, most of them given to her over the years, such as Japanese pinks, heliotrope, Canterbury bells, Sweet William, tea roses, larkspur, doubleleaf pansies, and Oriental poppies, and that it was a nip-and-tuck battle three seasons of the year to keep the soil loose and rich around them, keep the witchgrass and other weeds out, and to save roots, foliage, and blossoms from cutworms and countless insects so that the seed once sown, the plants set out, would flourish and spread to need thinning, dividing, and replanting elsewhere.

By the time I understood the intricacies of farm flower-gardening to the extent that I could be trusted alone among such precious specimens, I had already trudged so far in happy pursuit of wild flowers — Indian tobacco, purple and white violets, mayflowers, cowslips, wild fruit and berry blossoms, buttercups, daisies, devil's paintbrush, black-eyed Susans, pink laurel, lady's slippers, red sumac, and cat o' nine tails — that I knew the whole farm as thoroughly as the front yard or even the rooms of The House. Knew the Back Field, bounded by lane, main road, pasture, and House. Knew the Front Field where the kitchen garden was most likely to be and lilacs bloomed in a corner where a Warren blacksmith shop had once stood, and the Upper Meadow sloping down from it to the Lower Meadow. Seed sown on the slope was sure to do well at least at one end or the other, whatever the rainfall. The cabbage patch was fenced against the cows, for cabbages were not harvested until long after the cows were turned into the field in the fall. Cranberries grew along the ditches of the lower meadow; strawberries bloomed, set on, and ripened in both meadows. At the foot of the lower there were steep little twin hills, the front half of them mowed (sliding down one on a good crust of snow, a child rode nearly to the top of the other) and the back half grown up to hickory trees which bore what we called walnuts. When the frost had split their green burrs and turned them brown, we stained our fingers extracting the shells to put in baskets, took them home to dry, and later fed them into the mouth of the nutcracker my grandfather had made, so that we could pick out the slivers of meat with darning needles. Examining our stains, we remembered stories we had heard of how gypsies disguised with walnut juice children they had kidnapped and carried away in their wagons. Though we had never seen a gypsy we knew how their wagons creaked because when we sat on the porch steps on spring evenings and listened to the peepers in the marshes, one of the old ones often said, "Sounds like gypsy wagons coming over Rocky Hills." The marshes where the peepers sang were at the far edge of the pasture, west of the twin hills, bordering a winding brook which overflowed in fall rains to form a vast natural skating rink. Winter sunsets made it look, from the kitchen windows, like rainbows come to earth. They overflowed again in the spring and children built rafts to ride the inland sea; but in summer they were dry and when the fields had been cut the men mowed the marsh grass which was sharp as razors and fit only for mixing with sawdust for bedding for barn creatures with tough hides.

In the beginning was The House which gradually became and remained the hub, the center of our world. The hub was immovable, invulnerable, timeless, changeless. Secure in this knowledge, a child ventured forth on one spoke or another, balanced as when he walked a beam above a haymow, knowing that if he fell he would bounce with the smell of meadow sweetgrass eddying about him and either eagerly start over or dreamily go back to The House.

One spoke ran into the woods where the sawdust piles

were, and the huckleberries, raspberries, and blackberries; the pink ivory pips and the red checkerberries among thick dark green leaves; the tarpaper shanty which had sheltered the French woodchopper through the winter (though we could not speak his language nor he ours we had learned his favorite song, which sounded in our ears like "Paddy me for nor saw, Paddy me for nor saw; compare ici, compare ici, Paddy me for nor saw"); Warren's Pond where ice was cut in winter, waxy lilies bloomed in summer, my mother's step-father had drowned, my great-grandmother had seen a waterspout, and my brother dove off a ledge to astonish me by coming up far from where he went down.

Another spoke led to the church a mile away. On summer Sunday afternoons we walked there, passed from time to time by carriages of neighbors to the south and west of us. We knew all the passersby by their given names. Charles and Olive, Charles and Melissa, George Albert and Laura were of my grandfather's generation; Frank and Belle, George and Minnie, Will and Grace were of my parents'; Mabel, Harold, Leslie, Clyde, and Bernice were of my brother's and mine. My elders recognized the horses before they could distinguish the features of the passengers, and knew not only the horses' names — Max, Pacer, Pony, Whitey, Old Doll, Old Tom, Old Mutt, Old Tipperary — but their ages, dispositions, and how much they could pull. Most of the carriages were democrat wagons with front and rear seats (the rear seats were removable to make room for farm produce on market day) but there were also one-seated buggies, easier for riding than the wagons, and George and Minnie were distinguished by having a top buggy which shielded Minnie's pretty face from the sun and her pretty hat from a possible rain shower. We all, men, women, and children, wore hats and gloves to church. My mother and Aunt Vinnie made my hats. The first one I remember was a strip of yellow straw with white ribbons on the ends to tie under my chin; clusters of pink and blue velvet forget-me-nots attached to the straw were the jewels in my little crown.

I'm the child of a King, the child of a King!
With Jesus my Saviour, I'm the child of a King! . . .

O God, our help in ages past, our hope for years to come,
Our shelter from the stormy blast, And our eternal home . . .

We had come out of the lane into the main road, gone down Columby's Hill, crossed Warren's Brook, passed through Lafayette's Woods, and could hear the organ playing. We knew Aunt Lula, my mother's sister, had seated herself on the horsehair-covered stool, pulled out the stops, pressed the carpeted foot pedals, and spread her small, strong hands above the keys.

Still, still with Thee, when purple morning breaketh.
When the bird waketh, and the shadows flee;
Fairer than morning, lovelier than the daylight,
Dawns the sweet consciousness I am with Thee . . .

No one was singing but the summer birds, yet we heard the words.

At Nason's and at two Walker houses Lucy and Lizzie, Em and Frank and Lizy, Lois, Chase, Fred, Angie, Leah, Vera, and Doris, if they had not gone on ahead, were coming out to join us.

Faith of our fathers, living still . . .
We will be true to Thee till death . . .

Now we could see our church at the fork of the sandy roads. It had no spire, no belfry, no stained glass, but what it did not have I had never seen. It had a huge wineglass elm in front and a long, unroofed platform leading to two wide open doors through which the organ music was rolling out, as also through the open windows.

Nearer, my God, to Thee, nearer to Thee . . .
He leadeth me! He leadeth me! By His own hand He leadeth me . . .

Behind the church, horses were hitched to a board fence. Beyond horses, carriages, and fence the Newichewannock River flowed.

We shall gather at the river, the beautiful, the beautiful river,
Gather with the saints at the river that flows by the throne of God . . .

We went single file up the steep narrow path worn into the green turf by climbing feet. Reaching the platform my mother turned and took my hand. From there on none of us put any weight on our heels.

He leadeth me! He leadeth me! By His own hand He leadeth me . . .

The bare brown wood pews faced the open doors. Above their railings I saw what seemed to me a sea of brown faces all alike except that some were bearded, like my grandfather's, some were bareheaded, and some wore hats. If children were in the pews, they were completely obscured.

A hand scarcely larger than my own, but gloved in black silk, reached out to me from the first pew in the center row, and from its size I recognized it as my mother's mother's. I slipped in beside her, wriggled onto the seat, and Aunt Em reached across her to pat my white-stockinged knee. From my other side and over my head my mother whispered, "Hi, Mama," and "Hi, Aunt Em. How's Cathie?"

Aunt Em leaned toward us, smelling of sweet lavender, to whisper, "Fairly good this morning, dear. The heat yesterday was hard on her. A mite cooler today, though, praise the Lord." Her brown face, bright with thankfulness, smiled down at me.

This was the Brooks pew, and had been since the church

was built. My little Grammy and my Great-Aunt Em had sat in it as the daughters of James and Catherine Brooks and now that they were widows and grandparents it was theirs still. It was also the first of the singing seats, and faced the organ where my Aunt Lula was playing. From it I could see only her hat between two china bowls of garden flowers. She and Aunt Em's daughter Cathie took weekly turns at the organ. If Cathie had been able to come to church, one of them would have been with us in the Brooks pew. In that case the pew would have been filled and my brother would have followed my father, grandfather, and Aunt Vinnie to the Hasty pew, behind Uncle Gran and Aunt Phoebe. As it was, he sat beside my mother, next to the aisle, in the Brooks pew. If you were of Brooks descent, you sat in the Brooks pew if there was room for you, especially if you liked to sing; and Harold did.

Softly and tenderly Jesus is calling, calling for
you and for me;
See on the portals He's waiting and watching,
watching for you and for me . . .

The side portals to my right were the open windows looking down the sandy road past the Walker and Nason farms toward home. There was a big wall clock between them with a white face, brass figures, and a swinging pendulum. I could not tell the time. In one corner there were open shelves filled with Sunday school books. I could not read.

The side portals to my left were windows open on the Emery field, new-cut hay, apple trees, Aunt Em's house, and the foot of Neal's Hill down which Aunt Lula had driven her sorrel mare, Bridget, bringing my little Grammy to church, coming to play the organ.

The front portals were the two doors, open onto the sunny ends of the platform, the spreading shade of the big elm, and the sandy road. The floor space between these portals was filled by a platform with the pulpit in the center. I could see, past the organ, only the top half of the pulpit and the great Book on it. The Book was closed, but places in it were marked by heavy satin ribbons with fringed ends, one scarlet and one the color of gold. Behind and above the pulpit there was a high window brushed by leaves of the elm.

Sing them over again to me, wonderful words of Life . . .
Beautiful words, wonderful words, wonderful words of Life . . .

As the organ swept into the prelude to the Doxology, there was the rustle of everyone getting to his feet, and I saw The Shining Stranger come in from the portals where he had been waiting just out of sight. I called him Stranger because I did not know his name, not because I thought I had never seen him before, quite otherwise; but church was the only place I ever saw him where other people were, where everyone there could see him. I called him the Shining Stranger because that was how he looked, that was what I saw, a Shining so beautiful that I could hardly breathe. The most remarkable thing about seeing him at church was that there he was not just one Shining coming in at one portal. He came in at every portal, through both doors and every open window like a shower of stars, each with its own trail of light, swiftly converging behind the pulpit, and there almost seeming to go out. But didn't go out. Because as the Elder appeared behind the pulpit, so much taller than the tall pulpit, rested his arm on the great Book, and covered the edge of its pages tenderly with his big hand, I saw a halo behind his white head and knew the light came from the Shining which now filled the Elder and would speak through him.

Praise God, from whom all blessings flow;
Praise Him, all creatures here below;
Praise Him above, ye heavenly host;
Praise Father, Son, and Holy Ghost. Amen."

He said, "Brothers and sisters, let us pray."

After the Elder had talked to God, and to us, and after we had sung the last hymn, he asked God's blessing upon the congregation. Then he came down the pulpit steps and stood by the door to give each of us a special blessing with the touch of his big warm hand, the bright twinkle of his blue eyes, the gentleness of his bearded smile, and the tenderness of a few personal words.

Emerging into the sunshine of the platform, pausing in the shade of the elm tree, we saw one another with new eyes and began the coming week together, even though we separated at the foot of the path, some of us to spend the rest of the day at Grammy's or at Aunt Em's or at Cousin Minnie's, and the rest of us to our own homes, in a land where we felt we had a near neighbor if we could see his lamplight at night.

We Hastys were fortunate. We could see four lights at night, — Oliver's, Jim Earl's, Melissa's, and Deacon Dorr's — and spokes of our wheel, visible only in daylight, ran to and past their houses, sheds, and barns to those of more distant neighbors. Beyond a circle perhaps three miles or less in diameter lay another world, but of its existence, as small children, we were totally ignorant and for a long time afterward practically unaware. It lay somewhere to the southwest of the Junction on one side and over the Mountain to the east. It imported as many eggs, vegetables, wild berries, apples, and dressed fowls, as much butter, veal, salt pork, and firewood, as we could spare. It exported flour, sugar, tea, extracts, spices, raisins, an occasional piece of beef, and in our dire emergencies Dr. Ross.

When we were sent out along the spoke which led to the schoolhouse few of us knew that it could be extended to greater length than other spokes.

Our district schoolhouse stood beside a sandy road on a

patch of land fenced on three sides to keep us out of fields and pastures and the cattle from looking in our windows. East and west of the building, between it and the high board fence, there was a path leading to the woodshed behind which there were two toilets. In front of the building there was room enough, between it and the road, for fifteen or twenty children between the ages of five and fifteen to join hands and play drop the handkerchief, running back and forth across the long shadow of the peeled pine pole up which we pulled the flag every morning. The shadow of the flag billowed on the road.

Pole and building were painted stark white.

There was a door on each side of the pole, one opening into the boys' coatroom and the other into the girls'. In early fall and late spring, when we came barefoot and without jackets, these coatrooms held only the dinner pails of scholars who lived too far away to get home and back within the noon hour. In late fall and early spring we hung our caps and jackets on the hooks there and left our muddy rubber boots on the floor beneath. But in winter the coatrooms held only wood sawed into stove length, for we were wearing what we wore outside, and the dinner pails lined the zinc mat under the stove to keep the food in them from freezing.

Teacher sat in a captain's chair behind the long oak table with one drawer which was her desk, on a platform built between the walls of the coatrooms. There was a north window at her back, with the flagpole dividing it into two narrow sections. On her left was the red papier-mâché water pail on a shelf, a blue enamel cup hanging by its handle from a nail. On her right was the thick wooden box, painted dark green, which held the globe and sometimes served as a seat for a scholar needing special attention and close supervision. These, with blackboards between the windows on the east and west and all across the south wall, a big dictionary, a box of white chalk, the pencils, yellow scratch paper, and lined white paper in her drawer, the handled bell for calling us in, the tap-bell for signaling recitations, and a row of books between bookends constituted her equipment for the task she had undertaken.

The stove was set in the spare floor in front of her, and its black funnel went straight up to the ceiling and, resting on wires, ran back the length of the room to a hole above the long blackboard on the south wall and so into the chimney.

Beyond the stove from Teacher were the rows of individual desks and benches for her scholars. These were of heavy oak, screwed to iron frames riveted to the splintery floor, and graduated in size, the lowest in front for the smallest children, the highest in back for the big boys and girls. All were quite generous in width.

"Teacher, can Bernice and I set together?"

"*May* we *sit* together . . . Yes, you may, if you don't disturb anyone around you."

"Teacher, can I go out?"

"*May* I go out . . . Yes, you may, but don't linger."

"Teacher, can I get a drink?"

"*May* I get a drink . . . No, you've already had three since recess. If you have any more, you might float away."

All children while in school were scholars. On First Day Teacher had only to count noses, pointed, snub, and freckled, to know how many scholars she had.

We brought the water from Nason's pump up the road. We made our own ink to fill the small iron wells set into round holes in the corners of our desks. We washed the blackboards and swept the floor. We sawed and split the cordwood and brought it in from the shed. The boy about to be disciplined selected the withe and cut it with his own jackknife. And we learned to read, write, and cipher. For those who had done that, what we read and what we wrote and what problems we solved were the measure of our progress. We were ungraded. Our chronological ages were of no significance. Each of us was assigned the textbooks for which Teacher thought him ready, and read with those who had the same reader, figured with others who had the same arithmetic, recited history and geography and grammar with anyone whose books matched his.

Gradually we discovered that as we grew taller and moved farther from the stove there were seats waiting for us because others had also moved back and the biggest scholars of one year usually did not return the next. We saw sometimes former schoolmates who had reached the age of fifteen and gone to work on their fathers' farms, the boys perhaps soon to have farms of their own and the girls soon to marry; we saw less often those who went into the village or a nearby city to work, or who walked or bicycled or drove a horse from eight to a dozen miles a day to and from Berwick Academy. My brother walked or bicycled there, and I slowly began to understand the process by which he had come to want to make this effort to do such an extraordinary thing. He brought home books in which I could not read a single word, explaining to me that they were written in languages I had never even heard spoken. He studied about what was happening in the world *before* Columbus discovered America. He had notebooks in which he wrote up experiments he had performed that day in a *laboratory*.

I asked for a notebook like his and when it was given to me I took it to school and wrote in it whenever I had nothing else to do. Having no experiments to report, I wrote about everything going on around me and took it home daily for my mother to read. The day the notebook fell from my desk while I was out at recess, opened to the pages where I described Beulah's vain struggles to spell a long word correctly, and was picked up by Beulah, Teacher confiscated the notebook and gave me a new assignment. She would hand me a picture every morning and a large sheet of lined paper. I could not go home until I had covered both sides of that paper with a story suggested by the picture and placed it on her desk. It must be written neatly, in ink, and I must not use any word I could not spell correctly — but I might refer to the dictionary in the back of the room. She would check the punctuation, paragraphing, and sentence structure at night, and if there were mistakes I must copy it over the next morning before receiving that day's picture. From then on I was never with nothing to do.

In my thirteenth year Teacher sent word home that she thought I was ready for the Academy; the question was whether I would be going there in the fall or should she try to assemble more advanced material to occupy me until I was older. Suddenly The House shook with debate. My father and grandfather took no part in it. My brother, who had been graduated from the Academy three years before and now came home only weekends, strongly favored my entering the Academy. Auntie agreed with him. My mother thought it would be wonderful if I could but she did not see how it was possible. I was the Negative.

I did not want to go so far from The House. I did not want to leave Bernice from across the river who had been my constant playmate, and she was only ten; nor my other schoolmates. I was sure Teacher had numberless pictures I had not yet seen. I reminded them all that I could not ride a bicycle. My brother said he would teach me, and he tried; but I proved that I could not get on it and, if put on, promptly fell off. The Outer World had no charms for me. Oh, I would go to the Academy someday to learn to read and to speak the strange languages and to do experiments in the laboratory. But not yet. Not for a long time. A long, long time.

But the wheels were turning.

Auntie came to visit school and talked with Teacher throughout a recess which was ten minutes longer than usual. My father built a new stall in the barn, across from the twin stalls of Old Bell, my grandfather's workhorse, and her flighty daughter Bess who would draw no other wheeled vehicle than the red gig. He brought home Maud, a good, steady, gentle driving horse, and my mother said, "Now maybe I can get up to see Mama and Lula oftener." I watched him sponge and curry Maud until her coat shone, while I fed her froze'n'thaw apples. He loved horses . . . A girl I had never seen before came to spend the day. They said she was my cousin (distant) Eva. She had very dark, bright eyes, wore a red cashmere dress, and laughed easily. She said she was in the ninth grade in the grammar school in the village and would go to the Academy the next fall. We described our schools to each other and finally she said she liked hers better and I said I liked mine better. Then she went home and I never expected to see her again.

But that night they told me that everything had been settled. I need not go to the Academy unless I wanted to when the time came. But I could not make a sensible decision about that without more information than I had now. Therefore Teacher and Auntie had agreed that I should enter the village grammar school for the coming spring term, and Teacher had made the necessary arrangements. There I would get acquainted with those who would be my classmates if I did go to the Academy next fall, become accustomed to having classmates (I had had none for two years and never more than one), and have a chance to learn whatever they knew that I did not. If I did well enough I would graduate with them in June, and *then* I could decide whether to go on with them or come back to the district school for another year or two. That was fair, wasn't it? On schooldays my father would drive Maud instead of Bess so that I could ride with him. Harold had brought home, the weekend before, the material for two new dresses, and one piece was blue câshmere. My mother would cut out that dress the very next morning and was sure she could make it much like Eva's red one, even without a pattern, for she had taken particular notice. My mother's purple eyes shone; she loved dressmaking and very rarely had new material to use for me. Auntie's face was faintly flushed with pride. My grandfather lay on the kitchen couch asleep — or pretending to be — as no doubt he always had while womenfolk chattered about education for girls. My father was obscured by his newspaper, having curried, fed, and bedded down Maud in her new stall.

That's fair, isn't it? . . . No, it was not fair, I thought. They had undermined all my defenses with their love, their sweet reasonableness, their arrangements behind my back, their carpentry, their dress material, their shining eyes and proud faces.

I swallowed hard, said, "Well, I suppose I'll have to try it," and was ashamed of my own ungraciousness. But I did not want to leave where I was . . . I never would want to leave it. No more next year, or the year after or ever, than now . . .

Maud drew my father and me out of the yard early one March morning. My former schoolmates were still eating their breakfasts. Ours was the only team on the road. The schoolhouse yard was empty, the schoolhouse doors still closed and locked on the flag in its canvas bag, the globe in its green box, the unfilled water pail, the cold stove. It was like a dream of everything having stopped. We rode on past Nason's pump, down Goodwin's Hill, across the junction bridge and the railroad tracks.

At some corner Eva was waiting for us. My father pulled

up the horse and she climbed into the wagon. I moved to the middle of the seat, on its front edge, to make room for her, sitting between my father and her as I had often ridden between my parents on fall Sunday afternoons. She was wearing a brown velvet dress. I could see it between the flaps of her brown plaid coat with a fur collar. I remembered a coat my mother had once made for me of brown plush trimmed with brown velvet. The big girls at school had called me Teddy bear, and hugged me a lot. Eva's black kid boots were buttoned, with scalloped tops. My boots were brown and laced. My father and Eva talked about the weather, lumber sawed that winter, the spring work coming. I said nothing.

At the paint shop my father asked if I would leave my lunch pail there and come to eat with him at noon, or take it with me. I did not know where the grammar school was. I did not know whether I could find my way back to him. I said I would take my lunch with me. I went down the sidewalk with Eva. She turned a corner and I turned with her. I looked back and could no longer see my father, Maud, or the paint shop. I was alone in the outer world.

But a sign told me this was Goodwin Street. There were many Goodwins at home. I thought about them — Minnie, George, and Harold; Ed, Annie, Eliza, Lucy, and Edwin; Marcia, Greenleaf, Harvey, and Milton . . .

The grammar school was two stories high, a frame building painted yellow with brown trim. It had a narrow porch across the front, reached by broad, steep wooden steps. We went through open double doors and turned left to climb a very long staircase, Eva explaining that the sixth and seventh grades had the lower floor, the eighth and ninth the upper.

At the top she introduced me to the principal and went to find her friends outside. It must have been a very unrewarding morning for Eva. I hope I made up for it later, in some way.

The principal was a small, dark, nervous man whose name was Mr. Leazar. He seemed to have expected me, took me into a very large room filled with long rows of screwed-down desks and screwed-down chairs, told me which side was the ninth grade side, which chair had been assigned to me, and that the books I would need were in my desk. Then he took me across the hall to a smaller room and introduced me to the assistant principal, Mr. Bennett.

This was bewildering as Mr. Bennett was Clyde Bennett who had been my brother's classmate and closest friend at the Academy. He lived just below our schoolhouse. He and Harold had walked or bicycled to the Academy together for four years. Until now his three younger sisters had been my schoolmates. I had had no idea of finding Clyde here, and of course this was not really he. This was Mr. Bennett. We tried to avoid each other's eyes until Mr. Leazar told me I might go out now until time for school to begin.

I went out and stood on the porch until he came to ring the bell. Then I hurried back up the long staircase, hardly breathing until I had found my chair and none of the crowd following me claimed it. As soon as we had been called to order, Mr. Leazar said the ninth grade had a new member, her name was Gladys Hasty, and would Malvena show her where to leave her cap and coat. After that he read from the Bible, we repeated the Lord's Prayer, and he read off the spring term recitation schedule for us to copy down.

The wheels began to turn faster.

Teacher had already taught me all that was being taught by teachers in the grammar school that term, but as time went on I learned much from my contemporaries. From the girls, as we ate our lunches together in the only shady corner of the schoolyard, I learned that lunches should be carried in candy boxes or paper bags, never in tin pails, that curls could be made from winding hair around strips of cloth and sleeping on the bunches, and that the attentions of boys were desirable.

Once a week a Mrs. Goodwin came to give the eighth and ninth instruction in art and a Miss Gore in singing. At my age, I knew, my mother would have been ecstatic about both, but I could not draw so much as a convincing tulip and I had never been able to carry a tune. Still the high point of the week came when Miss Gore asked what we would like to sing together as the closing number. Dozens of hands always shot toward the ceiling, but regardless of where her nod pointed, the choice was almost certain to be the same, and we all shouted the words:

A capital ship for an ocean trip was the Walloping Window Blind
No wind that blew dismayed her crew or troubled the captain's mind —

We were the last undismayed generation.

My class taught me to love a world which seemed to me so crowded with my contemporaries that I was for three months scarcely aware of the few adults in it. Where I acquired — or how I retained — the capacity for attachment to places, to locations, I cannot say. But there it was. The closer we came to graduation day the more I felt that I could not leave the grammar school.

The Friday before we were to start a week of final examinations, my mother had nearly finished my dress of white seed voile, its many ruffles all edged with white satin ribbon. Auntie had given me a wide white satin ribbon for the sash, and white silk stockings. My brother had bought my long white silk gloves and my white canvas pumps with white satin rosettes. Nevertheless I drove myself to seek a private audience with the principal and asked, "If I should fail all my examinations next week, could I come back here next year?"

He asked me to repeat the question.

When I had, his answer was no. He amplified this to give me the clear impression that I was ready for the Academy, that final examinations were not given or read for scholars to make a mockery of, that he was a busy man and I was wasting his time; in short, that he would not have me in the grammar school another year.

So, somewhat sullenly, I went to the several rehearsals at the town hall, thankful only that, since Alice and Malvena were both shorter than I, I did not have to be the first one down the aisle, allowed myself to be arrayed in white for the sacrifice, was graduated, and returned to the solace of my family, The House, Shed, Barn, yard, fields, pastures, woods, and neighboring farms. There I put into a little pink box the rosebud which had been pinned to my graduation dress, identified on a bit of composition paper as "The rose I wore on the day I graduated from South Berwick Grammar School No. 5 on June 14, 1917. The rose was pinned on my dress by my music teacher, Miss Adeline Gore. The principal of the school was Mr. Herbert S. Leazar, the assistant principal Mr. Clyde D. Bennett, the drawing teacher Mrs. Jennie Goodwin, and the superintendent Mr. Blynn Allen."

It was the summer of 1917. My thirteenth birthday was a very hot day. My mother cut Hundredleaf roses and put them in her blue glass basket by my breakfast plate. She had cooked breakfast in the shedroom. There would be no fire in The House that day. Later I searched, as always, for my birthday gift and was a long time finding its hiding place, which was the cold oven of the kitchen stove. The gift was a large tintype of my mother when she was two years old, set in a heavy walnut frame. That afternoon my father and grandfather hauled in untrod loads of hay while I went across the river to Bernice's house. It was her birthday, too; she was eleven. Her father had left his haying to churn and pack a freezer of lemon ice cream, and her mother had baked us a cake with pink frosting and coconut. We had our party in the icehouse, sitting on cakes of ice thinly covered with damp sawdust. After that we waded in the brook and drifted over the surface of the Deep Hole in the canoe my brother had built and, when he went to live and work in Dover, New Hampshire, had sold to Bernice's brother. As we drifted, our heads were bent over notebooks, our braids (mine brown, hers blonde) often getting in our way. Each of us was writing the next installment in an endless story about her favorite family of paper dolls, long ago disintegrated but still very much alive and embarked upon fascinating adventures in our minds. When we separated, I would take her installment home to read, and she would keep mine. This was a custom established for the purpose of the enlargement of our libraries, still as meager in proportion to our growing need as they had ever been, though she had dozens of Bobbsey books, Ruth Fieldings, Camp Fire Girls, and L. T. Meades, while I had the Peppers, Dorothy Dales, Elsie Dinsmores, and L. T. Meades, all of which we read over and over and exchanged, along with our brothers' Horatio Algers, G. E. Hentys, J. T. Trowbridges, and James Fenimore Coopers.

But that summer, along with the days in the hayfields, on the planted pieces, and in the berry woods, with the evenings in the swingchair under the maples listening to my mother sing against the bass accompaniment of the frogs in the marshes, between Sunday church services and visits to my Aunt Hattie and Uncle George Webber in Eliot and to Sarah Jane's brother, my great-uncle Joe Brown and his wife, Aunt Lucia, where they camped on the Old Brown Place, I opened every book I could find, in The House and in all the houses up and down the road, and read it until I wanted more to read another. Leather bound, cloth bound, watered-silk bound, paper bound, if it was a book I opened it and read . . . Gene Stratton-Porter, Bertha M. Clay, Sarah Orne Jewett, Joseph C. Lincoln, Mary J. Holmes, the Brontës, Winston Churchill, Harold Bell Wright, Zane Grey, Zona Gale, Dickens, Whittier, Longfellow, James Whitcomb Riley, Coleridge, Shelley, Grace Livingston Hill, Temple Bailey, the Bible, Grace Richmond, the County Atlas, Thomas Bailey Aldrich, Kate Douglas Wiggin, Celia Thaxter, Shakespeare, Tennyson, Jane Austen, Mary E. Wilkins Freeman . . .

The United States had become an ally of Britain and France against the Kaiser in a European war which seemed always to have been going on, but it should soon be over now that we had joined in. In the meantime, it was at an incalculable distance from me. It was not my country's war. My country had won its wars and was free and united . . . I was at home. I was working. I was reading.

When the goldenrod and wild asters bloomed among the sweet fern and evening primroses along the banks of the lane I walked between them in the early morning chill and waited near the mailboxes beside the main road to listen for the sound of horses' hoofs and wagon wheels climbing Warren's Hill to the east. Christie Hooper and Chase Boston from the school district above ours were also entering the Academy that fall, and each had his own horse. One was usually close behind the other and when they were I rode with Christie because she was alone and Chase's sister, Lois, a sophomore that year, rode with him. But if the Bostons came first and had not seen Christie, I rode with them, lest she was not coming to school that day. None of us had telephones.

Lois guided three freshmen up Academy Hill to a great

stone building which looked to us like a medieval castle. The bell in its gilded tower was clanging a ten minute warning. We followed her through heavy doors and she pointed Chase toward the boys' basement where he was to leave his cap and lunch. Christie and I followed her up the stairs to the girls' coatroom where we left ours. It was filled with girls and if I had ever seen any of them before I did not recognize her. An inside bell rang and we spilled into a main room where by some magic we all found seats, freshmen in the front rows, and upperclassmen in proper sequence to the back. The desks and chairs of the main room were like those in the grammar school, and screwed to the floor, for which I was grateful. It was weeks before I felt secure anywhere in the Academy except when I sat in my own chair with my hands on my own desk.

But early each school-day afternoon I went back with Christie, Lois, and Chase down steep Academy Hill, along the uneven sidewalks of Academy Street to Hoyt's Stable, stowed bookbags under the wagon seat, helped fasten the horse between the shafts, and rode the sweet way back up Portland Street, out Agamenticus Road past the paint shop where my father waved from the door, past two peaceful cemeteries, through Old Swamps, across the railroad tracks and the bridge above the Newichewannock River, up Goodwin's Hill, past the end of Witchtrot Road, Nason's pump, and the district schoolhouse which now looked too small for so much to have happened — and to be still happening — inside it, down Nason's Hill, over White's Marsh Brook, and so to the end of the lane up which I hurried on foot, green felt bookbag bumping my knee. Home again!

And so, gradually, I became accustomed to leaving my chair and desk for recitations in the Latin room, the mathematics room, the history room and in a far corner of the main room where my Latin teacher taught us English; to the strange smells of the laboratory where we had general science; to religious exercises at noon instead of at the beginning of the day; to seeing lights flash on all over the building at the touch of a switch in the wall when the clouds were heavy outside; to the use of plumbing in the coatroom; to heat blowing up through lacy iron grates in the floor; to doing research in a library with great, arched, stained-glass windows; to the picture of blind Milton being read to by his daughters, to the statue of Mercury by the headmaster's office door, to portraits and marble heads of great writers and composers and early benefactors of the school. The Academy became my cathedral. I moved through it, only half believing, with deep reverence and with growing confidence.

But by then my family had another surprise for me.

My mother worried about snowstorms which often closed our roads for several days at a time, also about my tendency to have severe colds, and whether, in the periods I could not get to the Academy in winter, I could keep up with my class. Auntie was of the opinion that an Academy scholar missed many worthwhile opportunities by not being there for afternoon and evening activities; my brother agreed with her, and both spoke from experience. I said I could study at home when necessary, and could stay down overnight sometimes with Malvena if I wanted to. They shook their heads.

Mother, looking at Auntie, said, "If she stays down, one of us ought to be with her."

Auntie said, "No reason you can't go, Frank. I can see to things here."

My brother said, "I'll be glad to help with the cost of it."

My grandfather slept — or seemed to — on the couch. He had always said Vinnie put out the best food he ever sat down to, and had since she was ten years old; also that she had the lightest step around a kitchen of any woman of her size he ever knew.

My father folded his newspaper and went to bed. Within

a week he had found a house where my mother and I could stay in the village, and the first week of November we went there — she with my father in a loaded democrat wagon and I after school. I am unlikely ever to forget my feelings as I walked alone for the first time along the sidewalk of one of the three main streets of the village and turned in to cross the porch of a house which had been pointed out to me but into which I had never stepped.

I knocked at the door and my mother opened it. Though she looked suddenly small to me, there was not room for both of us in the narrow hall and she moved back into the kitchen as I came in. She had a wood fire crackling in the cookstove. There was a sink under the one window to the north, and a table and four chairs under the two windows to the west which faced the house next door, separated from it only by a graveled driveway to the stable attached to the house we were in, and there was a bedcouch along the dark south wall.

She said, "Keep your things on, dear, and I'll show you the other rooms. But first, look! See what we have in the sink!"

She grasped a long handle, moving it forward and back, and water spouted out of a faucet.

I had been told that the lady who owned the house went south in winter and left it furnished, just as she lived in it the rest of the year.

My mother opened a door into a dining room, nearly filled by a great, shining mahogany table, eight matching chairs, and a sideboard. I looked in for a minute, while she put on her coat, and then she closed this door and opened another into a living room furnished mostly in wicker. She closed this door behind us and we went on to look into a small bedroom which opened off it, and to go through a spacious hall to a parlor with a bay window facing the street. The parlor furniture was marble-topped tables, red and green velvet upholstery and Oriental rugs. We went upstairs to where all the bedrooms were locked except one — a large one with floor covered in straw matting and chamber set painted light brown with daisies and bluebells on the towering headboard of the bed. All the rooms had radiators and there was a coal furnace in the basement.

But we had no coal and should not have known what to do with it if we had. We went back to the kitchen, our shelter until April. When my father stayed down with us overnight, he and my mother slept in the small bedroom off the living room. My brother came for weekends and slept in the big bedroom upstairs. We had brought our beach rocks and sandbags for cold beds. But I always slept in the kitchen. Sometimes Christie or Lois stayed down and slept with me.

For I was no longer at home. I was Downtown. I was in the village. I could go to the library on Saturday nights and to the Baptist church and Sunday school and Young People's meetings on Sunday. I could go to school plays and parties and Chautauqua programs and sometimes to see a moving picture in a dark hall where dancing shadows moved in time to the pounding of a piano. I joined a Camp Fire group of which my English and Latin teacher was the Guardian; the Indian name she chose for me was Migwan (meaning Quill Pen) and I earned honors represented by embroidery on my cotton, leather-fringed Camp Fire dress and by large wooden beads strung on leather thongs to wear around my neck; I laboriously made an Indian headband of small beads.

My Uncle George Webber died that fall. I remember crossing the long cold porch, going through the small dark hall, and opening the door into the kitchen. It was such a dark day that my mother had lighted a lamp to sew by. She lifted her head and said, "Your Uncle George died last night . . . Poor Hattie!"

It was my father's sister's husband, Uncle George, who had once refused to speak to me until I said I was sorry I had campaigned for Teddy Roosevelt from the chopping block when I knew he favored Mr. Howard Taft. He had also taken me to York Beach in his new Hupmobile, and before that by horse and buggy to Kittery from the Webber farm in Eliot. From Kittery we had crossed the river to Portsmouth by ferry for an evening performance of *Everywoman* in which the girl who played Vice had red-lidded eyes. He and Aunt Hattie had had only one child. My cousin Roland. Aunt Hattie called him Roly.

I did not understand that winter why we did not go home for Christmas. I think now it was because my mother had waited a long time to have Christmas alone with her own family and thought she might not have another chance. The war we were to have ended was far from over. My brother enlisted in the Signal Corps and left early in the new year for the University of Vermont.

A few weeks after that Aunt Vinnie was in the Homeopathic Hospital in Boston. I had not known she was ill. She had told nobody. But one February day my father took my mother up home to see if she thought Vinnie was all right. That night my mother went to the drugstore and telephoned Aunt Hattie, who said she would be up on the ten o'clock train in the morning. The next afternoon my father put my aunts on the train for Boston where Sarah Jane's brother Joe and his wife, Lucia, met them in North Station and took Auntie straight to the hospital. After the operation Aunt Hattie went home to Roly, but Aunt Vinnie stayed many weeks. I wrote to her at the hospital and also through the spring at the address of my grandfather's sister, Aunt Annie Harriman, who lived on Harriman Avenue in Lawrence. Eventually Auntie wrote to me, telling me the length of the stems of the red roses Uncle Joe and Aunt Lou brought to her at the hospital; telling how the girls who were beginning to learn nursing wore pink uniforms and were called Pinkies, those who were more advanced wore blue uniforms and were called Bluies, and those who had finished the course wore pure white uniforms and caps and were called Graduate Nurses. It sounded like fairyland.

Meanwhile my father stayed nights at The House with my grandfather. My mother did their baking and sent it up by him. One day a week he took her up to clean and to bring back their laundry. I tried to imagine how The House looked to her when she rode into the yard, when she went into the kitchen, and how it felt to leave it, closing the door behind her, early enough on a winter afternoon for my father to take her to the village and get home again before dark.

I was scanning and trying to understand sonnets, memorizing declensions and conjugations, writing themes, making book reports, feeling the warm air from the Academy furnace fill out my pleated skirt like a balloon, learning my Sunday school lessons, leading Young People's meetings in my turn, adding wooden beads to my thongs, watching Ted Miller in basketball games and going with him to a Valentine party. I also had a piano. My brother had named me his service dependent, and directed that the checks which came each month make payments on a piano until it was paid for, and after that be put in a savings bank under his name and mine. I was taking piano lessons with a man who rapped my knuckles with a pencil when I made a mistake.

But at the end of March we went home, the piano with us. A place was found for it in the parlor, on the opposite side of the room from Aunt Vinnie's organ, at the foot of the guest bed.

We were there when Harold came on a three-day leave before going to Camp Sheridan near Montgomery, Alabama where, with what seemed to us amazing speed, he became a corporal and then a sergeant.

That summer while Aunt Vinnie was completing her convalescence at Aunt Hattie's in Eliot, Grammy came to live with us.

That summer I folded sheets of paper, sewed their folds together to make a binding, and wrote a "book" of short stories. One of them began:

> It was February and the snow was packing itself in solid heaps in every part of New England where constant travel did not keep it within bounds . . .

There were weeks for finishing the haying, for running back and forth across the river with Bernice, for going to the mailbox at the end of the lane every noon, taking out the Boston *Post* with its big black war headlines, hoping for a letter from Harold and — if it was there — taking it to my mother with fear growing at every step of what it might say. Meantime the Miss Paul who owned the house where we had stayed last winter had died and her house had been sold. My father made inquiries, found that a similar house on the same street was for rent, unfurnished, and took it for us, moving into it my piano and the furniture which Grammy had brought with her.

Auntie came home. I took my last drink of well water, and, months earlier than usual, just before school was opening, let myself be driven back to the village.

The Brackett house beyond the Soldiers Monument, on the North Berwick road, had a pump in the kitchen sink, but no faucets. It had no chilly, closed dining room. It had, off the kitchen, a small living room in which my father had put the piano, a secondhand chunk stove, and Grammy's bed-couch and platform rocker. Off the side of this living room there was a room with barely space enough to admit

Grammy's double bed and her two-drawer cherry nightstand for her lamp and Bible. I slept there with her. Off the south end of the living room there was a large room for which my father had bought a secondhand double bed and a bureau. This was my mother's room, and his when he stayed down overnight.

It was a strange fall.

We had an epidemic of Spanish influenza. Soldiers died by the hundreds in Army base hospitals. In every city and town the deathly ill were bedded down in Protestant churches and Jewish synagogues with Catholic sisters nursing them.

We could buy no white flour, and sugar only a pound at a time — by standing in line early in the morning once every two or three weeks. We packed boxes of baked bean sandwiches on johnnycake, to send to my brother in the Southland of fried chicken and watermelons, and Grammy made him cakes of cornmeal which my mother frosted with melted chocolate drops. Night and morning Navy Yard buses rolled through the streets carrying women who had never before worked outside their own homes, but now, to aid the war effort, had replaced men on the assembly line; some had become machinists. Their hands were cracked and their fingernails broken and ringed with black grease, and their faces were smudged from their hands, as they smiled and waved from the bus windows. These were the first buses I ever saw.

The daily newspapers gave us constant practice in endurance.

In October Bulgaria quit the war and Austria appealed for cessation of hostilities. A note from Germany was handed to President Wilson as he sat in his box at the Metropolitan Opera House in New York City. But still the fiercest fighting of the year continued on the Cambrai front, and German U-boats sank three American steamers with a loss of nine hundred lives.

Our President's reply to the note handed him was printed in the papers:

> At the very time that the German Government approaches the Government of the United States with proposals of peace its submarines are engaged in sinking passenger ships at sea, and not the ships alone, but the very boats in which their passengers seek to make their way to safety; and in their present enforced withdrawal from Flanders and France the German armies are pursuing a course of wanton destruction which has always been regarded as a direct violation to the rules and practices of civilized warfare . . .

Several times I had seen called out of class a schoolmate who did not return until a few days later, and we heard that an older brother had been reported killed or missing in action.

My brother wrote that his company had been alerted for shipment overseas and all their fighting equipment issued. He sent us a snapshot taken by a buddy; he had a full knapsack on his back and was sighting along the short barrel of a revolver. The only gun I had ever seen was my father's rifle with which he had shot only a few rabbits and partridges for my mother to fricassee, but with which Harold, when he was fourteen, had brought down a deer to provide us with fresh meat all that winter.

Meantime, I was reading Caesar's *Gallic War*, studying English history (The Wars of the Roses; the Thirty Years' War), and learning the French language.

Grammy and my mother spent a day each week at the town hall folding bandages for the Red Cross and brought home all the khaki yarn they could carry to knit into socks, mittens, scarves, sweaters, and wool helmets for the Red Cross to distribute to soldiers. Grammy knit almost constantly, even in half-light, often reading aloud as she worked, her small fingers flying. My mother knit whenever she could spare the time from the mending and dressmaking which paid for our kerosene, our cornmeal, our occasional pound of sugar, and the chocolate drops for frosting Harold's cakes.

And all the while, in this world of wars, past and present, I was an exile, a pilgrim wading through a morass, hoping only somehow to live — that we all would live — to get back home. Yet I knew, too — we all knew — that unless we kept putting one foot in front of the other, young men kept going into the trenches and over the top, women and old men kept the assembly lines moving, the Red Cross could meet its quotas on bandages and warm clothing, and schoolchildren learned to speak French and German and Spanish and to know the causes, course, and results of all the wars in recorded history, home as we had known it would not be there to get back to, and whatever might be left of it would not long endure.

Then suddenly our war was over. There had been rumors of a forthcoming armistice for several days but none of us believed them. We could not afford to believe them. The race had been too arduous and had gone on too long for anyone to take the chance of dropping out of it in what might be the last lap. But when the shoe shop whistle blew and then the sawmill whistles blew, and the church bells began to ring, and it was neither noon nor Sunday nor prayer-meeting night, there was no doubt in anyone's mind as to what it meant; there was only one meaning it could have. An armistice had been signed. The fighting had stopped. We were not and never would be the muted slaves of any dictator, nor need the people of any other country be, once they had tasted freedom, provided they had sufficient determination not to be.

The whistles blew freedom, the bells rang out freedom, and when they fell silent, the silence was pregnant with it, the air intoxicatingly fresh and sweet with it.

For a long time afterward at school we continued to sing the "Marseillaise" in French and "God Save the King" almost as often with almost as much fervor as we sang "America" and "The Star-Spangled Banner."

It was late spring before most of our boys came home, including my brother.

That was a fine summer. Grammy was on a long visit to her brother. Everything at home was just as I had always known it, except that my brother was there only on weekends. He had returned to become the assistant superintendant of the Williams belt factory in Dover where, after his graduation from the Academy and a year's home study of International Correspondence Courses, he had begun as a draftsman at $1.35 a day; and he had bought a motorcycle with a sidecar in which he arrived every Saturday for a late noon dinner my mother had kept on the back of the stove for him, and stayed until our bedtime Sunday night. In the forty hours between I trailed him as he inspected the barn and the planted pieces with my father and grandfather, served as his eager but awkward helper as he worked in my mother's garden, sat beside him at meals, often with my hand in his under the tablecloth, sat with my mother in the swingchairs while he lay in a hammock he had hung high above our heads among maple branches, talking and singing, on Sunday mornings walked with him through fields and pastures or went with him through the woods to the pond where we gathered lilies, and Sunday afternoons went to church with him to play the organ and sometimes to sing a duet with him, for now that I had learned to read music I could sing the alto part. In these duets I often had three or four words to his one, and this suited us both.

While he was gone I absorbed the world around me with all my mind and all my heart. I read little if at all that summer. I had no time for it. I hungered to live and realized now that only at home was I fully and intensely alive. I watched every movement, every expression of my parents, grandfather, and aunt, heard with quiet rapture not only what they said but exactly the words they used and their inflections. I went outside and watched the grass grow, the flowers bloom, the berries ripen. I heard the birds sing, the telephone wires hum, the wind blow, the rain fall, the crooning in the tops of tall pines, the running brook, the grinding of steel-rimmed wheels and the clink of horseshoes over stones, the distant whistle of trains on the eastern division of the Boston and Maine. I felt things with my hands and my bare feet, and what I could not press to my cheeks or my lips I pressed my lips or cheek against — the bark of trees, the great stones in the walls my grandfather had built, the soil of the planted pieces, vegetables, flowers, the pile of new-sawed boards, the splintery curb of the well, the horses, cows, hens, warm eggs, a nest blown from an apple tree, fence posts, hay, sand and gravel, clothes in the laundry basket and clothes on the line. I smelled the million smells of a Maine farm in summer, sweet and acrid in an infinite blend from which no fragrance or odor could ever be entirely separated from the rest. I knew now that Sarah Jane would not come back. Neither would the others who had gone, over the years: Aunt Lula, Aunt Nell, Uncle George, or Uncle Joe. But I was there, and in living I lived for them.

And I traveled. I walked the sandy roads, meeting people in wagons who stopped to speak to me. "Well, Gladie, good to see you round." I had been taught not to kiss any man who was not related to me, but I could climb up on the iron step of the wagons to hug my father's cousin who because he had married my Aunt Lula was my Uncle Clarence, or my mother's cousin, George Emery, or my grandfather's brother, Uncle Gran, and I did. I saw the sharp lines in their brown faces; if I knocked back their broad-rimmed hats I saw the white of their upper foreheads; I saw how dark Uncle Clarence's eyes were and how blue were Uncle Gran's and Cousin George's; I felt the gentleness of the touch of their work-hardened hands. But I could talk with anyone I met in a wagon or cart for I knew them all and they knew me — Will, Peter, Bennie, George Albert, Frank, Lafayette, Sam, Dave, Alfred, Len. I heard the beauty in their deep voices, the dear old words and phrases they used, their participles without *g*'s, their broad *a*'s. It was nearly always a man driving the horse I saw ahead or heard coming behind. Rare strangers passed in touring cars, bestowing smiles on me from below their goggles. We exchanged waves and they disappeared in clouds of dust on which long dust-colored veils floated. Then the dust subsided and I could trace the prints of their rubber tires, clearest in the damp clay near the everlasting springs which bubbled up here and there along the roadside.

I spent many hours with our close relatives and as many more with those more distantly related. There were family connections among all our neighbors.

That was the summer I was preparing a surprise for Bernice. I was filling a thick notebook with a collection of true stories about her and me, hoping that one day they would be printed. The central characters in the series were Vivian Emery and Winifred Dow, combining our middle names and our mothers' maiden names.

The introduction reads:

> These stories I have prepared in order that in future years they may be referred to by those who are interested. I hope that they will hold the interest and attention of the children, cause the memory of the elders to revert to the forgotten friends,

trips, and plays (games?) of childhood days, and will bring about thoughtfulness and patience in the characters of both ages. The stories are positively true and I hope you will care for them and profit by their teachings. Most affectionately I dedicate this book to Vivian, my dear friend and constant companion during childhood and girlhood.

I completed long accounts of "An Unlucky Incident," "The Hallowe'en Apparition" and "Amateur Theatricals," but, as I was reporting in sequence, I never reached what befell us in the course of what was perhaps our most fervent sharing of imagination and role-taking, when during the last fall and winter we were together in district school (she ten years old and I twelve) we used a hollow fence post as a mailbox in which we deposited and from which we withdrew letters to each other, under wholly assumed names, from two imaginary lovers.

One of these letters is still extant but it is no longer clear which of us wrote it.

Portland, Me.
Dec. 2, 1916

Dearest Edith,

Well, my pet, it is nearly time for you to come home. Gee Whiz, I'll be glad when you do. It has seemed like night with no moon or day with no sun since you went. There have been some splendid moons here too, but I didn't have the heart to look at them alone.

Lynn and I knocked at Maggie's door a few evenings ago and found the whole family in the dining room. After about 15 minutes Lynn and Maggie went out and left me there talking about the poor crop of potatoes, the way the presidential election went, and the high price of grain. A lot I cared about that! After I left I met Lynn and Mag-mag coming back. He was hugging her like everything and she had her head on his shoulder . . .

Maggie and Lynn, what they have been
And what they will be, makes a worry for me.
Edith and Ted, when we are wed,
How happy we'll be, Edith and me.

Now for a lovers' chat:

You're a little honeybunch, as sweet as the sweetest cell. The bee who sweetened you, sweetheart, must have carried the honey from many a flower. S'nough.

Say, Edith, before I'd send 16 pages of that mush through the mail!!!

I'm sending you a poem, 'Mr. Fisk's Friend Crazy Cal.' It's a sequel to the one I sent before 'Mr. Fish the Schoolmaster.' I think I'll have them printed in the Boston *Post* . . .

That was the summer Henry Earl came back for a week. He had grown up more on our place than on his father's across the lane from us. A year or two younger than Harold, he had hoed Harold's potatoes when he should have been hoeing his own. A charming, mischievous boy, he was a nuisance to district schoolteachers who burst into tears when forced to discipline him, and had not gone to school after the law no longer required it. Following his parents' death he had gone to Hopedale, Massachusetts, to live with a married sister and work in the Draper Mills with her husband, and we had not seen him since. But he had joined the navy when we went into the war, and now was back, briefly, a hero. His ship had been torpedoed and all hands lost, save only Henry and a few companions who survived twelve days in an open boat on icy Atlantic waters. He had been decorated for bravery.

Henry spent with us the days and the two weekends Harold was home. The other nights, but one, he stayed with other young men who had been his playmates when they were boys. That one night was mine. After an early supper I walked the five miles to the village with him and sat in the front row while he told the townspeople of his experiences. I heard the applause and saw the modesty with which he responded to it. There was a reception after his talk. Then he went home with the chairman of the committee and I with the postmaster's daughter. But the next morning before the dew was off the grass we were walking back together past the big cemeteries, through Old Swamps, over the Junction Bridge, up Goodwin's Hill, past the district schoolhouse where we had been scholars, over Nason's Hill, across White's Marsh Bridge, and up the lane.

I was sure I was in love with him, and not only because he was a hero. I traced my love back to when he had lain in bed puffed with poison ivy and I went every few minutes to look at him through the window because his bed was of a mysterious type which folded into a wardrobe at a touch and stood against the wall like a monstrous coffin on end. I was in agony for fear it might do so with him in it.

But on Sunday night Henry went back to Hopedale (we heard indirectly within the year that he had married a girl named Lena), and before Labor Day my mother and I returned to the village rooms my father had kept rented through the summer because our furnishings were there, including the piano, and in order to be sure we had a place to go to when the school year began. My grandmother joined us the next day.

During my last two years at the Academy I read Cicero and Virgil, continued with French and history, struggled with advanced algebra and solid geometry, but what I enjoyed most was reading, writing, and dramatics. I became a Torchbearer in Camp Fire. Ted helped me with mathematics, I helped him with Latin, and he took me to parties and play rehearsals.

The specter of college was approaching inexorably. No one from our neighborhood had ever gone, but Harold deeply regretted that he had not. The girl he was to marry, now teaching English and Latin at Sanborn Seminary, was a graduate of Colby College like my Camp Fire Guardian, who was also my English and Latin teacher. The wives of the owners of the belt factory were graduates of Wellesley. Several of my classmates were going to college and some of them were applying for scholarships. In the winter of my senior year my Camp Fire Guardian gave me forms to fill out, and I dutifully did so, then forgot about it. That was the winter my mother slipped on the ice and tore the ligaments in her shoulder. Before my mother's arm was out of the sling, Grammy had a stroke, lay near death on the bedcouch for days, and was completely helpless for many weeks. I was never marked absent while an Academy student, but for months of my Senior year I was hours late every day.

That spring I received a letter saying that I would be admitted to the entering class at Bates College in the fall if I would fill out the registration blank and send a matriculation fee of twenty-five dollars. I filled out the blank and Harold wrote the check.

By May I had been forced to the realization that I could not go home again to stay. I had been admitted to college and, whether I was granted a scholarship or not, I was to go to Lewiston, Maine, in September and stay as long as I could. Lewiston was thirty-some miles north of Portland. I had never been to Portland, never farther north in Maine than Wells, never farther south than Portsmouth, New Hampshire, except the time I went on the train with Harold to Lawrence, Massachusetts — where Aunt Vinnie was visiting Great-aunt Annie — for Aunt Vinnie to buy his graduation suit and have it fitted to him by a tailor. While I was in college, Harold would help with my bills; so would Auntie, from savings accumulated by teaching school at a salary of three dollars, then six dollars, and eventually nine dollars a week. But of course I must help myself as much as I could, so Auntie had ridden to the village with my father, taken me to Dover on the trolley, and helped me apply for a summer job in the office of the Pacific Mills. There was an opening for a switchboard operator. The pay was fifteen dollars a week. I was engaged. Auntie's eyes shone. Great-uncle Ezra and Great-aunt Mollie said I could board with them for two dollars a week.

Since I could not go home again, all I had left was the Academy, the church, and the village, and I would not have them long. Now, characteristically, I became intensely attached to them. Every day, from the predawn sound of the milkman running up a neighbor's path with his rack of clinking bottles to the last stroke I heard of the town clock at night, my nerve endings were exposed to the loveliness of everything about me and to the knowledge of how transient it all was for me. The uneven spots in the sidewalks, the shadows of the elms that lined the streets; they would be here but I would be gone. The greetings of the classmates who joined me, those ahead whom I knew by their backs, those behind whom I knew by their voices; a few weeks more and none of us would be traveling this way.

Climbing Academy Hill while the warning bell clanged (if I was on time), pushing open the heavy green door, running up the broad worn stairs, the coatroom buzz ("Guess who Ola's letter's from" . . . "Guess who's taking me to Senior Dance" . . . "Guess who . . ." and "Guess what . . ." and we all knew the answers), the headmaster's desk in the front of the main room, the row of chairs behind it where the faculty sat for devotional exercises, the seats and desks which had been ours and those of our special friends, the changing light rays as the sun moved across the sky, even the look and smell of the green powder with which Mr. Rose, the janitor, swept the room in the late afternoon . . .

The smell drifting down from the laboratory; I had never become really familiar with anything in it except its smell. Every classroom, every book-lined wall telling me they had much to teach me which now I might never know. The stage in the auditorium whispering the first lines of recitations I had given in speaking contests, halting words from my debate rebuttals, bits from *The French Maid and the Phonograph* (I had been the French maid) and other plays. Now the Academy motto, DEI TIMOR INITIUM SAPIENTIAE, was being temporarily replaced by the motto of the Class of '21, NON VESPERE SED MANE; we were sewing white letters to blue cambric. The Academy colors were blue and white. The arched windows of the auditorium through which we could see the playing field; the arched windows of the library through which we could see nothing because they were of stained glass and sunlight slipped through them veiled in Venetian colors.

And the arched and stained windows of the church, its cushioned pews, its carpeted aisles, its hymnbook numbers on a gilded scroll, the voice of the young minister who had come to us by a unanimous vote of the church membership, the beloved faces of those who were always there (and would be when I was not), the rustle of sitting and rising, the turning of thin pages and the bowing of reverent heads. The bare brown vestry from which we had marched by classes to the Sunday school rooms and where Young Peoples' and prayer meetings were held, and the suppers and socials and fairs. I had never seen Jesus there as I had in the church at home, but I was sure He was very close whenever the bell rang in the steeple . . .

The days grew warmer. The druggists, father and son, stood in their white coats in their doorway as did the meatmen, father and son, in their white aprons and straw hats in the doorway of the butcher shop, all nodding and smiling at us as we passed. We could buy a dill pickle from the grocer, candy peachstones of the town clerk at his penny counter if he was not behind a rusty green curtain making out a marriage license, or other penny candy at the paper store where we got fillers for our notebooks. But I was now too old to want to eat pickles or candy on the street and not nearly ready for a marriage license. I looked at the signs my father had lettered — WILLARD'S DRY GOODS, SOMERSET'S MENSWEAR, HUNTRESS'S LIVERY STABLE. I smelled the roses blooming across the picket fence of Sarah Orne Jewett's garden and went in and sat in her thatched summerhouse where her sister, Miss Mary, had told me she had often hidden away to write. Trolley cars — we called them electrics, which was also what Miss Mary called her automobile — came in from Dover and I watched sparks dripping off the lines as they stopped and started on again . . . From *Dover* . . .

Then suddenly it was Commencement Week. In accordion-pleated gray taffeta I went to Baccalaureate. In ruffled blue organdy I gave the Class Prophecy at Class Day, telling what I foresaw for us all forty years hence. In middy blouse and skirt I floated down Great Works River in a canoe which Ted had borrowed and we talked of what we could not foresee for the year ahead when he would be at Bowdoin and I at Bates. In white embroidered crepe de chine I sat on the stage in the auditorium for the last time, looking down at my parents, my Aunt Vinnie, and my Aunt Hattie who had come up from Eliot on the electrics. I was wearing a rose from a bouquet my brother had sent me; Aunt Vinnie had fastened it to my dress. I stood to acknowledge the scholarship the board of trustees had awarded to me. I went forward to receive the diploma — a roll of white parchment tied with a blue satin ribbon — which the president of the board held out to me. A benediction was said.

II

To Dover, New Hampshire
and
Lewiston, Maine

I WENT OUT of my school and out of my village where my church was. That weekend I helped my parents and my brother move their furniture and Grammy up home; Grammy was no longer able to go visiting. They went home, but Sunday night I went to Dover to board with Aunt Mollie and Uncle Ezra, and Monday morning I reported at the Pacific Mills office to learn to operate a switchboard, and to transfer from big ledgers to brown pay envelopes the name of every worker in the mills and the amount he had earned in the past week.

From Sunday night to Saturday noon I was in a new world. After supper in a dining room with a bay window, a rolltop desk, and a sideboard where an iridescent bowl in a silver frame was heaped with fruit, I helped Aunt Mollie with the dishes before we went out to stroll around the terraced gardens in which Uncle Ezra was always working, small black Jocko at his heels. Later she and I lay in the porch hammock, swinging to keep off the mosquitoes, and she told me about her girlhood, before she became Uncle Ezra's second wife. When the nine o'clock train whistled, she went in to set the table for breakfast and Uncle Ezra came to the porch from the parlor, where he had been reading, to get cooled off before going to bed. He talked about the night sky and taught me to recognize the constellations, telling me how they had come by their names. I slept in Aunt Mollie's sewing room and, thus inspired, soon began making blouses, skirts, and dresses to take to college with me, since Grammy's needs now left my mother no time to sew. I sat on the side of my bed, often until after midnight, cutting and basting what I would stitch before supper the next night when no one would be disturbed by the sound of the treadle machine.

Each morning after breakfast I followed a footpath through a hilly pasture, climbed the steep incline to the railroad track, crossed it, came out on Washington Street and continued on it until I came to Central Avenue. This was the way Uncle Ezra had always gone to his work until he retired, and the way my brother had gone to his when he first went to Dover and boarded with Uncle Ezra and Aunt Mollie until he could afford a boarding place nearer the business center. As I crossed the avenue the mill gates had not yet opened but the throng before them was growing. Many workers sat on benches. Others stood smoking their pipes. Those who noticed me going alone to the white office door in the brick wall waved and smiled. I wanted to stay with them. I have always wanted to stay where I was unless I was going home. But I had to unlock the white door and go into the silent office. The switchboard was expected to be open when the mill gates opened. Thus before my seventeenth birthday I was aware of a sense of personal importance which I felt was altogether out of proportion and which therefore embarrassed me; it seemed that each morning Number One, Number Two, and Number Three mills awaited my turning of a key — to set in motion machinery I had never seen and to admit the workers to earn the money which would be put into their pay envelopes for them to take home to provide food and shelter for hundreds of families.

When I spoke of this feeling, apologetically, to Uncle Ezra he nodded and said, "That is your key to turn. Each of us always has a key; not always the same key. Whether and when we turn it makes all the difference. A dead switchboard at opening time would cause delays and inconvenience. But a live switchboard is useless without superintendents and foremen to pick up their telephones. The machines would be useless without workers to operate them. The workers could do nothing if the machines were not kept in running condition, or if orders were not sought and received. All the keys must turn for the day's work to be done, the money earned, and the bills paid."

I was making friends. There were the other office girls — Lena, Leone, Scotty, Dot, Bessie — and Mr. Macdonald the janitor, Mr. Elwell the bookkeeper, Mr. Henderson the rose grower and manager of the office, Mr. Minnick the mill superintendent; also several of the foremen who often stopped at my window to leave a message. And there was Fred Tibbetts, near my own age, living across the street from Aunt Mollie and Uncle Ezra, who sometimes took me to an early movie and once to a carnival where I rode on a merry-go-round and a Ferris wheel for the first time. Aunt Mollie's nephew took her and me to Hampton Beach one evening and I thought I was in love with him (though he was a married man) because at her urging he tried to teach me to tango at the casino when moonlight put silver caps on the waves. I took my lunch to work and ate it in ten minutes in the ladies' room. Sometimes during the rest of my noon hour I had a tooth filled or extracted, for I was having my first dental appointments that summer, it being a requirement of the college that an entering freshman must bring a dentist's statement that his teeth were in good condition. Sometimes I shopped for patterns and dressmaking materials. But usually I sat on the stone steps leading to a small courtyard surrounded by the brick walls of the mills and worked on the first chapters of a novel. Its title was *If the Lilacs Bloom.*

I saw little of my brother in Dover. His work both began and ended later than mine, and he spent most of his evenings with the girl he was to marry in the early fall. I looked forward to passing each morning the house where he boarded on Washington Street, knowing he was there, and even to passing it again a little after five o'clock in the afternoon, knowing he would be there soon if only to shower and change.

The mills closed at noon on Saturday, but the switchboard had to be kept open at least until 12:30, and longer if any long-distance calls were out or expected. Whenever I emerged from the white door on Saturday, Uncle Ezra and Aunt Mollie were waiting in the Maxwell nearby, I climbed into the back seat beside whatever I had packed the night before, and I was driven home.

For twenty-four hours I sought to keep awareness of the coming week from my mind. My grandfather, unable now to get farther from his bed, sat on the porch, watching me come up the walk, and said, "Well, Gladie, you're back again." My mother kissed me and went with Aunt Mollie and Uncle Ezra into the parlor which was now Grammy's throne room. Aunt Vinnie took in lemonade and sugar cookies for the company and came back to the kitchen to fix my lunch of crisp salt pork slices between split sour milk biscuits. Sipping her lemonade she asked questions about the week past, and between bites I answered. When neither of us was speaking I heard the clock tick. Uncle Ezra and Aunt Mollie had usually gone and I had visited with Grammy before my father came in from the haying, which he now did with only a neighbor's boy to help. For supper there were baked beans, steamed brown bread, sliced cucumbers, deep cereal dishes of Boston lettuce dressed in vinegar, salt, pepper, and a dash of sugar, followed by berry pie. And we did dishes in the sinkroom, sat in the swing-chairs in the dark and sang, and listened to the whippoorwills. But Harold did not come now until we were all asleep. My mother had the sitting-room couch made up for his bed. I slept with Auntie.

Then there was Sunday morning . . . Sunday dinner like Saturday night supper except that the beans and brown bread were cold, not reheated as they would have been in winter . . . And by the time these dishes were done, the Maxwell was back in the yard. The coming week had begun. Uncle Ezra and Aunt Mollie left Harold at Jennie's house, and I went on with them to Dover. It was years before I appreciated what they had contributed to my earning fifteen dollars a week, and to the cushioning of my first separation from my family.

Yet at summer's end I did not want to leave Dover. I wanted to stay where I could go home every weekend. I was used to Uncle Ezra's house, to his terraced gardens, to Aunt Mollie's cooking, stories, and merry laughter, to wondering at supper whether Fred would come over and whether, if he asked me, I would go to the movies with him or keep the evening for sewing, for hearing the whistle of the nine o'clock train. I liked every step of my walks to and from work, calling good morning to the workers at the mill gates, turning my key in the white door, and opening the switchboard which had terrorized me at first with its flashing lights, its buzzing, its myriad of brass-tipped red rubber tubes, and the gear I wore to hear strange voices barking incomprehensible directions and to make some sort of response. Now it was all familiar, easy, and could have been automatic if I had not enjoyed it too much to let it be. Now when the first light went on I knew who had picked up his phone, that when I said, "Operator" to the superintendent's light, Mr. Minnick or his secretary was likely to say, "Get Lawrence on the line, please. Let me know when you have them." Lawrence was the parent mill. But "Operator" to Number Two mill's light was likely to elicit, "Hi, there, sweetheart. Top o' the mornin' to yer. Give me Tommy and don't spare your horses." That was Mr. Cassidy, wanting Number Three.

The day I left, Mr. Cassidy stopped by my window and

pushed across my little counter a pin he said he had found in the grass near the sidewalk on his way home the night before. But it looked brand new. The girls gave me a framed copy of Kipling's "If" to "take to college with you," a fountain pen "to finish your book with," a matching towel and facecloth set, bone hairpins "to hold that heavy figure eight" (I was wearing my hair up for the first time that summer), and perfumed stationery "to let us know what it's like when you get there." Mr. Henderson, who brought a bouquet of his roses for his desk every day and divided it among his girls at night, put a whole bouquet on my desk beside the switchboard that last morning. I was carrying it and the other gifts when I kissed them all goodbye — even Mr. Henderson himself — and ran in tears to the Maxwell. I had promised to come back the next summer, and every summer. But I was never inside that white door again.

For the next week everything at home seemed to center around my mother's dome-lidded trunk and Auntie's straw suitcase with leather corners, handle, and straps with buckles. My mother had brought the trunk with her when she came to The House as a bride. I suppose it was her hope chest. We re-covered the inside with sprigged wallpaper. We polished the filigreed metal which covered the top. My father varnished whatever wood was bare, and oiled the lock, warning me, whatever else I did, never, never to lose the brass key. Then the trunk was set, open, in the middle of the sitting room floor, the suitcase placed, open, on the sitting room couch, and the rest of the couch and all the sitting room chairs began to fill up with what they thought I would need until Thanksgiving. Bed pillow and blankets, bath towels, hand towels, facecloths, umbrella and rubbers, bathrobe, slippers, shoes, new clothes, "still good" clothes, all the graduation dresses, silk stockings, lisle stockings, soap, talcum powder, cold cream, an embroidered bureau scarf, sofa cushions, a bedside rug Sarah Jane had hooked from strips of her father's and brother's Civil War uniforms . . . I looked at the growing accumulation in despair.

"It will never go in, Mama . . . Mama, it would fill *three* trunks!"

"But there's nothing here you won't need . . . Except maybe the blue organdy —"

Auntie said, "You leave it to your mother. She'll fit it all in like the pieces of a puzzle."

Late the last night that was what she did. Having separated what I had to have on arrival from what it was hoped I could live a day or two without if by some most unlikely chance the trunk did not get transferred with me in Portland Union Station and so went on up the coast while I turned inland, I put a pillow on the floor for her to kneel on and ran back and forth at her direction to hand her what would fit in next. When the last piece was in place she closed the trunk cover (did she think of other times when she had closed it?) and put her hands on the edge to lift herself stiffly to her feet.

"Now you can lock it," she said. "Then put the key in your handbag right away. To be sure you don't forget."

It was too late to go out to the swingchairs. Too late to sing. The last whippoorwill had gone to wherever whippoorwills spend September.

We went upstairs to bed. When I crawled in beside Auntie she said nothing and lay very still but I knew she was not asleep so I couldn't cry.

The next morning we were all up early. My mother took Grammy's breakfast tray into the parlor and came back to sit with the rest of us at the kitchen table. My father finished quickly and went to the barn to harness the horse. I went to find my hat, gloves, and handbag. It was a warm morning and I carried my coat on my arm. The trunk and suitcase were already in the wagon.

Grammy said, "Be a good girl" . . . Grandpa said, "Come

home when you can" . . . Auntie said, getting wood from the box behind the shedroom stove, "Remember now. *Non vespere sed mane.* I guess you'll be here for Thanksgiving" . . . My mother said, "Oh — Gladie, dear —"

I got into the wagon beside my father and we rode down the lane, over the bridge, up the hill, past the district schoolhouse . . . past the grammar school . . . turned the opposite way from that which led to the Academy and the Baptist Church . . . At Salmon Falls railroad station he bought my ticket to Auburn, Maine, and checked the trunk. I don't know how he knew I should get off at the Auburn station instead of Lewiston. The Androscoggin River flows between these twin cities. Perhaps the Nutters told him. Dr. Nutter and his wife were at the Salmon Falls station, buying a ticket and checking a trunk for their daughter Ruth who had been my classmate at the Academy and would be my roommate at college.

"She'll be all right," Dr. Nutter told my father. "We're going as far as Portland with them to see they and the baggage get on the right train."

My father told me, "We'll be looking for you Thanksgiving. Let us know what time you'll get here." And he went away.

And he went away. Everything went away. Salmon Falls, South Berwick, North Berwick, Wells, Highpine, Kennebunk, Biddeford, Saco, even Portland. When Ruth and I got off the train at Auburn two girls, older than we, were waiting and said they were seniors at the college. I did not know until days later that one of them was the governor's daughter. They said seniors were meeting all passenger trains. They rode with us in the taxicab which had our trunks strapped to the back. Ruth said that was the reason we had not stayed on the train to cross the river to Lewiston — because there were always taxicabs at the Auburn station. I wondered how the Nutters knew that. I wonder now who paid my taxi fare and for the delivery of my trunk to the hall of Milliken House. I have no recollection of opening my handbag except to get out my trunk key until the next day when, after registering at Roger Williams, we went to Chase Hall to buy our books.

I was away the day my brother was married. I was at home for Thanksgiving, for Christmas, for Easter. Away when Aunt Vinnie died quite suddenly in the spring. At home all the next summer helping my mother care for Grammy, who was never again to be able to move from one place to another without the support of someone's steadying hand, and for Grandpa who still got by himself wherever he went, but went only from his bed to the sink and then to the table and from there to the kitchen couch, each day a little weaker than the day before, saying often, "I won't last much longer. I never thought to outlive Vinnie." At home again for Thanksgiving, a four-day college recess during which Grandpa died and was buried beside Sarah Jane.

The morning after he died, Grammy and her chair were brought out to the sitting room, the door was opened between his bedroom and the parlor, he was placed in his coffin, his bed was taken apart and carried to the shed-chamber, Grammy's bed replaced it, and the parlor became the funeral room. I slept the next few nights on the sitting-room couch to be near Grammy. It snowed the night before the funeral and the next day was gray with a gusty wind which blew the snow like icy pellets as we stood outside the front door waiting for the bearers to bring out the coffin. The neighbors and distant relatives who had sat with Grammy and been called out first looked stiff and pinched from standing in the cold. The undertaker called my cousin Roly and me first from the parlor, my brother and his wife followed;

then my Aunt Hattie, my father, and my mother together. Each group took its place at the head of the line as it emerged, so that as the coffin was carried down across the field, Grandpa's daughter, son, and daughter-in-law followed it closely, his firstborn grandson and wife were next, then his younger grandson and his granddaughter, his nieces and nephews and their families, and his friends. It was a modest gathering, as funeral corteges go, but it seemed a great many people to be walking in November across the whitened field through the biting wind and blowing snow.

Great changes had come to The House and the way of life there, and more were coming, yet everything it had ever been it still was. Home was like a curious kind of flower which cupped all who had lived there, all that had happened there, all that was said or even thought there, all the work, the music, the memories, the scents, the living, the growing, the dying, and never let it go, never would let it go, but held it secure forever. It was stronger than death, longer than time. It was reality and all else I knew gained reality only by being rubbed against it, as an electric lamp was lit by connecting it with a power line. And above all, for me, it was the center of peace.

I went back to college, now a sophomore, an English assistant, and a member of a creative writing club to which fifteen students from the three upper classes were elected. Wanting only to read (in Greek, Latin, and French as well as English) and to write (of going blind, of losing one's sanity, of wandering destitute on the Left Bank of the Seine, of whatever I knew nothing about) I waited on tables in the women's dining room, washed dishes in the kitchens, worked in the alumni office sending news of my fellow students to their hometown papers, sat with professors' children, struggled with required courses, won public speaking contests, hiked, played hockey, basketball, and soccer, learned to strum a ukulele, let my overshoes flap, went to a church of a different denomination each Sunday, kept the student government rules, counted my cuts, sang "The Sheik of Araby," "Yes, We Have No Bananas," and "Witch Hazel," enjoyed it all, and wrote home about it every day.

I also met the man I was going to marry.

That small country college founded by Baptists on the outskirts of a dark little industrial city in the northeast corner was to me in the 1920s an Elysian field. Looking back, I still see it so. As far as I knew it was to everyone there. We had nearly all, faculty and students alike, come from farms where a new book had been so rare as to fill us with ecstasy, and even the old books were a constant temptation to neglect obligations we knew must be met if the course of life was not to bog down like a cartwheel sunk to its hub in a muddy road. Here food, shelter, warmth was provided, as long as money was forthcoming to pay for it. Our first obligation was to find out what was in a bookstore and in a library filled with books and to report our findings on paper. What a heavenly assignment! We carried those books and papers with us to the brick and granite buildings, each set far enough from the next so that oaks and elm trees grew between, the sun swept through, and the rain, the snow, the northeast gales; we took them in the fall to Mount David, a wooded pinnacle on the edge of the campus, on snowshoes in winter to Pole Hill, and in spring to the bank of the Androscoggin River.

Also, on the farms from which we had come, most of us had lived with older generations, seeing our contemporaries only on school days or at programs planned for us or on occasional afternoons spent in one another's homes. At college we lived together, studied together, worked and played together, chose our own times and places for meeting. We were all young, all rich in energy and hope, all filled with excitement and love of life.

We had no luxuries. We had never had luxuries. We felt no need of luxuries. Even the girls who visited the governor's daughters at the Blaine Mansion in the state capital reported that it was like a dormitory with home-cooked food. We had opportunity and we had freedom, and so we had joy. Our cup ran over.

We read sometimes of speakeasies but our favorite spots for a treat were the Greek's (his daughter was a fellow student), the Chink's (he transported us to the mysterious Orient as soon as we reached the top of his stairway), and the ice cream parlor kept by an elderly Negro gentleman who, having been graduated from the college long ago, had chosen to stay on its fringes the rest of his life. We heard of ballroom dances which sounded to us exotic, but we were content with the waltz, the fox-trot, and an occasional tango. Once in a while Bowdoin boys in coonskin coats and berets rode past in a Stutz Bearcat, waving a silver flask, but on the whole we had a rather low opinion of the maturity of Bowdoin boys. Wherever we went we walked, except for the rare times when we took a streetcar or a train.

One of the senior members of the writing club in my sophomore year was rather older than most of the students. He had come off a western Massachusetts farm to work his way through high school; this had taken him six years, and he had enlisted in the Medical Corps some weeks before his high school graduation. After two years in the army, at the end of World War I, he had worked in a mill for a year to accumulate savings for college. He was twenty-five when I met him, waiting tables in a restaurant downtown for his main meal of each day, had assistantships for which the College paid twenty-five dollars each semester, held the Coe Scholarship as the highest ranking man in his class, and conducted services on Sunday in any of the surrounding villages where a Protestant church lacked a pastor and asked him to come. He was preparing to be a high school teacher of English, coach debate, dramatics, track, and tennis, and serve as a faculty adviser for school publications. He was a Greek major, managing editor of *The Student*, an indefatigable player of pool, a dangerous adversary at all-night penny-ante or five-and-ten. He also had a campus reputation as a Don Juan.

His name was Herbert Carroll. He went home with me for an April weekend and when we returned to college we were secretly engaged. I met his mother and three older sisters when they came to his Commencement. By then he had accepted an instructorship at James Millikin University in Decatur, Illinois and, after a summer pastorate in North Shapleigh, Maine, he spent a few days at home with me before I drove him to the train on which he left for the midwest. I was wearing a diamond and thus our engagement was no longer secret, but when I returned alone to college, friends dutifully pointed out that it was still a secret in Illinois.

That was the summer my father bought our first car, a Willys-Knight, on the distinct understanding that my mother would drive it; he still preferred his horse though Bell, Bess, and Maude had all been turned out to pasture to live as long as they could enjoy it and then die by one shot from his rifle, and he drove big gray Pony. My mother did drive the car in her own delightful and often hair-raising fashion, after Herbert taught her the rudiments, and I drove it exactly as I had been taught by my father, who would not touch the wheel himself. We all carried driver's licenses which were to be had by sending two dollars to the state capital with an application.

For my last two years in college "I wandered lonely as a

cloud" across a bright plateau. I had completed all required courses which were not to my liking. Funds left by Aunt Vinnie and my grandfather insured the payment of my basic bills. I needed to earn only that part of my spending money for which I did not feel justified in asking my father, and I did this by serving as proctor for my dormitory (collecting and counting sheets every Saturday morning and passing out clean ones, reporting stopped-up plumbing, and replacing blown fuses) and as head waitress in the women's dining room where I waited on the faculty and assigned student tables to the other girls who worked in two-week shifts. Looking forward to marriage at my Commencement time, I had a single ambition, to be a good wife and mother, therefore had no professional requirements to meet, no anxiety about an uncertain future. I wrote a long letter to Herbert every day, another long one home every other day. The rest of the time, week after long, lovely week, I wrote other things whenever I was not reading in the library stacks — that sweet, musty smell of treasured books — or doing whatever I liked best to do alone or with my friends, several of whom were members of the writing club, others members of my second favorite organization, the 4A Players, for which I either acted in or directed both original dramas and such popular one-acts as *Trifles* by Susan Glaspell and *The Monkey's Paw* by W. W. Jacobs. I was now an assistant in Public Speaking as well as in English, editor of *The Garnet*, women's editor of *The Student*, and House Senior of a sophomore dormitory. I joyfully counted among my friends Esther Kisk (long before we could suspect that she was to marry Dr. Robert Goddard, father of rocket ships which would take Americans to the moon), Erwin Canham (even before we knew he would be a Rhodes Scholar, to say nothing of Editor of the *Christian Science Monitor* and a leader in many national undertakings in the fields of religion, education, and business), Dorothy Clarke Wilson whose intellectual brilliance we recognized but whose breadth of vision, appreciation of the efforts of others, and willingness to travel anywhere in pursuit of elusive facts and impressions were not revealed until later, and many who would become, even if less widely known, key figures in their areas of the world — earnest teachers, devoted ministers, research scientists, gifted musicians, foreign missionaries, community leaders, parents of outstanding young people.

We were aware from reading, observation, and shared experience that much was wrong with the world, and we differed in our theories as to what most needed making right, but I knew no one who felt that changing its systems would automatically improve it. We gathered that people were what needed changing, some much more than others, and because of the infinite variety of human nature, people could be changed only one at a time. This, we realized, was going to be a long process by the human calendar, but we had faith that God would provide the time for our generation and those to follow to take the necessary steps, one after another. What mattered now, here, was for each of us to choose the trail best suited to him and prepare and equip himself to walk it, as much of a Samaritan as he could learn to be.

We heard from our Negro fellow students (we no more thought of them as black than of our Oriental classmates as yellow or of ourselves as white) something of what life was like for them in the South and we were glad they had come North and hoped they would stay where they were free, as we would seek to leave any part of the world where we were not. We hoped — and believed — that our country would never be involved in another war, but we knew this was not certain, since avarice and aggression were as human as the drive for freedom and security. We knew little of wealth and thought rarely of it, though one of our favorite talk-games was "If somebody sent you a dollar, what would you spend it for?" A fellow student was from a rich family if her mother could order three dresses sent from a department store for her to choose one from. He was rich — and his friends lucky — if his father sent him five dollars and said, "Take four of the fellows to dinner at the hotel after church." She was rich — and disadvantaged — if she was not considered by the administration to need the income from a campus job and so could not have one.

Most of us had known hardship, hunger, neglect, filth-bred disease, if not in our own lives, then at very close range in neighboring families, and we meant to escape it and help others to escape it. We deduced that we were here to learn how to do whatever we could do best, both for ourselves and for others, to learn how to be effective as leaders, to learn how to be truly Christian which we understood as the ultimate in humanitarianism . . . to learn . . . to learn . . .

I have described myself as "lonely," meaning it in a special sense. A single small white cloud is lonely only in that nothing touches it today except perhaps a breeze; whatever it has been attached to, what it will later attach itself to, is at a great distance. It is conscious of no pressure. It floats free. Its range is unlimited. Everything but this is past or future, memory or for by-and-by.

The sound of bells; the bell in Hathorn Tower clanging the class hours; the dormitory bells for rising, for meals, for study time, for calling someone to the telephone or the reception room, the end of visiting hours . . . The cinder paths and the shadows of great tree trunks striking black across the snow . . . The humming of the wires as the streetcar we call the Figure Eight comes around the loop . . . The light in the chapel entrance and in all the dormitory windows as we cross the campus at night from the library or the Little Theater under the bell tower . . . The Bates hello whenever we meet a fellow student; the voices we identify even in the dark . . . The singing late at night as Bates men come back from Twin City dances Bates women are not allowed to — and have no wish to — attend . . . The older men and women in dark suits, with serene faces and quiet voices, who have dedicated their lives to providing this atmosphere in which we are free to learn, if we will, all they know and more . . . The class meetings, council meetings, student government meetings, "Y" meetings, Athletic Association meetings, club meetings, committee meetings . . . The debates with Yale, Harvard, Oxford, Cambridge . . . The football rallies, intercollegiate and interclass games, the October and April air in the open stadium, the track meets, the snake dancing in the streets and bonfires on Mount David after victories . . . The early morning rush to the showers, the incoming mail spilled over the hall table, the dressing for dinner, the after-dinner singing around the piano, the nights we talked until dawn . . . the miles we walked, talking, while March thaws made a network of brooks around our feet . . . the books, the books, the books . . . strawberry shortcake for dessert, rhubarb ripening in the president's back lot, peonies budding beside the chapel walk . . .

I wrote my senior thesis on the Little Theater movement.

For four years we had seen ourselves as undergoing a slow, mysterious process by which we were being prepared, developed, improved, to the point where each of us would be ready to meet the world he was to serve, lacking only the experience which, on this foundation, would take him to the peak of his capacity for service. Then, suddenly again, as such changes always seemed to me, we were as ready to begin as we were going to be. It was time for doing our Greek play on the library steps, for Class Day exercises on Hathorn's steps (I gave the "Farewell to Halls and Campus") and for Commencement in the chapel. It was June, 1925.

My parents were there, for I had gone home by train to drive them down; they had not been sure they could find the way. The man I was to marry in the chapel the next day was there. The evening of Commencement day he and I went together to the Alumni Ball in Chase Hall, and the dean of the college, who was to conduct our ceremony, talked gently with us, between dances, of the privileges and obligations of married life. Two of Herbert's sisters and their husbands came the next day just in time for the wedding, as did my Aunt Hattie, and some of Herbert's closest college friends, including Elwin Wilson to whom my classmate, Dorothy Clarke, was engaged. Several of my classmates had stayed over, among these Dorothy, to be our organist, and my roommate for four years, classmate for eight, to be my maid of honor. It was a small wedding, making the chapel seem vast, and we had a small reception in the dormitory where I had been living. When my parents reached us to form the receiving line, my mother's purple eyes were as bright with pride and happiness as with love, but my father's shone with tears which ran unchecked down his ruddy cheeks.

That was the first summer of my life that I did not go home, the first summer since his early childhood that Herbert had not worked on a farm, in a factory, in an army hospital, as a church pastor, or as a camp counselor. We spent it in an abandoned hunting camp on the edge of a wilderness lake at the foot of Mount Bigelow near the trail by which Arnold had led his company of soldiers of the Revolution into Canada. To reach our nearest neighbors in a farmhouse three miles away we had to ford a river, but we went there every other day for milk, vegetables, and sometimes eggs. Two or three times we walked eight miles to the nearest village and eight miles back for meat, bread, crackers, sugar, and Herbert's coffee. Having no refrigerator, we sank perishable foods in the lake. Having no stove, we cooked over an open fire. Having no electricity, we studied and wrote by sunlight and lamplight. Plagued by mosquitoes and having no screens, we draped one end of our small porch in white cheesecloth, and slept there, though we could not afford enough cheesecloth for the whole porch and so the only way to reach our bed was by climbing through a cabin window. It did annoy us that bears brushed our shoulders in the night, rousing us both by touch and by the sound of their lumbering and snuffling, because we knew they were on their way to the raspberry patch on which we depended for desserts. It was by no means a lazy summer. For recreation we swam off a rotted pier, rowed around the lake in a leaky boat, walked and talked, talked and walked. When we returned to civilization in mid-August, to visit my family and his, we knew each other very well.

Herbert had resigned from his position at James Millikin and taken another as teacher of public speaking at Durfee High School in Fall River, Massachusetts, near enough to Providence, Rhode Island, so that he could do graduate work in education at Brown University.

III

To Fall River and Chicago

In the record or study of any individual part of the human experience it matters far less to whom something happened than that it happened; and far less that it happened than that we see how all the paths chosen led logically — though by no means inevitably — to confrontation with this happening.

Our first home in Fall River was on Hanover Street. We had a house all to ourselves, very small and set in the rear of the much larger home of the man who owned both. The furnishings we used belonged to him. We had a small living room with an upright piano and a studio couch; a smaller dining room; a tiny kitchen holding only sink, cupboards, breakfast table and two chairs; and a glassed-in side porch where the gas stove stood. Upstairs there was a small bedroom, a bath, and an alcove with a cot in it. We were surrounded by backyards, but had none of our own. Our house was set on the boundary line of a neighbor's backyard where she hung her laundry, our walk in from the street was on the boundary line between the two big houses which faced the street, and having passed between them the walk meandered past the kennel of our landlord's dog and between their two backyards where our landlord's wife and her neighbor hung their laundry. I hung mine in the cramped space between the porch windows and the side of our landlord's garage — and for a while I had a great deal to hang as part of my personal prescription for marital bliss was that not only our washable clothing but all the linen from bed, table, and bath must be laundered each morning. (I had no washing machine, only the help of a zinc tub, scrubboard, Fels Naptha soap, a covered boiler, and a wicker basket.) One of the four walls of our house had no windows. On any pleasant day, from any of the windows we did have, I looked out on a sea of laundry.

But there was an oasis. Brushing our living room and bedroom windows we had a large and flourishing crab apple tree. As long as it was in leaf it almost obscured the dog kennel, and during the month it was in bloom its color and fragrance filled our days and nights with glory.

Wedding gift money bought a secondhand desk to be placed end to the wall between the bedroom windows and used as with our roommates we had used the single desk provided for double rooms in college dormitories, one side for Herbert's work and the other for mine. Our study was in the heart of the crabapple tree.

I wrote while he studied. I wrote while he went by bus to Providence for his courses at Brown. Unless I went with him, to read at the public library, I wrote during the evenings he taught adult education classes to add to our income. (His annual salary was twenty-two hundred dollars.) I wrote while he typed, with two fingers on a machine he had bought secondhand while in college, the last story I had finished. It was the high point of our day if by midnight he had completed the perfect copy he required of himself, we scanned *The Author and Journalist* we had bought at a newsstand and selected what seemed either the most desirable magazine in which this effort might appear or the one most likely to print it, put it, folded together with a self-addressed, stamped envelope for return, into a heavy brown envelope, and finally walked slowly through the dark to the corner to post it before going to bed. There is no describing the feeling we had those nights of having drawn a magic bow and shot a shining arrow into the air.

I wrote stories we thought worthy of the magazines we respected most, *The Atlantic Monthly*, *Century*, *Harper's*,

Scribner's, The Dial and *The Forum;* and we debated long as to which to favor with the first chance to publish them. I wrote stories we considered had a bright touch, a romantic appeal, or a down-to-earth homeliness which made them better suited to the magazines we thought sophisticated — *Cosmopolitan, Redbook, Collier's* — or to the big women's magazines — *Ladies' Home Journal, Woman's Home Companion, The Delineator, The Pictorial Review, Good Housekeeping* — or to *The Saturday Evening Post, The Country Gentleman, The People's Home Journal, The American.* I wrote stories for the young, which we sent to *St. Nicholas, Youth's Companion, American Boy* and *American Girl.* I wrote stories and read them aloud to him; he typed them, and we mailed them out. And they came back to us. Again and again and again they came back to us, and as soon as they came back we huddled over the *Author and Journalist*, bundled them into new envelopes, and took another evening walk to the mailbox on the corner.

We were not in the least discouraged, for two reasons.

The first reason was that we had other interests which would have filled our lives if we had not had this one at all. Herbert's classroom teaching and graduate work were of primary importance, occupying five and a half of his days each week, and two evenings. Another evening, on occasion more, he assisted the Durfee High School debate coach, Mr. Chatto. While he was at Durfee I did my housekeeping — my baking, cleaning, and laundering (though I gradually ceased to be quite so meticulous as at first) — at which, I was surprised to find, I was neither very quick nor very skillful, only determined; I also shopped, wrestling with my budget, which allowed ten dollars a week for food, electricity, and telephone. There were grocery and drugstores around the corner on New Boston Road, but prices were lower downtown, two miles away, and I often went there for provisions. A streetcar passed the end of our walk regularly, and it looked tempting, especially when I saw it stop and start as I began the uphill trek home with a full paper bag in the curve of each arm; but the fare was a nickel and I was well able to walk, as Herbert was to walk the mile and a half between home and Durfee, and the two miles downtown to and from the Providence bus or his evening classes.

While he was with his debaters and on Saturday afternoons I was with my Camp Fire girls. I first served as Guardian for one group and later for two, each composed of fifteen Durfee students. Our separate activities combined very well. Each of my groups had an evening meeting every other week, we joined for hikes and cookouts on Saturday, and some of the girls came to my house after school nearly every day to get help with their handwork, to report progress toward advancement in Camp Fire, to rehearse for a program, or just to talk. I had great satisfaction in feeling I was continuing a part of what Mrs. Gray had done for me at Berwick Academy, and I had good times with those girls — Dorothy Guillotte, Shirley Ashton, Ida Cohen, Hazel Miller, Ruth and Grace Turner, Gilda Pacheco, and many others. They ranged in age from fourteen to eighteen and I was twenty-one; some of them were my closest friends that first year in Fall River.

Most, I believe all, of Herbert's professional associates were considerably older than he, and those I knew best had wives at least ten years my senior. These couples were established; had their own furniture if not their own homes; had school-age children; had cars which occasionally they could afford to use for pleasure, and some of them took us for a ride now and then — in the evening to see the Fall River or Boston boat go through the canal, on a Sunday to the Cape.

The unvarying social recreation of our friends on the Durfee faculty was for each couple (unless they were invited out) to invite in weekly another couple on Friday or

Saturday evening to play whist or bridge. There was always a little dish of hard candy or salted peanuts on the card table, and about ten thirty, as the game ended, the hostess served refreshments before her guests went home; sometimes cookies and punch, sometimes small sandwiches and coffee, sometimes creamed shrimp or salmon or Welsh rarebit on crackers with hot chocolate. I enjoyed the candy and peanuts, but I was poor at cards and had great difficulty keeping my mind on them, especially when we were out and I was wondering what the refreshments would be.

I was the junior member at these gatherings and seen and treated so; more junior there than I was senior at Camp Fire. I also entertained unmarried women teachers at tea and joined the local chapter of the Association of University Women, striving to be a good faculty wife; and at AAUW I met the wives of two young lawyers. These two couples, the Bogles and the Fullers, became our contemporary friends. We played bridge, picnicked, and went to Brockton Fair with the Bogles, had long hours of book talk with the Fullers.

And we were saving money and poring over catalogs with the intention of making sure that Herbert could add to his graduate credits during the summer. Having begun his work at Brown with the intention of becoming a school administrator, he was now veering toward the philosophy and psychology of education and we knew that in this field a master's degree would not be enough. He must eventually have his doctorate.

The other reason why we were not discouraged by the steady return of the manuscripts into which we put so much time and energy was that we had never expected instant recognition and success. The faint possibility danced before us like a mischievous star, but while we waited for the barely conceivable miracle of catching it we were content that I was writing what I wanted to write, in exciting variety, that Herbert's beautiful typed copies of what I wrote were traveling to New York, Boston, Philadelphia, and Chicago, and human hands at least took them from the envelopes and returned them for us to send out again. Not only that, but they enclosed slips. *We regret that the material you have sent us does not meet our present needs . . . The manuscript we are returning has had a careful reading but our editors do not feel justified in giving it space in the magazine . . . We have read this story with interest, but are at present overstocked with fiction. If in the future you have another manuscript you would like to submit for consideration, we should be glad to have you do so.* The very wording of the rejection brought us degrees of reward, and if the latter slip was printed under the letterhead of the magazine and had "The Editors" apparently written in ink below we felt we were almost on the threshold of Something Big. Magazines which made prompt returns rated high with us, the *Post* and the *Journal* at the top; they never kept a manuscript more than four days.

Then in the course of the fall other things began to happen.

In early November a stock company opened for the season in Fall River, to give a different play each week. To publicize the opening a prize was offered for the best review of their first play if left at the box office in an envelope with two ticket stubs. A professional play! A prize for a review of it! I had to be there. The following week I received two tickets to the second week's play. They were for a specific evening. If this was a consolation prize, I thought, I was fully consoled. We were going to see another play free!

At intermission it was announced that I had been awarded the prize and I was called to the stage to receive it. The prize was a check for ten dollars. I was delighted, of course, but would have suspected mine of being the only legible entry if it had not also been announced that honorable mention went to the Durfee dramatics coach.

I wrote home about it and wish I had now my mother's reply. She kept my next letter in which I said, "You never fail me . . . You said all the things I most wanted to hear from you. You knew I'd want to know not only of your happiness but that papa was interested, and to have the little pictures you drew of people who can't know . . . I only hope something will come of it — some chance to act or direct or review regularly . . . Herbert sent a note about it to the Bates alumni secretary (as we are asked to do, you know, when anything special happens to us) and yesterday I had a note from his secretary, congratulating me and asking if I am doing any other writing. How I wish I could place a story before long so we could tell them of that as proof I really am working! . . ."

In my next letter home I wrote, "Wednesday evening I sewed with Mrs. Giduz while our husbands were at night school. She spoke about that prize and asked if I wrote much, so I told her how interested in it I am. Then I found out that she was a college friend of Fannie Hurst (the short story writer who got that $200,000 prize — remember our reading about it while I was home this summer?). Mrs. Giduz took courses at Radcliffe in criticism of modern literature, and she has asked to see some of my manuscripts. I'm sure her advice will be very helpful and I am certainly going to avail myself of it . . . Mama, could you send me the rest of my Camp Fire things, *especially* my black serge bloomers for hiking? . . ."

We learned from the *Author and Journalist* that while there were few "quality" magazines to which to send the stories I carved out with joy and care, popular magazines occasionally accepted "quality" stories; there were many publications besides those on our newsstands publishing material similar to theirs; and *St. Nicholas, Youth's Companion, American Boy* and *American Girl* were not the only magazines carrying stories for children and the high school age.

There were *The Household Magazine* in Topeka, Kansas, *The Farmer's Wife* in St. Paul, Minnesota, *Woman's World*, *Modern Priscilla*, *Modern Homemaking*, *Holland's*, *The Christian Herald*, *Gentlewoman* publishing fiction about women, especially country and small-town women; and there were, it seemed, countless church publications seeking material suited to their magazines and story papers for children and young people. We gradually added all these addresses to our active list. We now kept a card file. For each story I printed a card (having learned quite elegant hand printing from my father the sign painter and my brother the draftsman) with, under the title, a column for the name of each magazine to which it was sent, one for the date of the sending, one for date of return, and one for the result. The "results" column was all blank until mid-December.

We had gone home for Thanksgiving. We were totally unexpected, as we had no money for unnecessary travel and were saving for Christmas when I regarded it as necessary that we should go home. But Herbert came in early from school on Wednesday with the news that the Chattos were leaving almost at once to drive to Maine and if we were ready when they came along we could ride with them as far as Dover and return with them to Fall River Sunday afternoon. We were ready.

In Dover the Chattos inquired where we were being met. We asked them to drop us off on the upper Square where we could take a bus to South Berwick. They did not know where my parents lived in South Berwick. Though there was now a telephone at home I had not called, both for lack of time and because my mother would insist on meeting us, though as far as we knew she had never driven with the car lights turned on. When the bus reached the village it was midnight. We walked the five miles past the Soldiers Monument and the two cemeteries, through Old Swamps, across the Junction Bridge, up and down Goodwin's Hill, past the end of Witchtrot Road and Number Ten Schoolhouse, past Nason's Eddy, across White's Marsh Bridge and up the lane.

Small suitcases in the skim of snow at our feet, we stood under the bedroom windows and I called, "Mama! Papa! . . . MAMA! We're home!" I can still hear my mother's sleepy, incredulous voice exclaiming, "Why, — that's Gladie!"

We had Thanksgiving Day . . . Friday . . . Saturday . . . And most of Sunday.

There was a mail slot beside our front door in the house on Hanover Street and when we opened the door late Sunday night the small hall space at the foot of the stairs was so littered with brown paper envelopes that we had to scoop them up like armfuls of firewood before we could get into the living room. While Herbert hurried downstairs to start the coal furnace, I opened the envelopes and extracted the slips which we studied and evaluated before we went to bed. The next night all the stories were ready to be taken back to the mailbox.

In mid-December a returning story brought with it a letter.

The
Farmer's Wife
Webb Publishing Company, Publishers
Saint Paul, Minnesota

A Magazine
for Farm Women
D. A. WALLACE, DIRECTING EDITOR
ADA MELVILLE SHAW, MANAGING EDITOR

December 11, 1925

Mrs. Herbert A. Carroll,
407 Hanover St.,
Fall River, Mass.

Dear Mrs. Carroll:

I am sorry that I must return your bright little story, *Of Course, Not Doug*. It is somewhat too slight in its bearing for our use. Sometime when you have another story which you think might suit us, we shall be glad to see it.

Very truly yours,
(signed) *Ada Melville Shaw*

When Herbert came home in the late afternoon I was wearing my wedding dress (no sweeping white gown with veil and orange blossoms but an embroidered powder blue crepe with a wide band of powder blue cashmere at the hem; this had become my going-away suit when I changed a white hat, scarf, gloves, and pumps for gray ones and added a matching cashmere coat to complete the "ensemble"). He blinked and asked, "What's this? Are we going out?"

I said, "No, but we're going to eat well. I've made an apple pie and there is a casserole in the oven. We're celebrating. Look what came in today's mail!"

That was the night we began our Red Letter Calendar, a kind of diary of Great-Days-in-our-Careers. The date of a Great Day would be typed in red, and a one line statement of the event would be added in black. "LETTER from the *Farmer's Wife* on *Of Course, Not Doug*." And in our file, on Doug's card, the result was entered: —LETTER. We also set up a program wherein, if another letter should come when Herbert was away, he would know what had happened as soon as he saw me because I would be in my wedding dress, *sitting down*. The significance of my sitting down was that someday some editor might accept one of the stories for publication. In that case, I would be in my wedding dress *standing up* when he came home! The dress now symbolized not only our marriage, but my part in what our partnership was enabling us to do.

I wrote to my mother that night, promising to bring Mrs. Shaw's letter when we came for Christmas.

That vacation was packed with excitement. We left Fall

River by train late on a Friday afternoon, carrying two suitcases filled with gifts, clothing, and manuscript, and Herbert's little old portable typewriter. In North Station in Boston we put the typewriter into a large (twenty-five cent) metal locker, transferred pajamas and toothbrushes to the battered typewriter case, pushed our suitcases into the locker, stowed away the locker key safely, and walked up the street. It seemed dark to me despite the street lights, and it was icy cold. At the first hotel sign we came to we went in and asked for a room. That is, Herbert asked for a room. I stayed well back. I had never been in a strange city at night before. Neither of us had ever stayed in a hotel before. And we came close to not staying in one that night. He was allowed to register, but the clerk looked with suspicion at what he had written, then asked where our luggage was. When told it was at the railroad station as we had brought with us only what we could put into the typewriter case, he asked to see our marriage certificate. It had never occurred to us to carry that about. In fact, we had found it rather embarrassing even to keep. It was inscribed in a booklet with flowers on the cover and several pages of illustrated prayers and inspirational poems. Herbert had to admit he did not have it with him. The clerk said, "With a wife as young as yours, you should never be without it. At least, when you want a hotel room." Herbert said, "She is twenty-one." The clerk shook his head and said, "Doesn't look it." I can imagine now that what I looked by then was aghast and insulted as well as young. When the clerk finally said he would take a chance on us, I was all in favor of leaving at once in what I intended to be high dudgeon, but Herbert sensibly reminded me that the night would be long on a North Station bench and I gave in. I still like to think that my incipient high dudgeon was what convinced the clerk that the chance he was taking was not great.

We stopped there only long enough to leave the typewriter case in the room, then went out for supper in a cafeteria and on to rear balcony seats for *No, No, Nanette*, the first production with its original cast that I had ever seen. I was entranced, and when it was over Herbert bought me the sheet music, on sale in the lobby, for "I Want To Be Happy" and "Tea for Two."

The next morning early we went back to North Station, repacked, and took a train for Salmon Falls. There was now too much snow and ice for my mother to get the car out. My father and Pony met us. At home he had set up in the parlor the tree he had cut on Long Hill, and we decorated it with strung popcorn and cranberries as always, but also with tinsel and bright bells my mother had bought. Mrs. Shaw's letter was nearly worn through, and everyone — including Harold and Jennie who came for Christmas Day — agreed that the most important part of it was ". . . when you have another story . . . we shall be glad to see it." I played "I Want to Be Happy" and "Tea for Two" over and over, and read my stories aloud to my mother and Grammy in the sitting room while Herbert sat by, glowing with approval of them, and my father lay on the kitchen couch. And while my mother and I cooked and did dishes, Herbert typed on the last stories I had finished. The House was filled with the heat of wood fires, the light of oil lamps, the smell of spruce, the steady nourishment of unquestioned love and faith, and the yeast of hope.

The night we returned to Fall River the little house behind the dog kennel was freezing cold, and there was a message from the landlord.

YOU HAVE NO WATER. YOU LET THE FURNACE GO OUT AND THE PIPES FROZE AND BURST. DON'T START THE FURNACE.

We lighted the gas stove on the porch and opened the

small mountain of manila envelopes which had accumulated. All slips.

It was three days before new pipes had been installed and we could start the furnace and run water. Then we owed the landlord some forty dollars in addition to the rent. But we had learned that fires go out unless someone tends them, and that when fires go out in winter weather, in houses which have plumbing, water freezes and pipes burst.

I wrote my mother:

. . . Mrs. Mullen (the landlord's wife) was worried about us. I guess she thought we couldn't get anything to eat for she kept sending over such things as hot rolls she had just taken out of the oven. It was lovely of her but we were comfortable and have had plenty to eat. Our eggs don't seem to have changed a bit, even though they did freeze . . . The hall was flooded with mail, including a cut-glass bud vase from Ruth Marsh — crushed into a thousand pieces! All the stories came back. I'm steaming ahead on the next one I want to send to Mrs. Shaw; "One of My Wayside Fires," about an old lady . . . We had our Camp Fire meeting at Shirley Ashton's to make the books in which we're going to paste poems and anecdotes to distribute to hospitals; also decided to give a play. I wish you could see the Ashton house. It is brand new, with set tubs, electric washer, breakfast nook, glass doors between the dining and living rooms, big square piano and huge fireplace, three bedrooms and a bath with the tub set into the floor so it doesn't have to be cleaned under. Mrs. Ashton served us ginger ale, cheese chips, and brownies. I was just putting on my hat to go home when Mr. Ashton opened the back door, coming back from his office. Mrs. Ashton snatched off my hat and said, "Stand right there a minute." When he came in she said, "Dear, tell me how old you think she is." He looked from me to the others and back to me and said, "Oh — sixteen?" She laughed and said, "This is *Mrs.* Carroll, the Camp Fire Guardian, and a college graduate." Maybe I shouldn't keep on being so mad at that hotel clerk in Boston . . .

In the course of January I wrote her:

". . . . This morning I hurried through the cleaning up, did my ironing, and was writing by 10:00. I had an idea and could hardly wait to get it down. Wrote steadily until after 2:00 and finished the story I started day before yesterday! It has John Henry Earle and Dr. Ross in it. I can imagine you all laugh at these lists of characters I send you, but they really come out all right combined on paper . . . I'm going to fricassee some meat for supper. My fricassees taste more like yours than anything else I make . . . Tonight Herbert is typing the last story I did before this. He thinks it is the best I have done yet and I guess I think so myself but I doubt if you would. It isn't gentle and homelike but pretty wild and tragic — I cried writing it . . . Yesterday I went over to the beauty shop on the corner and had my hair cut and shampooed. It feels like satin this morning. I'm going to try to have it done oftener . . . Saturday morning I finished "The Eclipse" (about 6000 words) and in the afternoon Herbert typed part of it. That evening we went over to play cards with the Cooks and while we played we listened to a Harvard-Yale debate by radio. They said that that night when we were home and heard McCormack sing they tried to get him but he just kept fading away. Their loudspeaker is built into the base of a floor lamp with electric lights at the top and a silk shade with fringe. It is pretty but I think maybe it muffles the sound. Or maybe battery sets like yours are better. . . . For the first time I'm writing a story I don't like at all. It's silly. The name of it is "His Wife's Position." Doesn't that sound enough like Charles Garvice or Laura Jean Libbey to be salable? We're running out of stamp money . . . My paper flowers came yesterday and they are perfectly lovely. I don't see how in the world you can make them look so real. I was glad I had just cleaned my kitchen. I put the yellow flowers in a yellow vase on the white breakfast cloth and they are like a spot of sunshine. I love my kitchen. We stood in the doorway tonight after we had finished the dishes and turned out the light and looked back at it by the light from the dining room. A storybook room with the table set for breakfast and the dishes gleaming through the glass doors of the cupboard! I keep having fears that the Mullen son and his family will suddenly decide to come back.

In February:

I just read a joke I like. In a courtroom: — *First man*: Judge, this feller owes me eight dollars for groceries. *Second man:* — It's not so, Your Honor. I never touched his dog. *Judge:* — Well, there's reason on both sides but she's your mother and you must take care of her . . . Yesterday my Doug story came back from *Christian Endeavor World* with a personal letter. That makes five personal letters I've had from four different magazines. Durfee students are writing radio plays and the best one will be broadcast by the Fall River station. I'm one of the three judges. One of the others is a Mrs. Lincoln who has a daughter Victoria at Radcliffe. Mrs. L. says Vicki likes to write. Isn't South Berwick progressive to have a snowmobile clearing the roads in the back part of town to keep them open for autos? You won't have those worries any more about what if anybody should need the doctor. I always thought it was wonderful to be blocked in at home, but you would say, "I hope nobody'll get sick" . . . Our next vacation begins three weeks from tomorrow. What do you really think about our coming home? I know company is trouble in the country in winter, even when they're not company but *are* extra people. We want to do just what will be best for all of you. You could never hurt our feelings. Tell us what you truly think . . . No school Friday and only two car lines running in the city because of snow-piled streets. It is a funny situation here, for they have only one snowplow which is the reason why we are blocked up so long, and there is no sidewalk plow at all. People are supposed to shovel the sidewalk in front of their property, so some shovel the whole width of the walk down to the concrete, and throw the snow into the street, others just make a sheep path, and where a house is unoccupied nothing is done. Everybody stands around helplessly and looks at it . . . Such a day as this has been! When we woke up this morning we couldn't see to the street for the whirling snow. All car lines are closed down and of course there was no school, but Herbert couldn't have gone anyway as he has a heavy cold in his chest. I went to the drugstore for medicine for him as early as I thought it would be open, and had to wade to my knees most of the way. I really don't think it is so much that there is a dreadful amount of snow as that Massachusetts could learn a lot from Maine about how to handle it, with or without snowmobiles . . . Such a sight as the snow is! I never saw it like this before — just stacks of dirt. I hate to think what we are breathing if all that and more is in the air . . . *I* have a new dress! I love it, and think you will when you see it. It is black georgette crepe with cut steel trimming and a silver leaf and flower on the shoulder. I have a black crepe de chine slip to go with it. It's for spring, of course, and makes me look very grown-up. I'll have a close metal hat, silver gray stockings and black patent leather pumps with silver buckles to wear with it . . . Mrs. Shaw kept "One of My Wayside Fires" so long at *The Farmer's Wife* that we really began to think she might take it, but it came back yesterday. She said it has an interesting slant but she doesn't think it "comes up" to their requirements. Last night when the Giduzes were here Mr. Giduz asked me if I would consider tutoring in French. He said he could send me all the students I would take. I was quite excited about it but Herbert doesn't want me to spare the time from writing. I don't know how he keeps his confidence when I haven't sold a thing, but he says he expects to get good interest on what he is investing. I finished a story yesterday (over 7000 words) and like it the best of anything I've done but have no idea it will ever be published . . . I had to stop to get an early supper and hurry off to our Camp Fire Valentine Ball.

We did go home for the March vacation, after which I wrote my mother:

You remember the debate Herbert was getting ready for while we were there? The one for the Men's Club at the church, Mr. Chatto and him against two lawyers? The audience voted on the merits of the question, not on debating skill, which was lucky for the lawyers! Practically all the men on the Durfee faculty and most of the lawyers in the city were there and ever so many from both professions said if there had been judges as to the debate the decision would have been unanimous for Chatto and Carroll. Mr. Seagraves, the oldest and most prominent Fall River lawyer, told Herbert his was "a masterly presentation." I stayed with Mrs. Giduz while our husbands were at the debate and read "John Crag" and "Louisa" to her. She said "John Crag" was very artistic but would be accepted only by one of the top literary magazines. She loved "Louisa" and is positive I'll place it — which is more than I am . . . Yesterday afternoon I wore my new dress to College Club. I met Mrs. Belisle, the superintendent's wife, and she asked me to sit with her during the program. She is delightful. The speaker was Bertrand K. Hart, literary editor of the Providence *Journal.* He talked on "What Everybody Is Reading," and I had read them all so was much interested in his comments. . . . I'm trying to get the house cleaned before Nellie Mae comes. The upstairs is finished (all white and smelling of Fels Naptha) and I'll start downstairs today. This afternoon my Camp Fire girls are giving a program at the Home for the Aged. I'm going to read something from Booth Tarkington. If Jennie goes to Washington, couldn't you get Harold to drive you up here the weekend she's away? I don't know just where we'd put him but we'd find a place. We'd love to see you both; better still, *all* . . . Everything has been cleaned through to the kitchen. I've washed all my yellow-and-white checked curtains. I soaked them in salted water, washed in Ivory, rinsed them twice, hung them in the shade, and they dried quick, — still the color ran! Not too bad, though. The hogshead cheese you sent is simply delicious. I don't know when anything has tasted so good to me . . . Monday night my Camp Fire girls put on an initiation banquet for the new members. . . . I *must* find another Guardian soon, for all the groups are now too big. . . . Nellie Mae came Friday to stay a week so was here to go to church with us Easter Sunday. . . . I had my wedding suit cleaned, shortened, and pressed. No, I didn't get a new hat. Sunday night Wally Fairbanks, Bates '24, now a buyer at Cherry and Webb's, called up and said Bernice Mayhew (my class) was coming in on the New York boat at 5:00 A.M. and he was going to meet her and bring her up here. So we all rose and shone before 5:00 and I had a big breakfast ready. It was lovely to see her but she had to leave in the afternoon to go home to the Vineyard.

Then APRIL:

No story checks yet so you hold right onto that surprise, whatever it is. But a letter came yesterday which made us happy. "John Crag," you know, has been drifting around *Century* and *Harper's* but a week ago we sent him to *Country Gentleman*, and yesterday a letter came from the editor saying they had all enjoyed reading it and he wished they could publish it, but he was afraid it was "too fragile" for his subscribers. I care far more about recognition for "John Crag" than for any of the others, because, you know, he is Grandpa. *Country Gentleman* is published by the same company as *Saturday Evening Post* which I read gets 1200 stories submitted each week, buys six, and writes letters on twelve. We played tennis all afternoon and my nose and the back of my neck are sunburned! . . . WELL — were you really surprised when I called you? I was so excited while I was waiting to get through! Wasn't it good to hear each other's voices? And it cost just forty cents! Did I tell you *which* story I had sold? It was "Of Course, Not Doug," the one Mrs. Shaw at *Farmer's Wife* wrote my first letter on — the one about the bride who lived with her husband's family and they didn't like her because she wasn't as athletic as they were but then she got a prize for a story she had written and they began to see there was something else in the world beside athletics. *Our Young People* is the name of the magazine that bought it. It is a Southern Methodist publication in Nashville, Tennessee. This was the first story I had ever sent there, and the associate editor, Mr. Edwin B. Chappell, Jr., sent me $25.00, saying they couldn't pay me as much as they "believed it to be worth" and "I shall be delighted if you care to submit additional manuscripts." (Do I ever care to!) You can imagine the day I had yesterday. The mailman brought this thin, *thin* envelope postmarked Nashville, Tenn. about 9:00 A.M. I opened it, stared at the check, read the letter, and had to do setting-up exercises to get my breath back. Then I called Mrs. Giduz and she rejoiced with me as if we were going to divide the profits! I had planned to start a new story but I just couldn't. I washed and I cleaned and nothing seemed to take any time. I thought Herbert would never get here, and when he did you can imagine how delighted he was! . . . I started my new story this morning and Herbert thinks it is going to be my best — but he always thinks that . . . I'm going to keep this letter to remind me of how pleased you all were by my first acceptance. I'll need it, especially if the first is the last. I'm sorry the news kept you awake. Mrs. Giduz says she slept better that night than she has for weeks because every time she woke up she thought, "Gladys has really sold a story just as I said she would," and that made her feel so good she went right back to sleep. I have to admit it didn't affect Herbert and me that way. I'm glad you told me what papa said. I wondered if it would really please him. We got a letter from the *Christian Herald* on "Old Lady" ("One of My Wayside Fires") yesterday. Before we send her out again I'm going to make quite a few changes and then Herbert will retype it. We think it is worth the trouble because she has been out nine times and brought five letters. I have about 1500 words done on the new story and I think the title is going to be "So Clyde Was Born." But I won't get much farther this week as this is Thursday and Bernice is coming from the Islands to spend the weekend and Monday. Wally will meet her at the train late tomorrow afternoon and will stay for dinner and the evening.

The surprise from my parents, in honor of my selling "Of Course, Not Doug," was a brand-new Corona portable.

So you and papa are really coming to see us at last! It seems almost too good to be true. Now you will get Grammy all settled a day or two before you start out, won't you? If she can't go until Thursday, you wait until Saturday. Because if you get here too worn out to enjoy yourself, I'll never forgive you. I want you to get started comfortably and have a nice trip. Remember, to cross Boston, just allow plenty of time and follow the signs in North Station to the elevated for South Station, which will be the *fourth* stop. Tell us soon just what connections you plan to make and I'll be on the platform whenever your train pulls into Fall River. Oh, I can hardly wait!

The crab-apple tree was in full bloom while they were there. My mother cooked all my favorite dishes. I played accompaniments for her to sing. They went with me to the little shops on New Boston Road and at the drugstore bought me a framed Maxfield Parrish print I had coveted all winter to hang above the piano. We climbed The Hill by day to see the houses which looked to us like mansions, each surrounded by gardens just coming into flower, and by night to look off at the city lights. Herbert took us on a tour of Durfee on a Saturday, and they came with me to a Camp Fire meeting, and they met our faculty friends who were halfway between their age and mine. We told them our plans for the summer. Because Herbert needed to take courses for which he would be credited at Brown and which thus would hasten the achievement of his master's degree and because I had fought homesickness all the year, we had decided that he must go to summer school and the summer school must be Bates where I would write industriously while he studied and hopefully sell more stories to help with the expenses.

They had hardly left to go home when our landlord knocked at my door with the news I had been dreading. Could we make other living arrangements at the end of this school year? His son who had once lived in our cottage was not returning with his growing family but a younger son had just been married and would like to move into it. I had difficulty keeping back the tears until Mr. Mullen left and I shed some every day from then until we returned the key to him. Only the knowledge that we were soon going home for a few weeks, then on to the campus I loved, and later home again for two weeks made the search for a new home bearable.

But the one we found was the setting of an unread fairy tale.

Once upon a time there was this old mill town where workers lived in the valley and the nobility had castles on the hill. These castles were built quite close together but separated from one another by spacious grounds, each castle and its grounds surrounded by a twelve-foot-high wall of beautiful blocks of granite. Within these walls the lords and ladies lived and entertained their neighbors, nannys pushed prams, governesses taught their charges, cooks used French recipes, upstairs and downstairs maids ran about in uniform, brides swept down the broad staircases to be married in the drawing rooms. But as the years went on the number of workers grew and they began to advance, the nobility to withdraw with dignity to a yet higher hill where they built new castles of modern design with modern equipment. Gradually the workers moved into the old castles and, since they had no experience with or desire for isolation, most of the walls were taken down and the beautiful granite crushed for street paving.

But on High Street, almost directly across the street from Durfee High School, in the late spring of 1926, one old castle remained with wall intact. Its owner, who had a men's store in the valley, lived on the first floor with his mother, his wife, and two little boys. They had the grand entrance, the drawing rooms, the vast dining room, the library, the serving room, and the huge kitchen with the castle stove which was of iron, set flat on the floor, and larger than any room in our cottage; but they had no uniformed maids or other help. The lady of the house was maid and cook, the grandmother the nanny and governess. They had rented the third floor to a family of three — its billiard room, tower room, fireplaces, view of Buzzard's Bay and all; but the second floor, having lately been made into two furnished apartments of equal size, a front one and a back one, each with three large, very high-ceilinged rooms and a bath of rose-pink tile, was just then advertised for rental for the first time.

We answered the advertisement.

The front apartment was exactly like the back apartment inside except that in the front apartment one had to cross the back hall to get to the kitchen. The back apartment looked out on a neighboring house, while the front apartment had a bay window overlooking the walled-in garden where the first magnolia tree I had ever seen was in bloom.

The rent for the front apartment was five dollars a month more than that for the back apartment but I had to have that wall, that ragged garden, that magnolia tree. The owners were very kind. They agreed to let us leave our few lares and penates there for the summer at half rent so that we would have it to come to in the fall.

We said goodbye to the cottage and the crab-apple tree (I never saw its apples set on), mailed all the manuscripts at the corner of New Boston Road for the last time, left a forwarding address with our mailman, and went home.

On June 16 the editor of *Our Young People* wrote that my story "Playing the Skirt" centered too much around a dance hall to permit of its being used by the Southern Methodists. We sent them "The Eclipse" by return mail. On June 17 Eunice Chapin of *The Forum* was writing me that "So Clyde Was Born" had a great deal of merit but didn't quite come off. We sent her "The John Crag Lot" and sent "So Clyde Was Born" to *Harper's*. We also sent a new story, "May in the Garden" to *Torchbearer*, another Southern Methodist publication. It was a kind of checker game. On June 19 Mrs. Shaw at *The Farmer's Wife* wrote that she couldn't tell exactly how I had improved "One of My Wayside Fires," but that it read very well now and she was glad to have it. She enclosed a check for eighty dollars. We sent her "Playing the Skirt." On June 29 Mr. Chappell accepted "The Eclipse" for *Our Young People*, and on July 2, Rebecca Caudill of the *Torchbearer* returned "May in the Garden" as "somewhat too mature for our readers; we always try to keep in mind the girl of fifteen or sixteen years." We sent "French Voile and Moonlight" to him and "The Period of Grace Anne" to her, scattered the other manuscripts, and went to Bates where my mother forwarded the mail which had been forwarded from Fall River.

At Bates we had the same room which had been mine with Ruth in our freshman year, and took our meals at the Rand Hall dining room where I had been head waitress. The familiarity of my surroundings and relief from household duties brought me both relaxation and buoyancy. Herbert was carrying a heavy course load; I was writing morning, afternoon and evening in the cool basement stacks of Coram Library. One night I was so involved there that I was much surprised when the door opened and a librarian told me I had been locked in at closing time and was now being rescued since it had occurred to her that she had not seen me leaving.

Mr. Chappell took "French Voile and Moonlight." Mrs. Shaw returned "Playing the Skirt." Miss Chapin of the *Forum* returned "The John Crag Lot" commenting, "3200 words would do the trick as well as the 5200 and would relieve the monotony which is inevitable in your pointillistic style. I think you would improve the story by lightening this style. You have too many clipped phrases." I meditated long on her advice but thought only cutting was possible. Miss

Caudill returned "The Period of Grace Anne," saying the last two pages "fell flat"; but I liked the last two pages. I took the dance hall out of "Playing the Skirt" and we sent that to her. In August she took it. "So Clyde Was Born" came back from *Harper's* with a slip and we sent them "The John Crag Lot," freshly cut.

Meanwhile our recreations were walking (to the riverbank, to Pole Hill, to the crags of Mount David where we had so many memories of undergraduate days), playing tennis (Herbert was rapidly working his way to the top in the summer school tournament), and the course I was "auditing."

I had quickly become too excited by this course in American Literature to remain a good auditor. The instructor was Professor Wilmot B. Mitchell of Bowdoin and his was an ideal course to audit — for anyone who could keep silent — because he wrote his hour-long lectures in most excellent English and delivered them, along with significant selections from his favorite American authors, in as effective a manner as that of Charles Laughton, whose reading I did not hear until many years later. I found Professor Mitchell so delightful and so challenging that from the first class meeting I felt obliged to stop at his desk every day to discuss what he had said and to ask questions. By the end of the week he asked why I was not taking the course for credit, since I was so interested in it; and I explained why I could not use the time that summer to do assigned reading or write assigned papers, adding that I did not need credit as I had no wish for a graduate degree. He asked if I had a recently completed story he might take home to Brunswick to read over the weekend. I was back within ten minutes with "So Clyde Was Born" and "The John Crag Lot." The following Monday, after class, he talked to me about them with such glowing enthusiasm as too few college professors are capable of, even when given much more reason for it than I had given him, and told me he would accept a story written during the session as a substitute for any assigned paper, that he gathered I was quite familiar with the work of the best American writers and thus might have already met his reading requirements, and that I had a good chance of passing his examinations as a result of previous reading and attention to lectures. He added that I should make a habit of seeking credit in whatever I did, whether or not I succeeded in getting it. I happily stopped in at the registrar's office on my way to the basement of Coram.

In early October, beside my bay window overlooking the walled-in garden, I wrote Professor Mitchell that Lee Foster Hartman, associate editor of *Harper's*, had returned "The John Crag Lot" saying, "There is a lot to admire in the workmanship . . . I am sending the manuscript back to you but I wish to thank you very much for allowing us to see it and I very much want you to try us again. I am sure you can do acceptable stories for the Magazine."

I added:

Yesterday I went to the first of a series of lectures on Modern American Literature by an M.I.T. professor; an extension course. I think he is basically a Babbitt, modified oddly by his academic associations. He says, "These fellows who grew up in the rigor of the Middle West, tramped the Mississippi valley, and finally dropped out of journalism into poetry and fiction are the real contributors to American literature. The Thomas Bailey Aldriches [my question: — how many of them were there?] aped the English and contributed nothing." When he says this his lips go flat together between his cheeks and his eyebrows shoot out above them like an umbrella going up. He says, "I wonder if I can find a few lines here as an example of what I mean," then leafs through a book to a page that has been *turned down* all the time. He did read *Come Up from the Fields, Father* quite nicely, but then flipped the book toward the table which it missed and fell to the floor, crumpling its pages. Part of what I carried away from you to give to a professor of literature I plan to build some day is the way you held books in your hands, tenderly, appreciatively, somehow wistfully.

That was the fall Mr. Chatto had left Durfee for Springfield where he became head of the English department and later principal of Classical High School; and Herbert had replaced him as the Durfee debate coach, also reluctantly added an English class to his public speaking program.

That was the fall I came to know the Top Floor Family, they of the tower room which overlooked both the garden and Buzzard's Bay; the billiard room, the book-lined study, the sewing-bedroom which matched the rose-pink bath and was like the heart of a rose, the kitchen which had always the lingering fragrance of warm gingerbread or brownies, and the fireplaces in which flames always crackled; Mr. West the genealogist; Mrs. West, the favorite "cover girl" of Haskell Coffin, the artist, and the designer as well as the maker of gowns such as I had until then seen only in dreams; and their daughter Dorothea whom they called Dolly and who came home on vacations from Barnard where she went to tea dances and to operas, plays, and the symphony.

The way of life of the Wests was a symphony in itself to me, and Mrs. West took me into it, much as fairy godmothers change pumpkins into golden coaches and mice into horses. She seemed oblivious to everything but beauty and graciousness and as far as I could see nothing else approached her. Where she was, even time did not intrude. The sun found her first in the morning and left her last at night, giving way to a brighter fire, friends climbing the grand staircase to join her at the spread tea table within drawn shades which, if separated, revealed the lights of the Fall River boat floating at dock or drifting out toward New York where Dolly was. She was neither separated from anything she loved nor fastened to it. Her sitting at her sewing, exquisite fabrics eddying about her, in some way spread life into the very material she touched, and in the perfection of her features, figure, and coloring, the shining serenity of her expression, she *was* an inspired painting. Dressing to go out or to receive guests was a ballet, dignified in concept but completely free in execution. She walked downtown like a young queen to her carriage. She might finish a gown in the morning, go to the shops to select crepe de chine, velvet, and ribbon for another, be back in time to make gingerbread for lunch, pose for Mr. Haskell in the afternoon, and be reading by the fire, tea table set and kettle bubbling, when her friends came at five o'clock. It was, it appeared, the easiest thing in the world always to be busy but never to be hurried, or late, or tired, or irritable.

Everything that had ever happened to her — and a great deal had — was out of a charming, often exciting storybook. Her childhood in Jamestown, Rhode Island, her large family with a long and distinguished background, the early years of her married life when she and Mr. West traveled constantly with his father (who was an actor) and wherever about the country she unpacked a trunk became home, the years of Dolly's childhood and growing up . . . She talked of it effortlessly in a voice like music, using words and phrases which fascinated me, never repeating herself, while moving about the billiard table swiftly cutting with a hand as sure as it was graceful lengths of sheer wool or shimmering satin into pieces to be combined into princess-style dresses with bands of fur at wrists and hem, or tunics with georgette sleeves. Meantime Mr. West, back from the historical library, looked in to nod and smile, and went on to his study to add another name to one of his genealogical charts and go through the day's mail from people who hoped he knew or could find out where they had come from.

Each time I went to my kitchen or emerged from it; I passed the staircase which led to the third floor. One short, familiar flight to Never-Neverland. Whenever I did not climb it, I underwent a stern exercise in self-discipline.

Yet I usually completed two short stories a week and, of this accumulation, perhaps one of three I considered a serious adult effort; the other two were intended to capture the interest of girls under the age of fifteen or of young people not over twenty. The serious stories continued to bring me frequent letters, from Eunice Chapin and Edith Walton of *The Forum*, Lee Foster Hartman and Frederick L. Allen of *Harper's*, Dorothy Chamberlain, Mary Brown, and W. F. Bigelow of *Good Housekeeping*, Maxwell Aley of *Woman's Home Companion*. One of these stories, written during the summer and praised by Professor Mitchell, titled "The Flame that Was Jan," after winning kind words from *Harper's*, *Smart Set*, and *People's Home Journal*, was accepted by a periodical called *Tales of Temptation* of which I had never heard except in the *Author and Journalist* listing and of which I have never heard since. But its editor liked and published my story and paid forty dollars for it.

The juvenile stories, however, were becoming reliable. Submission of a manuscript almost invariably brought a letter — so many that I had to forego wearing my wedding dress to proclaim them — and with increasing frequency small checks were enclosed.

From Rebecca Caudill of *The Torchbearer* in Nashville:

I am enclosing check for $20.00 for "Right Inside." We rarely use two-part stories but I shall be glad to examine such a manuscript of yours . . . Mr. Chappell asks that I send you the enclosed check for $25.00 for "The Girl in the Blue Middy." May I have a story or two for my summer issues? How is "Whitefeathers" coming? . . . I am always sorry to return a story of yours because all of them are above the average and I am glad of the privilege of publishing them. This story itself is not too mature, but is written from a viewpoint too mature for girls of fifteen. It should contain more action and less philosophy . . . Although this check represents *Our Young People* as well as *The Torchbearer* I asked the privilege of mailing it to you so that I might tell you that I think "Riding Boots" the best mystery story that has ever been in our office . . . I am enclosing a check for "Kitten and Katten" and looking forward to another story from you in the very near future . . . "Brass Bound" is quite the best story you have sent *The Torchbearer*.

From Edwin B. Chappell, Jr. of *Our Young People* in Nashville:

"Fran, Alumna" has just come back from the artist. I have no doubt there are a great many readers who appreciate this type of story, for we have found that there are about as many adults as young people who read *Our Young People*. However, I don't like to make a practice of using material such as this. Our paper is intended for young men and women of college age . . . I liked your story "The Old Shaw Place" very much and am accepting it . . . Very frankly, I can't make heads or tails of your story "Whom Fairies Love." At a time when you have just written such a splendid one for *The Torchbearer* it is hard to accept anything from you but the very best.

Clearly I was getting a firm grasp on the attributes and interests of the *Torchbearer* fifteen-year-old, having pinned her down as some three years younger than the average fifteen-year-old in my Camp Fire groups, while Mr. Chappell chafed under my bewilderment as to what young men and women of college age liked to find in their church story papers.

Youth, a Unity publication in Kansas City, accepted and published "The Period of Grace Anne," flat conclusion notwithstanding, paying $30.00 for it.

I wrote Lee Foster Hartman of *Harper's*:

> I am always wishing I could tell you how much I appreciate your criticism, but writing freely to an editor is a difficult thing. I wish you were just Anybody. I could tell Anybody a great deal. For instance, how I spend much of my time writing for children. How, when I try to do something more ambitious, the story itself is the last to come and often doesn't come at all. How I try very hard to conceal the essential weakness, and almost hide it from myself, then smile — though I confess to disappointment — when you find it all the same. How when I then send it to the *Forum* and the *Woman's Home Companion*, Miss Chapin or Miss Morris or Miss Walton and Mr. Aley tell me the same thing. How I honestly think I am gradually getting a better grip, in my own mind at least, and how I thank you for it.
>
> But I can't tell you because you're an editor, and though we know editors don't publish stories as a return for gratitude expressed we are everlastingly afraid you will think we think you will.

He replied, "Never be timid with editors. We are a very ordinary breed, really."

We went home for Christmas. We came back and began rehearsing for a Durfee faculty play. Mrs. West made the dresses (one of monkeyskin crepe with matching lace and one of pale green roshanara) which I wore in the part of the ingenue, and after the final performance the cast was entertained at one of the new mansions on the Highest Hill. Its third floor was a ballroom and on a grand piano the literary editor of the *Providence Journal* played and sang "Pale Hands I Love," all the while looking adoringly at his wife, Philomena, whom it would have been easy for anyone to adore. The hostess, introducing me to her, told Philomena that I wrote and published children's stories, told me that Philomena reviewed children's books for the *Journal*. Philomena, dark eyes dancing, told me, "Get a children's book published. So I'll have a nice one to review." I said I wished I could.

Then in early May I had a letter from Rebecca Caudill of *The Torchbearer*, enclosing a program for a three-day conference at the Vanderbilt Hotel in New York City of church story paper editors and contributors throughout the country, with speakers from the editorial staffs of all the leading children's magazines, several newsstand magazines, and some publishing houses. She asked if it would be possible for me to come. Were I now to be asked to take off tomorrow night for a controversial assembly in South Africa I should not be one tenth so startled.

We were saving every penny for Herbert's summer school course, harboring a dream of going away out west to Chicago for him to study under Judd. I had never been in New York. I had never traveled alone outside the State of Maine, and rarely there. Of course I could not go. But Herbert said I *must* go.

Those wheels, still inexorably turning!

I wrote that night to a Bates classmate who had been one of my closest college friends and a fellow member of the Spofford Literary Club, enclosing the program. She was at Columbia University, studying for her master's in English. I asked her if she would still be in New York May 23–26, if by any chance there would be an empty cot in her dormitory I could use if I should come down, and if where she lived was anywhere near the Vanderbilt.

I consulted Mrs. West the next morning and Philomena Hart in the afternoon. That night I wrote home about the invitation, adding:

Now the question before the House is whether or not I shall go. Herbert says *yes*, very positively, quite loudly, and extremely often. Mrs. Hart says I would be a very foolish girl to pass up such an opportunity. Mrs. West says I simply must and she will do everything she can to help me. She has already cut out a dinner dress for me from a piece of blue crepe with raised satin figures that she and I chose at a remnant sale in the winter. She has it all basted and I'm trying to run up the side seams. But I *can't* let anything interfere with my plans for Herbert's study this summer, so however many dinner dresses I fumble over until I fall asleep, I haven't decided yet that I'll go. Besides, we're expecting Mrs. Carroll's visit any day — she has already postponed it twice — and I'm not sure how long she'll stay. I think the apartment looks nice, but I'm not putting up the kitchen curtains until the day I know she's coming because the gas makes them sticky in just a few days; and I'm also saving the white spread for when I make up our bed for her.

Three days later I wrote my mother:

We had a letter yesterday from Mrs. Carroll saying she has given up all plans for coming. I know she is disappointed, and so are we. And food! I could entertain the governor and his council nicely if they were to drop in this minute. When her letter came I was so sure she and Walter would be here for dinner that I had a pie shell baked, pineapple filling and egg whites for meringue in the refrigerator, and the ham even stuck with cloves. I had already made a chocolate layer cake and there was a double quantity of waffle batter on the ice. As soon as the letter came I began sending out S.O.S. calls and, if you will believe me, I couldn't find a single mouth to feed. Lewis had gone home, Bob and Margaret were dining in Providence, the Giduzes were sick, and so on and on. So Herbert and I have been eating steadily for two days and wonder what objection anyone can have to just peacefully starving . . . About New York? Well, I'm still not sure. I haven't heard from Cookie yet. But I keep on with the dinner dress!

Two days later:

Dearest Mother, Dad, and Grandmother,

It is beautiful of you to offer to help me, and I love you for wanting to, but I know you all have plenty of uses for your money and I think I can manage. Cookie writes that she will be thrilled to have me with her on such an errand and because it is examination time and some graduate students have already finished, she can get a room near hers for me. That will be a great saving and very pleasant. She will meet my train. Herbert will put me on it in Providence (we'll go down by bus) and seems she is going to get me off, so you mustn't worry about me. She says she will show me how to get to the hotel where the conference is. I'll leave here Sunday noon and can use her iron to press my dresses when I get there. The meetings begin Monday morning. I'll take my green roshanara, the monkeyskin (that's rose-beige heavy crepe), my new blue (it's almost finished) for dinners, and wear my black georgette to travel in. Absolutely the only clothes I need that I don't have and so must buy are evening slippers and a dark kimono. I know Mrs. West would help me make the kimono if I can get downtown for the material, but I shouldn't let her because she is getting ready to go to N.Y. herself — for Dorothea's Commencement . . . Oh, yes, I'd love it too if Herbert could go with me — that would be perfect — but it is impossible both because of expense and because my husband is a busy man. He not only will be doing his regular teaching while I'm gone but the Director of the Education Extension Field of Rhode Island who is also the head of the Education Dept. at Brown has to be away and has asked Herbert to take over his classes! He (Prof. Jacobs) told Herbert he was much interested in his trying out college teaching and said, "As of now, I would give you the highest recommendation I have ever given to any man who has studied under me." ALSO the last night before I get back Durfee is holding a banquet to honor the school's undefeated debate team — and YOU KNOW WHO COACHED IT! I'm really heartbroken to miss that. Why does everything keep coming at once? There are such fine boys on those teams, and Herbert is so proud of them. The ones I know best are Norman Macdonald, the captain, Eugene Belisle, son of the Superintendent of Schools, and probably the most brilliant one of them all, Judge Hanify's son Edward who is only a sophomore . . . Now I want to read to Herbert what I have written today. Yesterday I finished a 4200-word story for *Youth*, and now I'm doing John Crag over again.

It was raining hard when I left Providence. Pressed into the corner of a dusty red plush-covered seat, with my feet on my suitcase, smiling and waving at Herbert through the grimy day coach window, I saw him on the other side of a thick dark curtain of rain. I *felt* wheels turning beneath me, faster and faster, and was trundled off toward the Altogether Unknown, the World, the After-Bates-What which I had often tried to contemplate from the security of the campus but had found little time to think of since. How evil would it be? How good? How tempting? How strong its tentacles?

Somewhere in wet, green Connecticut, a boarding passenger took the seat beside me which I had carefully left completely empty, holding my hat, bag, and gloves in my lap. We had paid for only one ticket, hadn't we? One ticket, one seat.

My companion was a neatly dressed, middle-aged man. He smiled at me and opened his crisp newspaper. As he did so, his arm touched mine and remained there even when I drew as much closer as I could to the window. As he opened the paper to the inside pages he tipped it as if to get a better light from the window and rested the side of his hand on my knee. I counted to ten while gathering courage to look at him, to see if he was actually reading. While I counted he took over a third of the seat we had paid for. He was not reading. He was staring at the margin at the top of the paper. I found that evil was not difficult to recognize. I stood up, clutching hat, bag, and gloves, and with my foot pushed my suitcase a little toward the aisle. He did not move. There were his feet, knees, arms, hands, and newspaper filling the space between me and release from the intolerable. The space had to be cleared. I cleared it. First I kicked him. Then I rammed my suitcase through. Then, passing him, I stamped on his feet. Finally, from the aisle, I kicked him again and much harder, since I had room for a longer swing.

A few rows forward I found an empty aisle seat and

slipped into it. As I sat there, my relief was gradually transformed into triumph. I had seen evil, confronted it, and defeated it. I had not screamed. I had not panicked. I had not burst into tears. I had not made a sound. But I had left my mark on it and I had escaped.

A few minutes later the conductor in his blue uniform with brass buttons stopped beside me and asked, "Did that man bother you, miss?"

I said, "He certainly did."

The conductor nodded. "I've suspected him for quite a while, but nobody said anything and I couldn't be sure. I'm sorry, miss. I'll see to it he never sits with a young girl again on my train."

My triumph grew. I had saved not only myself but who knew how many others? As we rode on through Connecticut, questions occurred to me which were less inflating, indeed were downright deflating. Miss? I was Mrs. Young girl? I would be twenty-three years old next month. And I was wearing my black georgette! By the time the train stopped at 125th Street and pulled out again, and I had watched the rain falling on the crowded squalor of a vast area I had no idea was called Harlem, I was aware that on my first venture into the World I had within a few hours encountered not only evil but good, and that no amount of kicking, ramming, and stamping would be of much use to any girl, young or old, were there no officials to notice who was bothered by whom, to make a close guess as to in what way, and to use their authority to protect the innocent.

Leaving the train in Pennsylvania Station I joined the throng climbing a long stairway. Cookie had said she would be at the gate. Would I see a gate? Would I know it was a gate? The only gates I knew were garden gates of white pickets. What if I did not come to a gate? What if I did and she was not there?

She was there. Cookie, though a Maine girl, came from

Presque Isle in rich Aroostook County, and had visited New York even while we were in college. Now she had lived there nearly a year. When I saw her, I knew I had arrived. I had reached New York. I was in the heart of the World.

We crossed Fifth Avenue in a heavy downpour and went upstairs to Mary Elizabeth's Restaurant. Perhaps because of the rain it was not crowded and we were given a table by a window overlooking the Avenue. I sat looking out into foggy dusk where great balloons of light floated. I floated with them. Mary Elizabeth's featured East Indian menus. Cookie ordered curried shrimp with rice and a tossed salad. I said I would have the same. I had never tasted curry before, and found it delicious. Surely, I thought, this was a dream.

Later we rode up the avenue, crosstown, and up Riverside Drive on the top deck of a bus. I could not see the Hudson River but I knew it was beside me. We got off at 116th Street and ran through the dark to a dormitory, arriving drenched. We talked; I met some of Cookie's friends. When I finally lay alone in a room near hers, listening to the rain and looking at the reflections of streetlights on the wall, I was still floating, still in a kind of dream. I was going to sleep — if I was not already asleep — on Morningside Heights in New York City.

It rained every minute of every hour, day and night, while I was there. New York was a city of warm silver rain with pockets of light in which people and Arabian Nights interiors appeared suddenly and sooner or later slowly vanished, drifting quietly back into the mist.

Cookie had said she had Monday morning free and would go with me to show me the way to the Vanderbilt and how to get back from there. We walked over 116th to Amsterdam and took the subway. I had never been in a subway before. The train was a Trojan worm tunneling at tremendous speed through the dark earth, stopping now and then to spew out people and swallow more. The Vanderbilt was a mass of stone, but the conference room was a pocket of light with deep carpet, French sofas, gilt chairs, small glass-topped tables, the walls hung round with tapestries. People were talking animatedly in small groups or running about with armfuls of papers. I gave my name and showed my invitation at the entrance and asked if Cookie might stay a while with me, since she had said she would like to. Then we sat down in a corner and waited for the program to begin.

No detailed record remains of that Monday. In the letter written home on the Wednesday of the following week I said:

I had finished telling you about Monday, hadn't I? Herbert says that in my first letter I talked too much about the scenery and the places I went, not enough about the people I met and what they said about my work. Well, I'm sure I told you that as soon as they found out I was there Miss Caudill of the *Torchbearer* and Mr. Chappell of *Our Young People* came to speak to me, and I liked them both enormously, and they introduced me to ever so many others. I'm a little embarrassed to repeat what they said in the introductions, like "I want you to meet Mrs. Carroll, our star contributor" and "No, Mrs. Carroll isn't Southern but we claim her," and "We shall hold onto Mrs. Carroll as long as we can but we have a feeling she won't be writing juveniles long," and "We're always afraid when we get a story from Mrs. Carroll that it is the last she will send us." I *don't* know where they get those ideas! The funny part was that they kept saying they were amazed to find I was so young, and all the time I was thinking I could hardly believe they were the editors who had been writing to me, because *they* were so young!

I told you that Monday night Cookie and I went to the Walter Hampden Theater to see *Caponsacchi*, a play made from *The Ring and The Book*. Tremendous! Tuesday Cookie had an exam so I went downtown by myself, and Rebecca took me to lunch at Alice Foote MacDougall's Coffee House on 46th Street. What a delightful place! Like a terrace in, maybe, Venice; all the tables for two, lit with candles, and the dishes heavy earthenware and pottery. I went to New York expecting to be overwhelmed by the size and brilliance of everything and came away with the impression that it is dim and exquisite. I was so fascinated by the *detail.* I mean, I learned not to be afraid to look straight into things for fear they were an illusion or a sham.

At lunch Rebecca said she couldn't get over being amazed that there could be so technically sure a touch in the pen of so young a writer, and asked me what responses I had had from other magazines than the Nashville group. I told her about the letters from *Harper's* and *The Forum* and she seemed very pleased and said, "That is the place we are not only willing but eager to give you up to, because we are very proud of and ambitious for you." Wasn't that wonderful? I love those Nashville people.

There was a talk on "Writing for Girls" in the afternoon and that, and the discussion which followed, was very interesting and helpful. That night Mrs. West had invited Cookie and me to dinner at Brooks Hall with her and Dorothea. We had a very pleasant time. And then what? Well, you never could guess what we did Tuesday night! Where *your daughter* was Tuesday night! BEHIND THE FOOTLIGHTS ON BROADWAY, that's where! I was indeed, and that's the truth. Trust *me* not to miss anything when *I* go to New York!

This is how it happened. The week before I came Cookie had met Kenyon Nicholson at a Writers' Club, and his play *The Barker* is running at the Biltmore. She had quite a long talk with him, and he told her, if she was interested in backstage local color, to go down to the Biltmore early any night, with a friend, and say he had sent them to take part in the "mob scene." She was dying to go and so was I as soon as I heard of it. So down we went, were welcomed cordially, made up, costumed, provided with peanuts, and sent onstage three times as people going to the circus, coming out of it, and going again the next season. You know how I would love that! I tried hard to steal those scenes, but Walter Huston held right onto them. He is the Barker and a marvelous actor, but a very real person too. Off-stage he reminded me of Uncle Clarence and Len. Before the play began he played the piano and sang in some dark corner and we all stood around and sang with him just like we do at home when Len plays his jewsharp in the barn. Everybody there was so nice to us, showing and explaining everything, including how they make rain and thunder and lightning, and treating us as if we really had joined the cast. I've always thought show people must be special and now I'm sure of it. Probably what I liked best was the half hour we had with the leading lady, Claudette Colbert, in her dressing room before curtain time. She talked to us all the while she was making up, read us her telegrams — and she is so beautiful, but doesn't seem aware of it at all! She couldn't have been more at ease or made us feel more at ease if she had been Helen or Alice or Euterpe from our class at Bates.

Wednesday morning at the Vanderbilt I heard a Mr. Thomson from *St. Nicholas* talk on "The Changing Demands in Juvenile Literature." Then enter Dr. Myers who owns the Methodist Publishing House, and his wife, both of whom I had met briefly the day before, to invite me to lunch with them. I accepted with pleasure, whereupon they swiftly collected Mr. Mudge, editor of all their Cincinnati (Northern Methodist) publications, Mr. Moore, editor of *The Classmate*, one of their young people's magazines, and some other editor, and off we go into the rain. First to the Near East Relief Headquarters with which Mrs. Myers is closely connected, where I was shown gorgeous embroideries, basketries, and potteries, heaped high with pamphlets, and assured that any time I might be interested in writing about the Near East the whole headquarters would be at my disposal. Then to the Publishing House where I met countless editors and was given a sample of every paper they publish and that's not a few, and where we had lunch — just the six of us — in a private dining room adjoining Dr. Myer's office. By the time we taxied merrily back to the conference I was feeling like the Star Boarder. But the best was yet to come!

That was the last session of the conference and I had invited Miss Caudill to dinner afterward. Before we could leave there was everyone to say goodbye to, and several asked for my address and wrote it down in little black books. Mr. Chappell asked if I could have lunch with him on Thursday and I said I was sorry but my train for home left before lunchtime. Then could I come downtown early enough to meet him for a talk in the Vanderbilt lobby before I had to go to the train? I said of course I could.

I took Rebecca to Mary Elizabeth's which I had liked so much with Cookie. And it was *still* raining so again we had a table by the window. We stayed at least two hours and talked about a million things, but if she knew what Mr. Chappell wanted to talk to me about she wouldn't tell me. Most of all she was urging me to go to see Mr. Hartman at *Harper's* and Miss Walton and the others at *The Forum*, insisting that they would be "ten times" as interested in my work after meeting me; but I doubted that; besides I didn't have time. When we had to go, I felt as if I were parting with an old friend. She has never seen Boston but hopes to come there next year. If she does, she will visit me.

Then Thursday.

Well, Thursday —

As best I can put it into a nutshell, this is what Mr. Chappell said to me: "I want to be sure you understand the light you are regarded in in our offices. We knew as soon as your 'Doug' came in that here was a writer with promise, and we have been keenly interested in the steady improvement in what you have been submitting since. I can't tell you how delighted my whole staff would be to hear that your work was being accepted by a much better magazine than any of ours, even though it meant that we never got another contribution from you, because we are excited about your potential. We shall appreciate it greatly if you will keep us informed of your responses from the quality group and if there is ever any way we can help you we shall be very happy to do so. Please just don't run the risk of injuring our feeling for you by offering material we could use to some other publication just because its rates are a little higher. If you can improve your literary position at all, or your financial situation appreciably, by taking your time from us and giving it elsewhere, do it, with our very best wishes, and we shall stand behind you as long as you write and we are a company. In the meantime, we'll come as near as we possibly can to the rates anybody in our field will pay you. For instance, our usual payment for a nine-part serial is about $150, but we are replacing *Our Young People* with a new publication, *The High Road*, in the fall (sixteen large pages on better stock, with an attractive cover) and if you will have a serial in my office in time to start it off, I'll pay $250 for it."

Then what do you suppose he did? He asked if I would consider coming to Nashville as editor of *The High Road*!! Of course I had to tell him instantly that I couldn't possibly (but what fun it would be, working every day with him and Rebecca!). He said well anyhow he wanted to fill the new magazine as full as possible of my work, and if I wrote so much for it that my name was appearing too often, I could choose a pen name or several pen names. So it looks as if how much I can garner toward Herbert's Ph.D. depends on how hard I work, doesn't it? The interview ended with his reminding me I had promised him the serial and our shaking hands on it and liking each other very much.

From the time I got on my train at Grand Central until I saw Herbert on the platform in Providence I saw almost nothing, being completely absorbed in working out a serial idea. I got it, too, and the nine sections outlined! It was so wonderful to see Herbert — he never looked so dear to me — and we had so much to tell each other we were still up talking at 2:00 A.M. The debate banquet was a real triumph with everybody singing praises of the first undefeated team in Durfee history, and his boys gave him a beautiful copy of Lawrence of Arabia's *The Revolt in the Desert*. His classes at Brown went very well, and — maybe what pleased us both most — you remember that sophomore class in English he so reluctantly agreed to take last fall (because he doesn't feel properly qualified to teach English)? Last week the class brought a petition to the principal's office, signed by every one of them, asking that they all have him as an English teacher next year!

But before morning! You remember what used to happen to

me when I went to the Webbers' and had a marvelous time, and that summer we went to Uncle Than's, and when we came back from a week at the beach with Harold and Jennie? Well, the same thing happened again. I don't stand intense excitement a bit better than I ever did. I don't show that I'm excited — Herbert says that psychologically it would be far better for me if I did — but how can I show what I don't feel? I don't *feel* excited — but if it goes on more than a day, or two days at most, I'm headed for being violently sick. I couldn't get out of bed all day Friday or until around noon Saturday. I liked to die, as the old ones used to say. Nevertheless, by Sunday I had the serial synopsis ready for Herbert to type and we mailed it to Mr. Chappell. Monday I could hold up my head long enough to write to you; yesterday I wrote a thousand words on the serial, and plan to finish the first section today.

Oh, dear family, I am so lucky and so happy and what in the world would I ever have been without you?

The next day I wrote:

I finished the first installment of the serial at 11:15 last night despite a long call from Mrs. Rocklin (our landlady) in the morning, and have done half of the second today despite Herbert's being home part of the morning with a headache from eyestrain after study for his exams, and despite a visit with Margaret on her way back from the dentist's. Did I tell you that since I got home I've had a check for $22.50 from *The Torchbearer* for that story I wrote about Grandpa Brooks's house, and one for $50.00 from *Youth* for another story written since I was home, the one I called "And They Saw"?

These, together with the $250 I'll almost certainly get soon after I finish the serial (which at this rate won't be long) has convinced us that we can make our dream come true of going to the University of Chicago summer session for Herbert to study under an international authority in his field. It will be great for him, and of course seeing the West will be a valuable experience for me. It may be the best and perhaps only chance we'll ever have.

This will change our vacation plans. We expect now to leave Boston for Chicago on the Minute Man Saturday, June 18, so I'll come home the Thursday before for a little while with you, then meet Herbert in Boston Saturday, reach Chicago Sunday night, be there six weeks, come back by way of Rowe, to visit the Carrolls, and then be home until about September 10. Doesn't that sound good? Five whole weeks!

The morning of the Sunday I left for New York Captain Charles A. Lindbergh, having flown the Atlantic alone in a light, single-engine plane, was waking up at the American Embassy in Paris and getting into a borrowed suit to receive the huzzas of an enthusiastically admiring France. News of his achievement filled the newspaper my seatmate in Connecticut was not reading. But I saw no newspapers while in New York, had no contact with radio, and people attending the conference took no time for discussion of current events. However, news, while traveling far more slowly in those days than now, lingered longer. In the rotogravure section of the Boston Sunday *Herald* of June 5 there was a full-page picture of "Our American Boy in France with His Ambassador," and I studied it a long time before sending it home. They stood on the steps of the embassy, front center in a group of perhaps a dozen men whom I took to be embassy officials, and Ambassador Herrick like all the others except the young captain had his wide open right hand flung as high as he could reach. All, including Captain Lindbergh, wore boyish, ecstatic grins which I could not doubt reflected those in the crowd before them. That Lindbergh's flight was seen as a victory not only for but by all mankind and as a tremendous leap forward into a joyful future was clear. I noticed that apparently there had not been time, either before or after it was borrowed, to get the captain's suit pressed and that he was still wearing army boots.

I wrote home:

Is Grammy interested in Lindbergh? From the looks and ways of him I'm sure she must be. In case you haven't seen this picture, I'm enclosing it. Don't you think he looks like Robert? Someone said the government ought to send him flying around over the world, representing America. Ambassador Herrick seems to me a very dramatic figure, too, just now — such an old man who has probably been through more than anybody knows trying to improve our relations with France, and now this boy comes flying in and fixes everything with his "Which way to Paris?" and his grin. But Lindbergh looks as if he didn't for a minute think he had done it *all*, just put the capsheaf on it. And Mr. Herrick looks so proud, doesn't he? . . . Yesterday I finished Chapter Three — 9000 words in five days; a third done! Now along with the writing comes packing. We've planned it so that I can leave here very early Wednesday morning (a week from this coming Wed.) and if I make good connections will get to Salmon Falls about 10:00 A.M. Standard Time. Our telephone will be disconnected soon so if you should need to reach me quickly call Mrs. West at 6429-W. . . I knew you would think it was fine for us to be going to Chicago even though it is so far away. Think of all the states I'll see, and Niagara Falls, and maybe on the way home we'll come partway on a lake boat . . . Did I tell you about my hat? How there were merchandise prizes offered by one of the big department stores here for 150 words on "Why McWhirrs has grown in 50 years to be one of the leading stores in southern New England," and I sent in my tuppenceworth? Well, the day before I left for New York someone called up from the store to say I had won my choice of the $5.00 hats in stock. Of course I didn't have a minute to go downtown then, but now I've been and have a darling — pink — in that crocheted straw you can roll up and put in your suitcase. Perfect for this summer! . . . Last night I spent the evening with one of my Camp Fire girls, helping her with the delivery of her valedictory. I'm pretty proud that one of mine has the highest average among this year's 475 Durfee graduates. There are six seniors in our group and four of them are on the Honor Roll of the graduating class . . . The serial steams on. I'm now in the middle of the fifth chapter; just halfway through. Had a letter from Mr. Chappell yesterday, approving the outline. It was nice. I'll bring it home with me Wednesday — a week from today!!

On June 3 he had written:

I'm right proud of you, honestly. That outline reached Nashville on the same train that I did, and we came into the office together.

You have a good plot on which to work. Don't forget all the mothers who will read *The High Road*. There are a flock of them. But if you handle these situations as skillfully as I believe you can, there should be no trouble.

Do you think you can make this story interesting to a sixteen-year-old girl? I know you will say that in that case it should go to the *Torchbearer*, but let me explain. I saw Mr. Shepherd of *Collier's* again after I left you and he was most emphatic on one point. "Don't," he said, "put anything in your young people's paper that would make tough reading for a nineteen-year-old boy or girl. We never use anything in *Collier's* that a high school graduate of twenty or twenty-one could not catch immediately."

I want stories for *The High Road* that will appeal both to young folks and adults. Everybody (the *Forum* family excepted) will read any interesting fiction if it is written in clear, simple form. Pick out some girl acquaintance who is just averagely intelligent — if you have any like that — and ask yourself if she would appreciate and feel a lively interest in your story. *But without writing down to her.*

If you can write this story so that it makes a hit with girls as well as their mothers, I think I can place it with a New York publisher. He has already accepted two that I have sent him. I talked to him about you the other day and he said, "Tell her I want to bring that story out as a book for girls." So jump right on this serial, and you will be getting the check for it in Chicago.

Monday morning I wrote home:

See you day after tomorrow! You don't mind that these last letters are so short, do you? I just don't dare give time to them, much as I have to say and would like to. Besides, it's a fact that my writing muscles really are getting a little strained. They still have some way to go, though. I have just started the eighth chapter, and that means over 5000 words to do in the next two days — among other things.

Painters are going to redecorate our apartment this summer, so we have to lock up in two big closets everything we value. We did a good deal of it together yesterday, and packed our trunk as far as we could, so today is free for writing. Tomorrow we'll finish the trunk and my suitcase, as when I go to bed tomorrow night I'll have to be all ready for an early start. Yes, I'll bring copies of all my new stories.

Tuesday night I wrote Mr. Chappell:

Done. A serial. Nine parts. Typing has begun. And I'm off (via Maine) at 7:00 in the morning for the land of the gangster and the machine gun. I feel as if I had made a good-sized earth with several moons whirling around it, and the possibility of ever developing it into a universe (to make a book-length) seems far from me tonight. Nevertheless, if you like it, maybe I shall. Even the Lord had to rest.

I read and reread your letter and honestly tried to meet your manifold requirements, keeping in mind, whenever I could, average girls, average mothers, *The High Road*, the New York publisher, and Mr. Edwin B. Chappell, Jr., who always may say as he did once before, "Very frankly, I can't make heads or tails of your story." If you don't buy "Playmate House" we may not be able to get back to New England. The nice part about that would be that I'd be in the vicinity of your conference in Dayton next spring.

At 7:15 P.M. of June 18 I was writing home on a postcard:

All power to the Minute Man, but doesn't she sway! When

I try to wash up, the water *will not* stay in the bowl. I might be in the middle of the Atlantic . . . It was exciting going through the Hoosac Tunnel — smelled earthy. Now, in the near-twilight, the Berkshires are beautiful. Only wish you were with me. I can't tell you my feelings as I looked back at you from the train this morning.

At eight thirty the following morning, in Cleveland, Ohio:

We're having breakfast in the dining car. Herbert almost got left while mailing you a card in Albany last night. He just caught the last coach and had to walk the whole length of the train after it started. It seemed like an hour before I saw him. I was *sure* he had missed it! Even though a berth is pretty narrow for two people, it's fun sleeping on a train. No swaying in this country — somebody sat on it.

Pulling slowly into Chicago Union Station through the city's East Side we stared in disbelief at collapsing buildings crowded close together, leaning against one another as if in some desperate hope of support, and all as alive with people as we had ever seen a disturbed anthill with ants. People hanging out or taking in laundry on rooftops, people airing bedding from windows and leaning on the bedding to see what was going on below, people filling sagging porches, people sitting on broken steps and stairways as if on grand-stands, people playing games in the narrow streets, lying on sidewalks, eating, drinking, fighting, making love — all as far as the eye could see in every direction. In the late afternoon of a June Sunday they seemed to be living outdoors, and still must be gasping for air. What happened there when night came? What happened there in winter cold and storms?

We had traveled enough now to know that nobody lived near a railroad who could move away from its smoke and soot, away from the rumbling, snorting, whistling which country people loved to hear in the distance. But in Maine, between Boston and Providence, even in New York and all the way west, we had seen nothing like this.

In the station, while Herbert inquired at Travelers Aid for a clean, low-priced hotel near the university, I waited in a cloud of depression. What could be done for, with, in a world where so many had no clean beds, no stout walls against the wind, no stout roof against the rain and snow, no shade between them and the sun, no grass, no flowers, no *privacy*?

We were directed to the Del Prado on the Midway Plaisance and went there. It was three stories high, possibly four, and had a broad veranda all across the front, facing the green Midway. I stood there, thirsty for chlorophyll, while Herbert registered, and watched a few old women digging dandelions. Shortly after going to our room I was back to watch them until they left at dusk, walking slowly, carrying their baskets and pails. They worked as my grandmother and her sister had when gathering greens in the fields and woods at home, or when picking wild strawberries or low-bush blueberries, not daring to kneel for fear they could not get up again, bending from the waist. From behind them one saw only the broad hips in faded dark cotton skirts with hems which touched the ground cover. I wondered where they would clean their dandelions. At home we always put them first under the spout of the pump in the yard. When rushing spring water had done all it could, we carried pails full of it into the house, and finishing the cleaning at the sink took another hour or more, depending on how many greens we had. But when they had been cooked with salt pork and whole peeled potatoes we had a dish — a full main course — fit for a king.

The next morning, while Herbert went to the university to find out where he would register for courses and to get a promised list of private homes offering rooms for rent, I went looking for souvenirs of Chicago to send to my family. Finding no shops on either side of the hotel, I crossed the broad green strip of the Midway. It was a good excuse. My feet had been longing to feel it. I wished I dared take off my shoes. I wondered if the old women digging dandelions had been barefoot under their skirts. I supposed not. I had never seen anyone beyond the age of twelve barefoot, except at the beach, though until that age most of us had worn shoes only to church from early May until the end of October.

I was pleased to find a business district on the other side, where I window-shopped for a while, careful to keep the Midway in sight lest I should get lost Out West, and then went into a department store. Of the salesgirl just inside I asked about souvenirs and was directed to them. It was not until I happened to notice that the girl at the souvenir counter was a Negro that I realized the first girl I had spoken to had been too, and then that all the salespeople and all the customers were Negro, and finally that all the people I had seen on the street had been. Yet this awareness must have been growing without my knowledge; otherwise I should not have noted the complexion of the souvenir salesgirl. She was interested that I had just come from as far east as the state of Maine and helped me choose a cup and saucer for my mother, a comb for Grammy, and a tray for my father's pipe. We put the tray and comb in the bottom of a bag which had the name of the store on the side, and the cup and saucer, carefully wrapped, on top.

At the hotel, when I asked for my key at the desk, the room clerk saw the bag I was carrying and raised his eyebrows.

"Have you been over there?"

I said yes. His expression suggested I might have done something wrong. I shouldn't have walked on the grass? But last night women were digging dandelions there —

"Did you go alone?"

"Yes . . . Why?"

He shook his head, pushing the key toward me.

As he turned away he said, "You shouldn't have gone there alone."

He had not told me why. I had seen no reason. If he had a reason, I wish he had told me what it was.

That afternoon Herbert and I registered for courses at the university, he for four, and I for one in appreciation of architecture in the School of Fine Arts. From there we went looking for a room and engaged the first one we saw. On the list he had been given it was the nearest to the campus. It was the front room on the second floor of a brick block, and had a bay window overhanging the street and the little shops below. This was its only window. Along one wall a studio couch opened into a double bed, but the room was so narrow that when the bed was open it blocked the doorway into the hall. The opposite wall was formed by sliding doors which separated our room from that rented by someone else. At the foot of the couch there was a bureau. In the bay window there was a desk. Off the dark hall, wide enough for two to pass only by turning sideways, there were two rented bedrooms, and a bathroom with no window used by all occupants of the apartment. Beyond the two rented bedrooms, with one small window each, there was a corner room with cross-ventilation, where our landlady's white-bearded husband was bedridden, and at its side was our little old landlady's kitchen. She had two windows, side by side, facing another brick building. We moved in before nightfall.

The next day classes began. We noticed that the other tenants locked their doors when they went out but we left ours open to let the air through, for our own sakes and for our landlady's. But when we came in we closed our door. As the hot summer wore on, learning what we paid for this privacy we cherished, we felt guilty that our landlady was also paying for it in the same coin.

By Sunday I had had mail from home and I wrote my mother:

You didn't want to come with me a bit more than I wanted you to. All the way to the station and as we waited for the train and as the train was pulling out, I could hardly think of anything except, if I had to go, how I wished you and papa were coming with me. Of course I always wish it, but never so much as this time, I suppose because I was going so far, and wanted you both to be seeing and doing and feeling whatever I did.

Thanks ever so much for the remailing. Did you notice that two of the letters were from Nashville? One was from Mr. Chappell, enclosing a check for $25.00 for "Wee Jock" which had brought letters from *People's Home Journal, Farmer's Wife*, and *American Needlewoman* and which I had sent him as soon as I got back from New York, and saying, "How is the serial coming?" The other, from Rebecca, written a few days later, says, "I hear your serial arrived today, and since you wrote it in such an unbelievably short time I shall be looking for the story about the American girl and the English boy and the white heron about the day after tomorrow. And how about the story in which a child of foreign birth is the principal character? If you intend to make a schoolgirl of her could you write it for me just as soon as possible so that I may publish it in the issue of Sept. 4? Something reminds me every day of how pleasant it is to know you . . ."

I'm so glad papa got some medicine that helps and just hope the cold stretch you've had didn't set him back. The weather here is BAD. So hot one day I can't even eat and cold enough the next that I need a coat if I go out as I have to do to eat — when I can eat! Every cold night I have your tomatoes on my mind. If they do get frozen be sure to let me know. I'll be sorry, but at least I'll stop worrying.

I finished "Whitefeathers" for Rebecca late Friday night and shall start another for her in the morning — about a little Russian girl.

Yesterday I had a very interesting experience. There was a bus tour of the slums and the leading Settlement and Neighborhood Houses there, and even though Herbert couldn't go, I went. We left Mandel Hall at 8:00 A.M., and my seatmate was a girl from Iowa. We rode through some beautiful parks and along a fine residential street and then on to the West Side. The University of Chicago Settlement House is near the stockyards so we got real Chicago "atmosphere." Most of those who live and work there are Mexicans and Poles. Italians, they told us, won't stay where there is an odor; they would literally rather starve. We visited the University House which seemed to me bare and cold, but children swarmed around it, peering in at every window, waiting for it to open. Then we went to a Neighborhood House run by a church. That had had many big, airy, comfortably furnished rooms, and a day nursery full of starchy-rompered, shining-haired babies with surprise in their eyes. Finally we reached Hull House. You must have heard of that — a really great establishment built out of nothing by Jane Addams. It fills a whole block in the Italian district; has a day nursery, a school, a cafeteria, a circulating library, a Little Theater, rooms for girls — everything one could ask for. Miss Addams talked to us charmingly, though she must now be past 80. On our way back we rode through the Greek Quarter and Chicago's Chinatown, both very interesting.

This morning we went to church at the University Chapel. The dean of the Divinity School gave the sermon and it was broadcast from WLS. Do you ever get that station?

We made it a two-meal day by having a good breakfast and an early dinner. It takes so much time (as well as money) to go out to eat three times every day. After dinner we took a walk in Jackson Park and were so surprised to find Lake Michigan within three blocks of our own door! But there it was, blue-green as the ocean, and with seven big ships in full view and ever so many dots out on the horizon. It must get deep very suddenly for though many were bathing just off the beach, there was a long line of red-uniformed lifeguards in bright yellow boats not more than fifteen or twenty feet out and a lake steamer coming to dock not far beyond. We walked at least a mile up the beach which is an artificial one with a brick-laid bottom and imported sand. This much open space inside a city amazes me. It even has golf courses and what looks like a river though it is actually a branch of the lake, dug out like a canal for rowing and canoeing; it was alive with boats tonight. We passed one of the buildings put up for the Chicago World's Fair and now crumbling, though only thirty years old. It must have been jerrybuilt. On the way back we stopped at a stand for hot dogs which out here they call red hots.

Which reminds me that when it is hot I'm always thirsty because I can't get any Moxie. The first time I asked for it as I would for bread, and the boy at the fountain was dreadfully fussed. He conferred with the druggist and came back, very apologetic, to say, "We don't know how to make that that you ordered, lady. If you can tell us how we'll be glad to mix it for you." I had to tell him the secret has not been disclosed to me. Now, whenever we go for a drink, I just say wistfully, "I suppose of course you don't have a bottled drink called M-O-X-I-E, do you?" And boys shake their heads. However, yesterday one did say brightly, "No, but I've heard of it. A cross between ginger ale and root beer. A great drink back Ohio-way, isn't it?" And they call tonic "pop"!

It's been a lovely day, but I couldn't think of it as my birthday. I have to be home to really have a birthday.

I keep wondering whether it is right for so much space to be kept as parks where people have to live jammed together as I saw them when our train was coming in and as I saw them yesterday. But maybe it is. It does give everybody places to escape to which I didn't know, at first, that they had. But what a choice to have to make! And even if nice places to go are worth living in crowded quarters, at least the crowded buildings should be well reinforced and kept in repair. I wonder what you and papa would say to see what I've seen. So many times he has told me, "Keep the sills dry and the roof tight, building will stand forever."

As I write, Herbert is typing a paper and I wish you could have seen him, a few minutes ago, stop suddenly to put a hand on each side of the typewriter as if it were a dog's head, and heard him say, "I don't know what I'd do without this." I'm sure I don't know what either of us would do without it. It has had a big part in all that has happened to us both this last year, and will stand us in good stead for years to come.

While waiting to hear from Rebecca on "Whitefeathers," I finished the story about Ekaterina which I called "Dark Forests" and Herbert liked it so much that he prevailed upon me to send it first to *St. Nicholas*, whereupon I immediately began writing one about Ming Toi for Rebecca. This was finished but not typed when we left Chicago for the weekend of the Fourth.

I wrote home from Wisconsin:

> You should see us now, camped beside a sandy road like a couple of gypsies, a few miles out of Sturtevant, the little town where we spent last night. It is about 11:00 A.M., a wonderful day for hiking, and we have been going up one road and down another for three hours, Herbert in his gray flannels and white tennis shirt, I in my old blue middy, tan skirt, and oxfords.
>
> We left our room about eight o'clock Saturday morning and took a trolley to the Michigan Avenue Bridge Pier which is on the other side of the Loop. There we went on board the *Christopher Columbus* which took us up Lake Michigan to Milwaukee, a five and a half hour ride . . . There was a high wind and the water was extremely rough. Well over half the passengers were deathly sick. One woman fainted and when we docked people were still trying to bring her to. But we weren't a bit sick and loved every minute. The whole ship was like one of the fun houses at Old Orchard, tipping first one way and then the other and everything sliding that wasn't chained down.
>
> When we got to Milwaukee we went first to the railroad station for a Wisconsin Line timetable. Then we had dinner — frantically hungry since everyone had been advised against eating anything on the boat. While we gobbled our chicken and cherry pie we decided on Sturtevant, on the way toward Chicago, as the place where we would leave the train and spend the night. After dinner we walked miles around Milwaukee and saw most of the places pictured in the booklet I sent Papa, but a city

is a city, and I've been longing for the country ever since I left it. So we left for Sturtevant at six o'clock.

Wisconsin looks more like Indiana and so more like New England than Illinois does, but still not *much* like New England. Right now there is a smell of sweet clover here that makes me homesick.

We got a double room for $1.50 at the Schlitz Hotel near the station, went straight to bed, and slept the clock around. When I woke up I was in the Wisconsin of flat land, little houses, and big barns. They gave us two mugs of lukewarm coffee, a plate of bread, and four fried eggs for breakfast. At least, they said the eggs were fried but they weren't a bit brown anywhere. They looked like hard-cooked poached eggs, but they were greasy. I can't imagine *how* they were cooked. Anyway, we left there as soon as we paid the bill, put our bag in the station locker, and started walking. We've taken lots of pictures for you. Hope they come out well.

Maybe what has interested us most today is the hangar with airships which we came upon about a mile out of town. There are six planes in it and with one they've been taking people up. Through a megaphone they kept calling, "Fly with us! Three dollars over the field, five dollars over Racine!" We wanted to go, but $6.00 we didn't have, so we contented ourselves with watching four takeoffs and landings. So graceful! Being a pilot must be the most fascinating work in the world. IF I knew my serial was sold, I'd have seen Wisconsin from the air by now.

When we got back to our bay window, Rebecca had taken "Whitefeathers," Herbert finished typing "The Mystery of Ming Toi," and we sent it to her in time for her September 4 issue. I wrote her:

It's new and fun to be asked for a special kind of story and to meet a deadline! . . . I love my course in architecture, the more because the instructor — Dr. Ward — admits that his own special delight is in Colonial American, which of course is what I grew up with . . . I do sometimes wonder what Mr. Chappell thinks of my serial and wish he would tell me.

On July 8 she was writing me:

> I can't tell you what Mr. Chappell thinks of your serial because I don't know. When I got back to the office after the holiday weekend I discovered from the notes on my desk that he had departed for Lake Junaluska and would not return for a week or more. But one of the notes concerned you and your serial, and the check I am enclosing is the result. I know he will write you as soon as he returns for he has been quite excited about this undertaking and has visions — is it an old man or a young man who has visions? — of your becoming one of the foremost fiction writers of America.

On July 13 she sent me a check for "Ming Toi," saying, "I like her a great deal and I think *Torchbearer* readers will like her, too. And it is such a relief to know that somewhere in all the great number of boarding school stories there's one dean who is human. Thanks a lot for that . . ."

St. Nicholas returned "Dark Forests" with a cordial letter and we sent it to *Youth's Companion* even though the market list said that magazine was overstocked with fiction.

On August 4 Mr. Chappell wrote me, enclosing the final payment on the serial:

> I enjoyed reading this story. You've taken a very shallow plot and actually made something of it. That's not easy. The style is lovely, and you have slipped in a little humor once in a while . . . No, I wouldn't recommend it for book publication. It wouldn't appeal to a juvenile audience and as a piece of adult fiction it would be a flop. In fine, you have written a delightful story for the *High Road*, and as editor of that periodical I should be very happy. I suppose I am. But I had hoped you would go a little bit further. With my very best wishes for you . . .

Meditating on this letter, and rereading his of June 3, I found that my original suspicion had become a conviction. It was impossible for me to write a story interesting to "a sixteen-year-old girl," likewise to her mother, which any high school graduate of nineteen would "catch immediately" and which would not be "a flop" if published as a book. If "Playmate House" was "a delightful story for the *High Road*," I was reasonably content and wished its editor would be. One thing at a time.

I was deep in a serious story I called "Outcrop" a few days later when another letter came from Mr. Chappell asking if I could get a Thanksgiving story to him before the end of the month. The close of the six-week Chicago summer session was by then so near that I put aside "Outcrop" (the only time, I believe, I ever did that to a serious story). I wrote "Thank Not Robin," and sent it off to Mr. Chappell before we left Chicago for our end-of-summer vacation.

At The House a letter from Rebecca was waiting for me.

> I would like a mystery story for the November 13 issue of the *Torchbearer*. Can you get it to me not later than August 31? I should also like a story for the December 18 issue. I have a Christmas story for December 25, but if you care to give a Christmas atmosphere to yours, I shall not object at all.
>
> The Thanksgiving story arrived just as Mr. Chappell was leaving for Vermont. I have read it and like it immensely, but it is too long unless it can be published in two installments. I can't say of course what he will decide, and he won't be back in the office until September 4. I have written him about it.

I replied:

> I'll surely do a story for your December 18 issue, but don't see how I could get one done and off to you before the end of this month. It is now August 20 and every day is full, every minute precious between now and September 5 when we go back to Fall River.

Every day was full and every minute was precious indeed, getting Grammy out into the sun and washing her silvery hair, coiling it to hide her wen; pumping and bringing in water; running to the woodpile for wood with which to build fires to cook in the shedroom the food we kept in the oven and tank of the cold kitchen stove to protect it from ants — which ran in streamers like red ribbons to anything sweet or greasy they found; feeding the chickens; petting Old Pony and the cats; talking and reading and singing; looking and listening and touching and smelling; walking in the woods; watching with the cats the fishman dressing fish on the tail-piece of his cart; picking blackberries and swamp huckleberries; snapping beans, slicing warm tomatoes, going out to find slender green cucumbers among the fat ones turning yellow for my mother to make into what people who did not know would think was watermelon pickle, seeing the barberries which, when they were ripe, she would cook with pumpkin cubes or sweet apples for barberry sauce; trying to see at least once all my relatives and neighbors who were still there for me to see, and staying with each as long as I could; going to York Beach and Wells to swim in the surf and picnic on the sand . . .

And another school year began. It appeared that it might be our last in Fall River, for Herbert expected his master's degree from Brown in June and hoped to begin study for his doctorate at Columbia in the fall of 1928. Only one more year with Durfee, his debaters, my Camp Fire girls, our garden wall and magnolia tree, the Wests, Bob and Margaret, Bill and Ethel, Bert and Merle, Philomena? The Giduzes had already left for the University of North Carolina. My secondary ache was beginning. The longing for my first home, whenever I was not there, was always primary; that for Bates, which had been secondary for two years, was now receding, as had that for the life of our village earlier, though I should never be entirely free of either, but the next, for Fall River, was sending warning signals ahead.

On September 19 Harford Powell, Jr., editor of *Youth's Companion* wrote me:

> It is true we have the accumulation of one complete century and, worse luck, we have just changed into a monthly magazine which makes it impossible to take a new short story.
>
> "Dark Forests" is a very fine story. I don't think you will have any difficulty whatever in interesting women's magazines in it, though some editors would think it only a character study.

On the same day Rebecca, mailing a check for the story I had written for her December 18 issue, added a postscript to her letter: "I see you're on next week's checklist for 'Thank Not Robin.' "

We sent "Dark Forests" to *Woman's Home Companion* and to the *High Road* a story called "Reestablishing Candace" which had already been out several times and brought us letters from *People's Home Journal* and *Modern Priscilla.*

In mid-October one of my Bates classmates came to visit. Early the following evening, Herbert took the Fall River Line to New York, for interviews at Columbia, and Eleanor and I went with him as far as Newport on the *Priscilla.* I wrote home:

> I was thrilled from the minute Herbert told the cab driver, "The wharf"! The boat is really palatial and we were all over it before it started. We had dinner on board and I felt just the way you did, Mother, when you went to visit the Harwoods in Lynn when you were a little girl and they took you to lunch at the Parker House. You said the food was delicious but you couldn't eat because of the chandeliers overhead and the elegant Negro waiter behind your chair. I think the *Priscilla* may have the Parker House chandeliers and that the same waiter stood behind my chair as stood behind yours. I'm sure his line is royal, his uniform was majestic, and his way of dealing with the white napkin or towel or whatever it was he had over his arm must be the envy of every bride who ever tried to cope with a wedding

veil. After dinner we sat in deck chairs, listening to the music, and watching the shore lights. Later the little while that there were no lights to see, just the blue dark and the swish of water, we liked best of all. Then we were at Newport and had to say goodbye to Herbert. Wally Fairbanks was waiting for us at the end of the gangplank and drove us home.

Eleanor caught the 7:14 A.M. train for Boston Sunday morning and Herbert returned from New York by train and bus in the afternoon. That evening I was writing home:

> Herbert is just back from Columbia, very pleased with the prospects there. Did I tell you about the letter he had from the University of Chicago the first of the week? Seems everyone in his field had to take some intelligence test last summer and was told he would be given his score in October as a guide to future plans. All I know about the scoring is that if one got under 20 he probably couldn't get a master's degree at U. of Chicago; if 50 his presence there to work toward any graduate degree was much desired. Herbert's was 91! So, as you might guess, U. of Chicago is in hot pursuit of him. However, rest easy. With things looking as bright as they do at Columbia, I'm sure he won't go out of the East for his doctorate . . . By the way I insert here immodestly that Herbert isn't the *only* one to get H's (for 'unusual distinction') from U. of Chicago. Your daughter got one, too, in her one course! But all mine means is that I have real feeling for Colonial architecture. How could I help having that unless I had been blind all my life? . . .
>
> Did I tell you that Tuesday before Eleanor came I finished the story I've been working on for three weeks? It is one of what we call my "heavy" stories. Tell papa the name of it is "Columby Maples." And did I tell you we got a very nice letter from the fiction editor of *Woman's Home Companion* on the Russian story?

On October 21 Mr. Chappell returned "Reestablishing Candace," saying he did not think it would "make a good impression amongst folks who inhabit Sunday schools" and adding that he expected "Playmate House," now running, to "please our family immensely." And on the twenty-fifth Rebecca wrote asking me to "try your hand at an outline for a girls' serial with a view to bringing it out in book form later."

We sent Candace to Mr. Mudge of *Northern Methodist Publications* in Cincinnati, whom I had met at the conference, and his assistant returned it saying that "the family wrangles give it an unpleasant note we should not care to bring to our readers." We sent Candace to *Farm Life* (where a bit of family wrangling might be endured with reasonable equanimity?) and between short stories I made the "outline" Rebecca had asked for, though probably not in the form she expected.

For the first time in my life I was thinking in terms of a fictional manuscript of book length and I discovered — as it has been ever since — that for me all such advance thinking is concentrated on the people with whom the story will begin, their background, and the setting in which I find them. I come to know everything about the leading characters that they know about themselves and some things they don't and as much about the minor characters as one knows about lifelong neighbors or close relatives. By the time I feel ready to begin to write the story I have researched these lives carefully, observed and sympathized with them up to the point where the story starts, but of what the story is to be I have no more knowledge than I have of what changes may occur in my neighbors or in myself in coming days, weeks, and years, what new elements may be introduced into our lives and how we shall react to them, or what that we have long forgotten we may suddenly be reminded of and forced to take into account. It is the people who live the story; they show and tell it to me.

I wrote Rebecca that I had a rocky Maine farm on which an old, very Yankee couple lived with their young granddaughter whose name was Opal, whose inseparable and practically only friend and confidante was a huge, ancient white cockatoo, and who was as unlike her grandparents as if she had come from another world. A long-deserted nearby farmhouse was about to be occupied for the summer by a family from the city with children near Opal's age. The story would be about the events of that summer. This would presumably run to about half a book-length. If then, as I expected, there was more to tell I would tell it in a second half. The title of the book, if there should be one, was *Cockatoo.*

November had come in. Herbert was busy with his debate team and his master's thesis. I was training Camp Fire Guardians. And the day before we left for Thanksgiving at home I had a letter from Rebecca saying that the more she thought about my idea for a serial the more possibilities she saw in it "in your hands." She concluded, "So go ahead with it and I'll be anxiously awaiting the outcome."

I sent a story called "Song in the Tub" to the magazine section of the *New York World* and went ahead with "Cockatoo" as soon as we returned to Fall River, continuing until my mother and father came in mid-December for a month's holiday while Grammy visited my brother and his wife. Our bedroom became the guest room; Herbert and I slept on cot and divan by the bay window in the living room; my mother and I cooked up banquets in the kitchen, served them at stoveside, and sang together as we did the dishes at the white enamel sink from which even she could not get out the brown stain deposited by a leaky faucet; my father walked, stopping to rest and talk at every corner grocery, barber shop, and shoe repair center, and soon had more friends in Fall River than I did.

We celebrated Christmas early, in the evening of the last day of school, and my parents' gift to us was a trip to Washington where none of us had ever been. We left the next evening on the Fall River boat and that night I didn't have to get off at Newport! We lay down, each in his own bunk, in adjoining staterooms, but slept little. At six the next morning, in the December dark and cold, I saw New York Harbor as I had often seen the sunset on the marshes at home, with my back against my father's body and his arms around me; my head scarcely reached his chest. We said nothing for our shared excitement was beyond expression. We were thinking, "Is this us? Is this really us?" *We* were on a boat coming into New York Harbor in the winter of 1927–28?

We took a cab to the McAlpin Hotel for breakfast and spent the morning on a sightseeing bus tour — which was a great disappointment since I never caught and so could not convey a trace of all that had so charmed me in the city in May and was still calling me back to what now seemed to be some other city. None of us chose to mention the probability that by another fall Herbert and I would be walking the maze of these cold, dark, noisy, crowded, dirty streets. At noon, with great relief, we boarded a train for the Nation's Capital.

My father said, "They ought to have this railroad station right at the dock. I've seen all I ever want to see of New York."

But Christmas week in Washington — the snow-white of the government buildings, the grandeur especially of the Department of Justice, the public rooms of the White House, the wedding gowns of the First Ladies in the Smithsonian, the balconies of the House and Senate, the peaceful beauty of Mount Vernon! The first time we went to the Capitol, part of a busload of sightseers being hurried into and through it, while Herbert and I were trying to keep close behind my parents, not to become separated from them, in the rotunda my father looked back at me, though moving almost at a run, his face flushed and his blue eyes shining, and said, "Gladie!

Did you ever think we'd be here?" I shook my head. I was so *glad*—glad our country had this splendid building, glad my parents could see it, glad they and we had the joy of their being able to bring us to see it. No, I had never thought we would be there, the four of us together. What a Christmas!

There were bright trees in hotel lobbies, and smaller but no less twinkling ones in house and apartment windows, the laughing faces of children who jumped up from their marbles in sunny sidewalk corners and danced for us, the blocks and blocks of souvenir shops along Pennsylvania Avenue where we strolled, looking in the windows as at a Maine beach in summertime. On the same avenue where inauguration parades passed, my father bought Japanese tea sets for my mother and me. Mine was in soft shades of blue and brown, with raised dragons. Our favorite restaurant was the Occidental Cafe. We had never tasted such delicious food—nor known that food could cost so much money.

We went to church on Sunday and from the balcony saw President and Mrs. Coolidge seated below us. My father whispered, "There he is. There's the President." We could see only the backs of their heads, but his said, "Vermont" and hers said, "Massachusetts." We were at church with them, and felt at home.

At the flying field where we had gone to watch the planes, Herbert and I decided to take our first ride in the sky. My heart went out to my parents when we told them. (What would become of them, standing there at the edge of the field, if we plummeted to earth at their feet?) . . . But the temptation was too strong to deny. We had not paid three dollars each to see Sturtevant, Wisconsin from the air, much less five dollars to fly over Racine. It cost only five dollars to fly over Washington. Charles Lindbergh had crossed the Atlantic in a plane like this. They nodded and smiled but my mother paled. We climbed into the seat barely wide enough for two, our knees pressed against the back of the pilot's seat, the propeller whirled, the engine roared, we waved, and up we went. At first we could see streaks of ground in cracks beneath our feet, but when we looked up the wind stung our eyes until they streamed tears and we could see nothing. A few minutes, and we were down again. My parents hurried toward us.

"How did things look from up there?" asked my father, cheerily.

My mother said, "Thank the Lord . . . Thank the good Lord . . ."

All the rest of that day my mother kept looking at me oddly. I knew what she was thinking, but finally I asked, "What are you thinking, Mama?" And she said, "How thankful I am you're back on terra firma."

I thought it couldn't be easy to be a parent of grown children.

We returned to Fall River closer united by having shared so many new experiences. My mother liked to go to movies; my father didn't. Herbert took my mother to movies and my father and I tramped the streets. Once when we thought they would soon be coming out of a movie my father paid our admission to go in, find them, and sit behind them until they rose to leave and discovered us. He told Herbert we wanted to find out if they were holding hands. This was a reminder of a family joke which had its origin one night, before Herbert and I were married, when he was taking my mother and me for a ride in her car. I sat between them, in the dark my mother put her hand over mine in my lap, and a few minutes later Herbert covered hers with his and did not know hers was not mine until she and I could no longer contain our amusement. He had asked me later if I was hurt that he did not know at once and I said no, I hoped it meant that my hands were a little like hers for I had always thought hers the loveliest I ever saw.

One bitterly cold night toward the end of their visit the

whole center of the city burned down. Herbert and my father went to the fire. My mother and I watched the shooting flames from her bedroom window. The next morning we all went down to see the ruins encased in walls of ice.

My mother shivered and said, "I wish you were coming home with us."

I said, "But the fire's out. It will soon be spring. We'll come in the spring."

We went home for Easter. Before the end of February we had sent "Cockatoo" in the recommended serial length to Rebecca and I was going straight on, as if I had never reached a stopping place, into a second serial I called "Captives" and which was the second half of my book-length. This time there was no uncertainty, no hesitation in me. I knew exactly what I was doing. I should be more than delighted to sell two serials — or even one serial — to the *Torchbearer*; but I was writing a book. I was writing a story I would have read and reread when I was ten years old, about a mysterious and lovely girl of fifteen who lived on a Maine farm, strangely attached to a big white cockatoo she called Family, whose only friends were her inarticulate grandfather and a kind Negro woman who lived down the road apiece with her little boy, Washington, and whose dreamworld was first brushed by and then gradually combined with the real world of a girl who would have been warmly welcomed into our Camp Fire groups, and of her brothers. I felt I knew Opal and that I knew Nan, Andy, Chris, and small Peter equally well. I was fascinated by the relationships between Opal and each of her new neighbors. They were telling me the story of an extraordinary summer; such a summer as any isolated country girl longs for, whether she knows it or not, and such a summer as any high-spirited city girl would never forget. I was only writing it down as the long, sweet days passed.

On March 14 I wrote Rebecca that I was sure she knew how pleased I was that she liked "Cockatoo" and thought I would have no difficulty in placing it for book publication, adding that I was midway into the next to the last chapter of "Captives" and that it should get off to her the first of the following week. "I have two recent letters which I reread when I feel tired. One is yours and the other is from Mr. Hartman of *Harper's* to whom I had sent a note to explain my long silence. He says that my long-story venture interests him and that he believes their juvenile department would be glad to read it with a view to book publication; also that if I will send him the manuscript when it is finished he will see that it gets prompt and careful attention from Miss Kirkus, head of that department. Nice? . . ."

We came back from the Easter holiday to find that Rebecca was equally satisfied with my second half. Three serials had now been accepted for publication, and I had written a book. There was no longer any doubt that we would go to Columbia in the fall. I rushed into the production of short stories to finance a summer session at Harvard. Herbert's master's thesis had been approved. The *Durfee Hilltop* hailed editorially the state debating champions, undefeated for two years and victors over New Bedford, Melrose, Hope Street (Providence) High Schools, St. John's Prep, and Worcester Classical, who had otherwise been undefeated for four years. The lead story in the same issue which carried the editorial was on the second of the Hilltoppers' debates with Worcester, and said:

> One of the judges said the Hilltoppers' was the best high school debate team he had ever heard . . . Chernock laid a solid foundation for the affirmative case . . . McDonald, president of the senior class, as usual electrified the audience with his clean-cut rebuttal. Edward Hanify's analysis of both the affirmative and negative sides of the question would have done credit to a college debator. His persuasive eloquence in the final rebuttal swept away all doubt as to the victors in the discussion.

It was a spring almost feverish with last times — last

classes, last tennis games with the Fullers, last bridge games with the Cooks, last rolling on the dunes at Horseneck Beach with the Bogles, last rides and picnics, the farewell Camp Fire banquet, last mornings upstairs with Mrs. West who was happily preparing for the wedding of their Dolly, last cocktail parties at the Harts'. And I spent many hours on the streets of Fall River, studying the faces and the figures, convinced — and I was right — that I would never again see so many wrapped in black shawls.

Cockatoo came back from Harper's juvenile department with a pleasant letter and was sent off next day to Doubleday, Doran. We sent a short story called "Blanket Blood" to Mr. Powell at *Youth's Companion* who had liked "Dark Forests," and other stories were going and coming — or staying — in all directions. "Song in the Tub" had come back with letters from the *New York World*, *Woman's Home Companion*, *McClure's*, and the *People's Home Journal*.

My father came for a week and crated our bits of furniture for shipment home — the dressing table and bench he had made for me, the desk we had bought with money the Nutters gave us as a wedding gift, the bamboo bookcase Herbert had brought from his room in the Carroll home in Rowe. He also found barrels in which he helped me pack my dishes, silver, and small electrical appliances, and boxes for the books and papers. We had nothing else except what would go with us in trunk, suitcases, and typewriter case. The last night and morning he was there we ate from paper plates with cardboard forks and spoons, and drank from cracked jelly glasses, as Herbert and I continued to do after he had gone.

We sent "Song in the Tub" back to the *New York World*.

I wrote home:

> The annual Durfee debate banquet was held at the Mellon Hotel last night and turned into a farewell dinner to Herbert. Really I couldn't help thinking he got such tributes as most

people must wait for until their obituaries, if they ever get them. One boy said, "We don't think of him as just a debate coach. We feel like we're losing a friend." Another said, "You folks don't know what Mr. Carroll does down there in the library. I do, but I don't know how to describe it. You see, we don't just prepare speeches. We talk about *everything*." The captain of the squad said, "Mr. Carroll is more than a man of character. He is a builder of character. What he has made of us in these two years, we are going to be." Mr. Wallace, the vice principal said, "Everything you young people have seen in Mr. Carroll the faculty has recognized and appreciated in a different relationship with him. That same keenness of mind, breadth of vision, modesty, diligence, and fine sense of values that you have admired and respected we have admired and respected. Durfee has splendid ideals and traditions to uphold but I believe no man or woman has ever lived up more truly to the very best." That is just what they said (and lots more) for I hung on every word and memorized them. His debaters gave him a beautiful set of William James, whom he considers the greatest psychologist that ever lived . . . I went downtown and had a water wave for the dinner. The hairdresser was a man and he just set the wave with a comb and his fingers and dried it with still, warm air. Of course it isn't like a marcel and I didn't want it to be. This is just a slight, natural wave and I love it. I wore my red dress and sat beside Mr. Wallace and had a happy, happy time. There was nothing to wish for but that all Herbert's folks and all my folks could have been there.

Then came the day when I watched Herbert in cap and gown receive his master's degree from Brown University. This was a real milestone as he had begun his graduate studies in education with the intention of becoming a school administrator, but had increasingly been taking courses in psychology and now all his future work would be in that field.

One morning I ran upstairs to say goodbye to Mrs. West and came down in tears. We picked up our suitcases and typewriter case, returned our key to the Rocklins, and followed our trunk to the taxi, with a long last look at the magnolia tree and the garden wall in the shadow of Durfee. We were leaving Fall River, but going home for a week. While we were there I received a check for $100 from the *New York World* for "Song in the Tub."

The summer at Harvard was idyllic. Crossing the Yard I always felt I was in heaven, and I crossed it many times every day. We had a student suite in a homelike house on a leafy Cambridge street, and as we came and went we passed a door always open into a studio where a young man was painting. He said he liked an audience when he worked and I often provided it. Sometimes the work did not go well, and he would drop his brushes and go out to an open car which always waited for him. He said he had to feel the wind in his hair before he could go on. We ate at a cafeteria in Harvard Square and from there went through the gates into the Yard on our way to classes or to the library or to sit on the grass and feed the pigeons. Herbert was taking two courses, one with Dr. Ross Finney of the University of Minnesota and another with Sir John Adams of the University of London. I was taking one in Victorian poetry with Dr. Charles Swain Thomas of Harvard, and his assistant was a graduate student named Frederic McCreary who had published a book of poems called *The Northeast Corner*. Emboldened by the indulgence of Professor Mitchell of Bowdoin during our summer at Bates, I asked and was accorded the same by Dr. Thomas and Mr. McCreary — a piece of creative writing of the required length would be acceptable as a substitute for any assigned paper. My first admission to the stacks in Widener Library led me straight back to the desk to ask if I might be assigned a cubicle in which to write every day and leave my materials overnight. Permission was granted. It was the most ideal place for working that I have ever had. I wrote voluminously, and handed in all my "serious" stories. Dr. Thomas read and made notations on them, and Mr. McCreary held conferences with me and criticized the work at length.

Being at Harvard I wrote, among other things, a four-part story for young people called "Coxing the Crew," though I had never seen a crew race.

We also took lessons in ballroom dancing at a school in Boston, and I went one night a week, by subway, for a swimming lesson at the "Y" in Kendall Square. Bob and Margaret Bogle came up from Fall River and we all went to Olympic trials in the Harvard Stadium and to Norumbega Park canoeing, where Bob had courted Margaret when he was a student at Harvard Law. Now he was clerk of courts in his home city.

Toward the end of July "Blanket Blood" came back from *Youth's Companion* with a letter from Eric Hodgins, the managing editor, who said, "It has the third dimension. I admire the style of this story very much. It is clear and straightforward and has none of the fudge and titters that so many girls' pieces suffer from, and there are occasional glints of humor . . ." However, it was a summer story and "all our efforts now are bent toward the fall and winter." Had I any Thanksgiving or Christmas material? I wrote him a Christmas story and he returned it saying, "I like 'Tawdry Town.' The change of key in the last few pages is unexpected and refreshing. I can't find a place for it largely because in spite of its excellent and O. Henryesque conclusion there is a tinge of old-fashionedness in it someplace . . . But there is a style in your prose that is welcome to the half-drugged reader and I hope I may see more samples of it."

We sent Mr. Hodgins "Coxing the Crew," which had already gone to *Youth* and been returned, and went home for summer's end. There *Cockatoo* came back to me from

Doubleday, Doran with a letter from May Massee who said:

> I hesitated about sending *Cockatoo* back because, judging from the promise in this, I want to be sure of a chance at your next book. But I am afraid this would not sell enough copies to pay expenses, and we cannot afford to take a chance on it. But I hope you will let us see anything else you may write.

I wrote Rebecca Caudill:

> You asked me for two stories. Well, I wrote them, one bloodying the heels of the other. That is, I wrote and sent you "Cinderella Chooses Boots," and finished another so soon afterward that I let Mr. Hodgins of *Youth's Companion* see it. He said he liked it, but couldn't use it, so here it is and what do you think of it? I had meant to do you another right away but then Mr. Chappell's "distress signal" came and I went at a serial for him — "The Grayson Gargoyle" which may be in his office by now . . . When do you plan to publish "Cockatoo"? My copy is back from Doubleday, Doran and I shall keep it until I get to New York and can hand-deliver it to Miss Seaman at Macmillan. I'm sure you have been right all along that she is the editor most likely to appreciate it.

Two weeks later Mr. Chappell bought "The Grayson Gargoyle" and a short story, "Berry Time," on which I had had letters from *Woman's Home Companion*, *McClure's*, *Modern Priscilla*, and *People's Home Journal*. *Youth* took "Rhinestone Heels." Harold and Jennie had a little boy they named Richard Spencer. And we left Maine again, this time for Bancroft Hall, a Columbia dormitory for married graduate students at 509 West 121st Street, in New York.

IV

To New York

OUR APARTMENT was on the sixth floor and had a study, bedroom, bath, and kitchenette. The large rooms were separated by a very wide, uncurtained archway and furnished with two cots, two dressers, two straight chairs, a flat-top desk, and bookshelves. The small rooms were windowless and with only enough floor space for one person; the kitchenette had a sink about the size of a handbowl, shelves above it for dishes, three gas burners with a cupboard below for cooking utensils, and a closet for the dumbwaiter which one pulled up by ropes from the basement, loaded with trash and garbage, and let down again. The only windows in the apartment were both on the same side, a French window in the study and another in the bedroom, both opening in, and looking out on 121st Street and the brick wall of the building opposite.

It all seemed very dark to me, and very dirty. Our dishes and most of what other household equipment we had were still on the way, coming by express. Our trunk which had traveled with us had cleaning cloths in it, and sheets — but no pillows or blankets; luckily it was a warm September. We went over to Amsterdam Avenue for soap and scouring powder, found a plain little restaurant where we had dinner, and came back with reviving courage. Mine was dashed when I ran to the windows and found that from them we could get no glimpse of the lights of New York. How could I live here and never see them? How could I remember where I was? I ran in some desperation down the hall, past several open doors — we must have been the first arrivals on that floor — noting that none of the apartments had a more distant view than ours, and was sobbing when I reached the fire escape.

But from there I could see myriad lights, most of them below me, all the way to the skyline — I suppose they were the lights of Harlem — and I huddled there and looked and looked and was comforted. I told myself that I would spend part of every evening on the fire escape and on pleasant days would sit there with pad and pencil.

After a while I went back to the apartment and scrubbed, and Herbert helped me. Later, as we were going to sleep, a strange rattling and clicking in the kitchenette continued until we got up and turned on the light there. By then a dozen or so extraordinary small creatures, the like of which we had never seen before, were scrambling into dark cracks in the plaster and floor and around the dumbwaiter closet door, and an instant afterward all was still. We did not know until much later that they were cockroaches. We closed the kitchenette door tight and went back to bed and to sleep.

But within two days we had walked in Riverside Park and identified with the Hudson and its boats whose whistles charmed us at night, looked off from Morningside Heights, and ridden on the top deck of a Fifth Avenue bus to Washington Square and back. I wrote home:

> Our express came yesterday afternoon. I longed to keep the big stout box and the crating but there is no place for it so it had to go. Our banners are up, our hooked rug down, our bookcase filled, our dishes washed, and our card table set up for our first home-cooked meals since we left you. I have to alter my draperies before I can put them up, but at least the windows are clean. We bring out one of the cots every morning to use as a couch in the study, and my Bates couch cover and pillows are on that. Did you happen to come across the top to our bridge lamp? It wasn't in any of the boxes. Herbert thinks it may have been left in the shedroom. If you do find it, please send it. Meantime the ship shade rests interestingly on the stem of the lamp. There's no lighting it, but it's good to see . . . *Didn't* we have happy hours

together? And we're going to have lots more. I'm almost sure we'll come Christmas; we always have been able to find fare money. And I do hope you and Papa can come down some time this year. Surely you will. It would give you a very different idea of New York than you get from what you read or from what we saw on that awful tour. It really is a big, splendid, shining city — shows you a million things waiting to be done and makes you eager to do them . . . Classes don't begin until Thursday, but such a process as registration is you can't imagine! One walks miles. But Herbert loves it all. I've never seen him so enthusiastic about anything, though as you know he is far from stingy with his enthusiasm. He has now added advanced German to his list of courses as his work next semester will deal largely with psychological studies in Germany, under a professor from the University of Leipzig . . . We thought of going downtown to a play tonight but it looks as if it might rain and it's getting cold, so maybe we'll hang pictures instead. How thankful I am our blankets and pillows have come! Such luxury! . . . P.S. We have to ask a great favor. There's no especial hurry but when he can will Papa open those two boxes of books out in the shop and send us all the German books he can find? He will know the boxes from the others because they're marked BOOKS and he will know the German from any other language there because the printing letters aren't like the ones we use. And could you send me some cleaning cloths with the books? Mine are going *so* fast! We'll both be very grateful. It is late afternoon now. We put up the pictures last night. It is cold and rainy again and getting dark. I'll do the curtains tonight for the radiators are singing hot, the lights are soft, the couch is comfortable, and Herbert will read to me. We only wish you were here.

In almost the first mail we received at Bancroft there was a letter from the Fall River Teachers Association asking Herbert to come back to be the speaker at their first meeting of the school year. He would not have left me alone in New York — we did not yet have even acquaintances, much less friends — and I could hardly have endured not sharing his opportunity to see Fall River again; but as the fee offered would cover travel expenses for both of us, he replied that he would be there.

Before the end of September I took the manuscript of "Cockatoo" under my arm, rode the subway from 116th to 14th Street, and walked through the maze of the garment district to turn a corner onto lower Fifth Avenue and see before me the marble building which was the Macmillan Company, Publishers.

I had no appointment. I was prepared to leave the manuscript with anyone who would take it. But when I had climbed the steps, passed between the pillars, crossed the threshold, and walked down the dim lobby to a desk at the end I told the girl who sat there that I had brought a manuscript for Miss Louise Seaman.

"Oh? Is she expecting you?"

"No."

"What is your name?"

"Mrs. Carroll. Gladys Hasty Carroll."

"Just a minute, please . . . A Mrs. Carroll — Gladys Hasty Carroll — to see Miss Seaman . . ."

She put down the receiver, smiled brightly, and said, "Go right in."

I looked about me inquiringly. There appeared to me to be no egress from this dark, paneled hall except the opening to the street and a stairway. If I went by the stairway, surely it would be "up," not "in."

The receptionist said, "You haven't been here before?"

I most certainly hadn't.

She rose indulgently and traveled some distance to open a door. When I had gone through the opening, she closed it behind me. I was at one end of a long, narrow room with two rows of desks its whole length, on either side of an aisle. Every desk overflowed with papers and at each either a typewriter was racing or someone was talking on a telephone. I stood where I was until a girl at one of the front desks looked at me.

"Miss Seaman?" I asked. For all I knew, *she* was Miss Seaman.

"Fourth office down. On your left." She began rolling a fresh sheet of paper into her machine.

I went to the fourth open door on my left. Inside, at an overflowing desk a stunning woman was talking on the telephone. She motioned to me to come in, and went on talking. I sat with my manuscript in a typing paper box on my lap and listened to her, enthralled. She talked very fast, using phrases, expletives, endearments I had never heard spoken before, in a lively range of inflections I had always associated with the stage, and with dramatic changes of facial expression and bodily posture as if thousands were watching her instead of only me. But no great star ever had a more absorbed and appreciative audience.

Finally she said, "Fine. Just don't forget where you're meeting me *this* time," (who could?) dropped the receiver onto the hook, and whirled toward me. I caught my breath as I always do when the curtain goes down; but it did not go down.

She said, "Mrs. Carroll? You write for Rebecca Caudill, don't you? She has told me about you. I'm tremendously interested in her paper. She prints delightful stuff. So — what have you brought me?"

I put the box on a corner of her desk and said it was a *Torchbearer* serial, probably to appear there in the winter.

"Do you think it's book-length? Great! We'll give it a very prompt reading. Is your address on it? Fine. If it's entirely unavailable it will be returned to you within the week. If I keep it two weeks it will mean *I* like it and I'm after other people to agree with me. In that case I'll try to give you a ring. You're in town? Have a telephone number?

Write it on the box. The longer I keep it the better, remember. Marvelous. Terribly nice of you to come in. Do hope we can use this. I'll take it home with me tonight —"

I was out in the aisle between the desks. She was back on the telephone.

I was out of the Macmillan building, crossing Fifth Avenue, waiting for the bus in front of the Brevoort. It would cost a nickle to go back to Columbia underground, a dime to ride up Fifth Avenue to Columbus Circle and crosstown to Riverside Drive and along the Hudson. But I was in no mood to go underground. I had just left a book manuscript with the Macmillan Company and talked with the editor of the juvenile department. For the moment, New York was mine. I would survey Manhattan Island from the top deck of a bus, like a queen. That night I started my second book.

A few nights later we were riding out of Long Island Sound into open ocean and going through Cape Cod Canal on our way to Fall River. We had only the one day there but it began early and was filled until we had to go back to the wharf. Herbert spent it all with his former associates at Durfee. I had the morning with Mrs. West, lunch with Margaret at the Johnnycake Shop, and the afternoon at the Teachers Association meeting. Then it was over. The bay, the canal, the sea, the Sound were shrouded in fog that night, and there was a fog of loneliness in my heart; someone else had my magnolia tree. In the chill, damp early morning the New York skyline was obscured. Herbert went back to his classes and I to my card table. There was one bright note — no package in the mail from the Macmillan Company.

On October 20 I wrote two letters.

The first was to Eric Hodgins of *Youth's Companion*:

I am inquiring in a hushed voice for my story "Coxing the Crew" which I sent to you from Cambridge. Understand that it is a *very* hushed voice. But I have had so many different addresses since then, and actually lost several pieces of mail, including one story! This, then, is all I ask. If you did not receive from me a four-part story, or if, having received it, you have returned it or otherwise reported, would you let me know? And isn't it a funny, brown, warm October?

The second was to Rebecca:

Nothing yet from Miss Seaman! She did say the longer she kept it the better, but she also said she would try to call me within two weeks and it has been nearly four. I can't help worrying that maybe she is ill, or abroad, and a grey-legged spider is weaving an intricate web over the corner of "Cockatoo." I want to do a new story for you and have an idea but can't quite get to it. Right now I'm launched on a book-length to enter the Longmans, Green contest. Not that I suppose I have a chance of winning, but in case I have I couldn't let it go by without even fluttering my handkerchief. When I don't get the prize, (which covers, you know, serialization in some juvenile magazine), would you care to see my *Land Spell*? And is that a good title?

Now I was off and running. I was not writing a serial, or two connected serials. I was writing a book addressed to young girl readers, with no ghosts, no hidden treasure, no startling adventures. It was about life on a Maine farm like those I had known and the characters were Mark Shaw, his second wife, Cora, their young son, his older children by his first wife and her two daughters by her first husband. The chief character was his fifteen-year-old daughter, Jen, who had been his housekeeper since her mother's death, and was still, though he had married again. My only concession to current expectations of books for "the teen-age" was a thread of mystery as to the identity of a girl who appeared at the Shaw kitchen door asking for shelter on a stormy winter night. This took up relatively little space. I was writing chiefly about the Maine countryside, Maine weather, and the personal relationships in an isolated family. While I worked on it, I was at home, and happy.

Rebecca was in Europe. Mr. Chappell was on a six-month leave of absence.

On October 25, Eric Hodgins wrote:

> Your hushed voice has thundered in my conscience. "Coxing the Crew" is at the moment resting in a pile of manuscript about two and a half feet deep. I shall have to go to New York shortly to apply cold compresses to the brow of the foreman of the composing room but when that is over I shall turn literary with a promptness that will surprise you. If you can give me another week, I shall come to grips with Connie and write you of the result. It is indeed a funny brown warm October. So am I, after these weeks of battle. I hope you are having a better opportunity to enjoy the season than any of us desk bound wage slaves.

I put away the letter and went on with *Land Spell.*

Three weeks later he returned "Coxing the Crew," saying:

> Now I feel very badly indeed. Connie can't quite make the team. The story is a bit too soft for us. Though your college atmosphere is finely developed, the ring of authenticity in the sporting episodes is not there. I can't see that this is any fault of yours. I don't believe anyone could put it there who hasn't actually rowed in the varsity shell of a man's college. I wonder if you read "Soldier! Soldier!" by Jonathan Brooks in our September issue. That story has created more discussion and enthusiasm than any other long piece we've published in two years and I think its unrelenting realism and completely truthful picture of the battles of the football field were what put it over . . . I am sending you a copy of our Christmas issue under separate cover.

I sent "Coxing the Crew" to a Mr. Simpson who was editing *The High Road* in Mr. Chappell's absence, and wrote Mr. Hodgins:

You needn't have felt very badly indeed. You needn't have felt badly at all. If you honestly are going to put out a magazine that uses stories of "unrelenting realism" and "completely truthful pictures," and if this Christmas number is the first step in a long flight of stairs in that direction, don't feel badly about anything. *I* don't . . . I didn't read "Soldier! Soldier!" Frankly, I hadn't seen the *Companion* since it was a weekly. But I read this, and it's good . . . Now let me talk to you. Christmas is over, as far as you are concerned. Surely you can waste a few minutes. Are you in earnest? I mean, about the completely truthful pictures? Yes, you are going to give them to boys. Are you going to give them to girls? Because if you are you will be in a class quite by yourself, and I want to have a try at you.

That makes you smile. You say, "That's what I've been trying so gently to tell her. She writes prettily about little girls who find it's best to keep the rules, little girls who run their worlds by making everybody love them." If I do, it's because I'm trying to help my husband to his doctorate and I've learned from experience that the editors of girls' magazines think — or hope — all girls are endlessly improving their dispositions or the disposition of someone else except when they take time off to hunt for treasure. Of course they're not, any more than boys are. Now listen to me, Mr. Hodgins. You had two girls' stories in your Christmas number, didn't you? And what were they about? One was about a search for golden bowls, silver trays, and pewter, and the other was about a happifier!

How grand I sound! As if I always wrote sense myself! But I know what girls are. I know what they do. I know girls under ten will read about dispositions and treasures if that is all that's put before them. And I know girls over that — intelligent girls — won't. Girls have as varying ages and interests and as much concern about what is ahead in their lives as boys have; and at least as much sense. *Give* them "realism" and "completely truthful pictures." I promise it won't frighten them. I promise it won't bore them. If I can't write it, all hail those who can!

On the back of the carbon copy of one of the two sheets on

which this letter was typed, I had written in pen, "Land Spell, Chapter VII. After supper Stephanie stood in the shed-room." On the back of the other is written, "Land Spell, Chapter VII. That night after supper Jen and Olly and Stephanie went through the barn and by way of the tie-up door into the pasture lane. The grass was so wet that they climbed the fence and sat in a row on the top rail. They talked in low voices. None of them noticed the loud peeping of the frogs, not even Jen."

I was having trouble beginning that seventh chapter, and saving for other use the yellow sheets on which I made false starts.

Mr. Hodgins responded promptly:

> Many thanks for your delightful letter. Of course you have scored a palpable hit. In extenuation, all I can say is that it isn't possible to remold a magazine to the heart's desire all at once . . . The objection I had to your last story was not its prettiness but the absence of firsthand knowledge of college rowing. This often happens. We are just beginning a new serial of the sea by a woman author. It is a splendid piece, but after all she has never lived in a fo'castle. Her atmosphere, then, is a little less realistic than Eugene O'Neill's. Not that I am suggesting him as the ideal *Companion* author. In another decade he may be, for all I know . . . I am putting your name on the list to receive the *Companion* regularly and whenever you have any scalding comments to make I should be delighted to have them. You mingle bouquets and brickbats very effectively.
>
> I took the liberty of mentioning your name today to Antrim Crawford who has just taken over the editorship of Senator Capper's woman's magazine, *The Household*. He was gunning for authors and I think you may have something which will be very interesting to him.

There was still no word from Miss Seaman on *Cockatoo* and those who were sitting in for Mr. Chappell and Rebecca Caudill were not buying the stories I sent them. I was still getting letters from *Harper's*, the *Forum*, the *Dial*, and an occasional acceptance from *Youth*. Herbert was working very hard and not feeling well. I was increasingly anxious both about his health and about how the remainder of the college year would be financed.

I wrote Mr. Hodgins:

> The prospect of having the *Companion* regularly is enjoyable. I promise to read and sit in judgment, for the value of which last I hold no brief.
>
> Your letter suggests some dozen things I should like to say. And I have a problem of my own which I'd most gratefully see your thoughts turned upon. I expect to go through Boston about the 18th on my way to Christmas in Maine. The 18th is a Tuesday. Could you give me a little time about three o'clock that day? If not, would the same hour on Monday or Wednesday be better? I could change my date for leaving here . . . "Gunning for authors" has a gruesome sound, but I trust Mr. Crawford is a humane man.

Rebecca came back and wrote me that it was very doubtful she could use another full book-length story within the coming year but Wilma McFarland, editor of the *Portal*, the Northern Methodists' girls' paper, liked *Cockatoo* so much that she had bought second-serial rights to it from the *Torchbearer*, and maybe she could afford to buy *Land Spell* as she syndicated *Portal* material to many girls' papers.

On December 14 I wrote Rebecca:

> I'm so glad to know you're home . . . You asked me to tell you when Miss Seaman made her decision on *Cockatoo*, and that day is not yet. She *has* called me recently, asking my patience — which remains strong since she was kind enough to say she is very much interested. The manuscript is now in Boston for what she says is a final reading by the children's librarian at the Public Library, and will be there, perhaps, for a couple of weeks . . .

Did I tell you I'm taking a course in writing for juveniles at the Columbia School of Journalism? One evening a week. You may have heard of the course as it considers itself to be rather widely known — restricted to fifteen who write and publish for children material which is of a grade to interest the instructor, Dr. Mabel Robinson who publishes with Dutton. We are all women, I'm much the youngest member, and I won't be there after this semester. I admit to being grievously disappointed. I brim over with ideas which seem absolute heresy to ladies who judge all by their own long-past youth. The coals of fire I've seen heaped on wicked heads this fall would have fueled your vessel to Europe and back . . . When is it that you are to start *Cockatoo? Land Spell* is nearly done.

In fact, I finished *Land Spell* the next day and Herbert, on his way to an afternoon class, left it at the tailor shop on the corner to be typed by the tailor's daughter during our Christmas holidays. I was resolved that he should take no work with him when we went to Maine.

When he came back from that class he looked so ill that I was frightened. I put him to bed, went down to the desk in the lobby to ask for the name of a doctor, and telephoned the number given me. The doctor came to our apartment at dusk. After an examination he gave us his opinion that Herbert had an intestinal ulcer, at least an incipient one, wrote out prescriptions, also a very strict diet list, and said the patient must remain in bed for at least two weeks.

Herbert said, "But we were leaving next Tuesday for a vacation in Maine!"

The doctor sat in silence, thinking.

Finally he said, "That might be the best thing in the world for you, if you will stay in bed here until Tuesday, stop overnight at a quiet hotel in Boston and go to bed as soon as you get there, and can stay in bed while you are wherever you are going. But get started on these medications and this diet *at once*. Don't lift anything — not even a book. Don't walk — not even a block. Climb no stairs. And be sure you stay in bed whenever you are where there is a bed; don't even leave it to eat. I shall want to check you again as soon as you get back."

Clutching the prescriptions, I went down in the elevator with the doctor, and ran through the icy dark to the nearest drugstore. The druggist was in a bad mood. When I asked breathlessly, "How soon can you fill these?" he said, "Be half an hour, maybe longer, before I can get to it. You don't think you're the only one who needs prescriptions filled, do you?" I snapped, "Give them back to me!" and ran sobbing to the next drugstore. The druggist there was less busy and more sympathetic. When I asked him, "Can you fill these right away?" he said, "Yes, but I hate to tell you there's no rush, lady. I took this stuff myself for three months and then had to go have my stomach removed."

Mr. Hodgins had written, "I am delighted to know that you will be in Boston. My time is fully at your disposal . . ."

I was at 8 Arlington Street at 3:00 on Tuesday, December 18, having packed our suitcases, carried them to the taxi and from the taxi to the train (a process which distressed Herbert), bought our round-trip tickets, and seen my invalid settled in as quiet a hotel as Boston had.

I had climbed an incredibly long, narrow, steep, dark, winding flight of stairs to an incredibly small, dark, crowded office at the top where the *Companion*'s big, young, dark, engaging managing editor peered at me from across an incredibly littered and high-piled desk.

He stood up carefully as if he expected — as I did — that he might hit his head on the ceiling, and we shook hands.

He said, "So you're Gladys Carroll."

I said, "And you're Eric Hodgins."

We sat down and talked for an hour. He talked about an editor's problems, I talked about a beginning writer's problems, and it was fun. I hadn't had so much sheer fun since the story paper editors' conference that rainy May week in New York. All our problems seemed to turn out to be hilarious. I told him more about what was wrong with his magazine and he agreed. He told me more about what was wrong with my stories and I agreed. I told him a publisher was seriously considering bringing out *Cockatoo*; he wished me well. I told him about *Land Spell*; he said he would like to read it. He asked me if I had anything I could offer Mr. Crawford; I said yes, but shouldn't I wait until he asked for it. He said, "Good Lord, no. Send it along." I said I would send Mr. Crawford something as soon as I got back to New York, when I would also send Eric a carbon of *Land Spell*. By the time I left, I felt that we were fellow conspirators against the status quo in the field of publishing for young readers.

If my mother was startled, when we reached home, by my saying that Herbert had to go to bed at once and stay there until we returned to New York, she did not show it.

She asked my father to open the bedcouch in the sitting room, and brought sheets and quilts for me to make it up while she put our noon dinner on the kitchen table and found two trays for me to fill, one for Grammy in the parlor and one for Herbert in the sitting room.

There was a chunk stove in the parlor, another in the sitting room; these two also warmed Grammy's bedroom. There was the kitchen cookstove, and a small tank-type wood stove in the chamber where my mother and father slept and where a bell tinkled if Grammy needed someone to help her in the night. The only way to the parlor from the kitchen was through Grammy's bedroom because the front hall was unheated and so the doors at the ends of it had to be kept closed. My mother had a Beacon blanket bathrobe to wear over her cotton flannel nightgown when she answered Grammy's bell, but I told her that while I was sleeping in the room next to Grammy's I would hear her if she spoke to me and would help her with whatever she needed.

Herbert was taking a small portion of half-and-half (milk and cream) every waking hour, and a powder dissolved in milk fifteen minutes before each meal.

My father brought in the Christmas tree and we set it in the corner of the sitting room, against the closed door into the front hall. We decorated it as we always had, with strung popcorn and cranberries, painted English walnuts, and a small collection of bright balls. My mother had a cat of the family called "lucky" or "money cats," three-colored, and she had two small yellow kittens. The kittens were charmed by the Christmas tree, and played in, around, and through it for hours every day, becoming its liveliest decorations.

We stayed ten days, five miles from a village doctor, ten miles from a hospital; and for three of those days we were snowbound. But there was not a minute that I did not feel safe and know that Herbert was steadily getting better. We were at home. We were together.

When we arrived back at Bancroft Hall we had exactly seven dollars in the world, part of it in Herbert's billfold and the rest in my handbag.

However, mail was waiting for us, and in it we found not only a check for $150 for a three-part story but a contract from Macmillan for the publication of *Cockatoo*. On the signing of this contract by "the negotiating parties" I would receive a $250 advance on 10 percent of the royalties. I put my signature to the contract that night, and mailed it to Miss Seaman the next morning.

That was the day Herbert had the checkup with his doctor and they agreed that he was sufficiently improved so that he could return to his studies but must continue the medication and the diet of no meat but lamb and chicken, no raw, fibrous, or acid vegetables, no uncooked fruit, only milk desserts, only poached eggs, no drink except milk and water, little or no seasoning, and no fats. As we had no oven, our closed kitchenette door began emitting clouds of steam and the cockroaches thrived on the humidity.

That night I sent all the good news home, sent Rebecca and Eric the good news of *Cockatoo*, and sent Eric a typed copy of *Land Spell*.

Rebecca replied:

> I am overjoyed that Miss Seaman is publishing *Cockatoo*. I consider the Macmillan juvenile department the very finest one going, and to have a *Torchbearer* story taken by them is almost as much gratification to me as it is to you to have your own selected . . . And I agree with you unreservedly about your course in writing. I have heard no little of it and am not surprised at what you say. Because I am so in the minority in my judgment of juvenile literature, I almost decide I'm in the wrong, but with you aiding and abetting me I'll be all right.

Eric replied:

> My first chance to read *Land Spell* came a few days ago. It is a fine story and reminds me of a canvas by Meissonier in the extent to which it covers every square inch of surface with true, well-observed, and faithfully recorded detail. The characterization is simply superb. Macmillan will have a fine book. It is practicality that rules it out of the *Companion*. You are right in your suspicion that it cannot be serialized. I suppose it might be used as a novelette — a misnomer so violent that I have stopped using it — but that would mean eliminating everything which makes the story really fine . . . Now I have another idea. It is so vague and nebulous that I shall not commit it to paper, but I'd like to discuss it with you some time. I expect to be in New York in a few weeks and I wonder if you will tell me how I can best get in touch with you. Mr. Powel, by the way, has retired from active editorial direction of the magazine.

I took the first copy of *Land Spell* to Miss Seaman, sent the carbon to Miss MacFarland in Cincinnati, and wrote Eric:

Thank you for reading *Land Spell.* You like it but not as much as I do. Here is honesty, since we enjoy honesty. If I were the editor of a juvenile magazine I should publish that story in toto, simply because I think it is good. But I'm not an editor and you are — which must have some significance! And that you are the new editor of the *Companion* I am tremendously glad. You are going to do remarkable things in Juvenilia. I can hardly wait to see what. In the meantime it is into the ear of The Editor Himself that I can breathe my not-so-subtle poisons. Still, the seriousness of this last letter from you makes me a bit fearful. Now that you're Editor, can't you play anymore?

Your "vague and nebulous idea" intrigues me. Please don't fail to encourage it by whatever means nebulae are encouraged, and I shall be happy to hear of it when you come to New York. You have my address. My telephone number is University 8800 — Ext. 368. If there is time, do come up and have tea. We are easily reached by the Broadway-Seventh Avenue train to Columbia University station. If you are too rushed for that, give me a ring and I can very likely meet you downtown. It wouldn't be the first time I have seen a nebula evolve in a hotel lobby . . . Now your January and February numbers . . .

I devoted three typing sheets, single-spaced, to criticizing everything addressed to girls in those two issues.

I'm not going to say this story had a tiresome title and how overwhelmed I was that everything a reporter might have in his notebook happened to this one girl. I'll just say thanks for a girl who was alive and did something . . . *Two* happifiers this time . . . "Lubber's Luck" ought to be a girls' story. Rod hasn't done one thing a girl couldn't do. I like the style. It is swinging and sturdy, like wind on a close day . . . From the G.Y.C. sports page: "When Ruth's father saw how much she liked the horse he gave it to her. Ruth loves Robin Hood dearly and has never used a whip on him." From the Y.C. (boys) sports page: "But by placing the scanning disc, identical in number of holes with that used at the transmitter, and rotating at exactly the same speed and in step with the transmitting disc, between the neon tube and our eye . . ." Please compare the two. Is something wrong? . . . Other articles for girls — "Can a Girl Make Herself Popular?", "When You Go Ice-Box Exploring" (recipes), "February for Parties" (recipes), "Girls Enjoy Music" (So-and-So has an entire orchestra in her own family; so who cares but So-and-So and her family?), and "Fashions for the Girl of Charm." If you say most girls are interested in popularity, clothes, and food, I say all right, and who isn't? But don't be so exclusive. If there is anything for a girl to aspire to being *except* pretty, popular, and a good hostess, why not let your girls hear about it? I read the other day about a Spanish girl who has been given sole direction of many miles of railroad in her country! . . . In my peculiar advisory capacity, I suggest discouragement of the exchange of personal commentaries — all this business of "So-and-So in Utah plays the violin" and "So-and-So of Long Island earned $243. 47 in 6 mos., 3 wks., and 5 da." and "So-and-So way out in India had a baby brother for a Christmas present." *Really*, do you think a girl who can read is going to read that? Why no descriptions of women's and coeducational colleges and the life, activities, and challenges there? And I mean laboratories and ski jumping, for instance, not just daisy chains . . . And that on page 26. That about betting. "Father, is it wrong, father — very wrong, I mean, father?" and "Well, son; listen, son—" Well, shall we just pass over the *Companion* on betting?

On February 1 Eric replied:

I brought your letter of January 23 to New York with me last Friday and telephoned thrice to University 8800, Extension 368. Silence was my answer. A great disappointment.

Your letter was nothing short of magnificent. It is the most penetrating critique that I have yet read, and I agree with almost everything you say. I hope to be in New York again soon, when I can give you notice, and we can go over it in detail.

Yes, by all manner of means, pass over the betting. I didn't write it and I wasn't really in charge then; but I did pass it because after all it had been only a few weeks since a tragic and heartbreaking overconfidence in the matter of Mr. Smith's ability to carry the state of New York had all but broken my spirit. My feeling on the morning of November 7 was that it *was* wrong; *very* wrong. I shall try not to parade my personal griefs again.

As to the rest of your letter, my own prose cannot deal with it. It is oratory I shall have to fall back on. But just wait!

I found it the easier to wait because we had just been evicted from our apartment. Not — as we had several times been in imminent danger of — for nonpayment of rent, but because Bancroft Hall had finally had to be turned over to the ministrations of a company whose specialty was extermination. All human occupants had been evicted first; then it was the cockroaches' turn; after that, as soon as the building could be re-entered, crews of workmen moved in to patch and paint plaster, sand floors, and varnish floors and woodwork in all apartments. We stayed several nights in a high, dark room in the King's Crown Hotel on 116th Street, and spent the days in classrooms, libraries, and going from neighborhood restaurant to neighborhood restaurant in pursuit of chicken, lamb, mashed or baked potato, stewed fruit, and milk puddings.

It had turned out that Miss McFarland did not have space for both "Cockatoo" serials, after her sudden decision to buy them from the *Torchbearer*, and so had written asking me if I would write her a new closing chapter, covering the material in the second half. I had done this, with some difficulty which I could solve only by adding material from earlier chapters.

We returned to our shining — and silent! — apartment to find a letter from Miss McFarland, enclosing a check for $75 to cover the additions, and saying, "You are an angel. I am also paying Miss Caudill for the extra chapter and buying an illustration from her for it, and I am more than happy to get out of a rather tangled situation so easily . . ." She went on to say she was delighted with *Land Spell* and would put through a check for $500 for it in March.

How broad seemed Fortune's smile!

We read the letter, took one long look at the shining but bare apartment, walked to the nearest furniture store, and bought the first new furnishings we had ever owned — a daybed (so that a cot need no longer be dragged out of the bedroom every morning and back every night, and we could have an overnight guest, or even two) and a scoop-bottom chair with an upholstered seat and an upholstered panel in the back (chiefly for Eric to sit in when he came, but also for our own self-indulgence when we had no guest to make comfortable; there is nothing harder than a reproduced Windsor).

Fortune continued to smile on us. In March Miss Seaman sent me a contract for *Land Spell* with a $250 advance on a slightly increased royalty: I was to get 10 percent of the list price on each copy sold up to 5000 and 12½ percent of sales after that. And Antrim Crawford of *Household* sent a check for $150 for "Whom Fairies Love" on its thirty-second journey to an editorial office. It had been returned to us with regrets thirty-one times in two years!

Eric wrote he was "bogged down."

On March 11 I wrote him:

How about transferring the *Companion*, bag, baggage and editor to a permanent location in New York: Though of course if it's too inconvenient —

I think I have a scrap of something now. The thought came like this:

Good letters. Fun to get, especially if your correspondent has some sparkle and writes mostly about you. (Pause here. No mental activity whatever. Then suddenly —) *Companion.* Girls. Departments. Why not a very human and racy series of letters from say, a professional girl in her early twenties to a younger sister or to any one of two or three younger sisters whose fortunes she has somewhat at heart? Well, well, I don't know. What would she write about? (Another pause. Concentration.) Jobs — hers and suggestions for theirs. Vacations — what to do with them; travel, sports, friends, expenses. Reversals in luck. Men, all ages. Clothes, yes. No recipes — give the Domestic Sister a cookbook, pat her on the head, and move her out of the way. (All *this* Big Sister knows how to do now anyway is stew lamb, stew chicken, stew fruit, and boil potatoes). But again and with emphasis, jobs! What there is to do, what you want to do, how to find out what you want to do, how to get ready to do it. What do you think? Does it make sense? How long should such a letter be? Would you like to see a sample? . . . You may not like the story I am enclosing but I defy you to pass up a heroine with that name.

The heroine's name was Erica.

He replied within the week:

I think yes. It does make sense. It should be a thousand words long. I would indeed . . . You are hitting close now to something I shall be forced to purchase from you regularly. Lively, personal, straightforward, uncondescending and to the point. Easy. Every subject you mention is an interesting possibility. Try one on men as a starter. The G.Y.C. has never ventured into this field and, thus is drawn the cosmic plan, it is the best of all . . . The only objection to transferring the *Companion* and its staff to New York City is that it would cut down the supply of interesting letters by about one hundred percent. Save for that, I'm all for it . . . I'd like to use the story about my alter-ego, but I can't. Still a trifle too soft. Leave this on the fire for another five minutes until well browned on both sides and you will have an extremely tasty morsel. Among our college boys, lieutenant commanders on submarines, aviators, football players, firemen, steel workers . . . the little rural schoolteacher is a bit too frail to stand up under the elbowing . . .

I sent Erica to the *Household* and wrote Eric on March 26:

I consider your comment on my story absolutely annihilating and obviously written with wicked malice aforethought. "Leave this on the fire until browned on both sides" indeed! Any smart little rural schoolteacher could put down most of your football players, submarine commanders, firemen, steel workers — if you didn't think she had to do it with her *elbows*. . . . So here are three Letters from Jan. Why three? Partly because I didn't like the first one but think it may be necessary to give an air of dignity and dependability to what may sometimes seem to some a rather irresponsible correspondence; partly because three will give you the general plan . . . Elinor for the pretty creatures of the upper teens, Peg for the fourteen-year-old ducklings, all their friends for those who aren't either Elinors or Pegs, and a clever older sister having one idea a month . . . If some of these are satisfactory to you and others not, you can set me right at the start. But no culinary terms, please! . . . P.S. Do you know about Mrs. Margaret C. Goodman of Brooklyn, World's Only Woman Deep-sea Diver? Has raised $300,000's worth of copper out of Lake Huron and innumerable ships from all over the place. Still is raising, I hear. She ought to be hard enough for you — even with her elbows!

On March 30 he wrote:

> Please forgive me. Actually, for the moment I had forgotten your culinary phobia . . . The three Jan Letters are admirable and just what I had hoped for. Would you like to do one for me once a month? And will you revise these first three so they can run in June, July, and August? . . . I am just dashing off on a Middle Western junket to be gone about two weeks, which explains the sketchy inadequacy of this letter. I am really extremely enthusiastic.

Eureka! I was *employed* again, for the first time since my summer in the office of the Pacific Mills in Dover. Though this was solitary employment, it did give promise of being a steady job with an income we could count on. Also I felt sure it would put me in contact again with girls like my Fall River Camp Fire girls, wherever the *Companion* went. And both for this reason and because of Eric I knew it would be fun.

I wrote a long letter home every Sunday.

I'm sorry the new pump isn't satisfactory. Did you get one of the copper ones? They were guaranteed, weren't they? Don't give up until you get one that is right. What a change raising the sink and putting in drawers will make! I love that old flour barrel but I can bear parting with it if that makes things easier for you. Speaking of the pump and the sinkroom — what I'd give for just one glass of that water! You thought the Fall River water was bad — you should just *taste* this! And of course there's no Moxie anywhere. I'd ask Papa to send me some but I don't have ice to keep it on. What are the Boston papers saying about the election? The same as the New York papers, I suppose. Our news here reads as if Al Smith were already elected. How I long for the sight of a midwestern headline to cheer me up! I read the other day a lot of things Mrs. Smith had "confided to a reporter." What a choice of a "confidante"! . . . Herbert sits here typing a term paper on "Cultures By Way of Philosophies and the Interpretative Social Sciences." He is working tremendously hard and his professors seem much pleased . . . I was going to tell you about my lunch with Cornelia Strassburg of the *World*, wasn't I? I went down to Park Place between 12:00 and 1:00. Oh, I am so anxious to take you down there. There's a little old park around City Hall with its mullioned windows; the buildings, some so old and some so new, but all tall and slender with towers; the newsboys and the old Greek women selling pastry rings hung like hoops over their arms. And newspapers, newspapers, newspapers everywhere — on sale at stands, under boys' arms, in baskets, in trucks, just everywhere! It is so exciting to me I could stand for hours watching, but everyone seems in a great hurry and people look at you in a queer way if you loiter. After I got to Miss Strassburg's office we had to wait a few minutes for her secretary to come back. She is very striking and talks with a lovely drawl. As I sat across from her I looked at her sleek, dark head outlined against a window that looks out on the red or gray towers of other buildings or down twelve stories on the newsboys and the Greek women with their crusty, golden hoops, and I thought, "This is New York." When she was free we went down the twelve stories and through Park Place to John Street which is narrow and old and partly wooden. What you say as you walk there seems to bounce against the walls and have an echo. On this street there is an old eating place called The Dutch Tavern which is a favorite of the newspaper people. I *wish* I could tell you how it looked to me. A long, dark, narrow room three steps below the street and lit by lanterns hung along the walls and from the ceiling. Hundreds of small tables crowded with men — a few women, but mostly men — all talking loudly, waving pencils and notebooks or printed sheets; and the air thick blue and dim with smoke. The waiter told us what was "good" that day and we had baked scrod with lemon sauce, and afterward black coffee in big cups. Miss Strassburg knew many of the people there and some came over to our table to talk. But by 2:00 nearly everyone else had gone and it was quiet, so we really talked ourselves; about magazines, books, writers, writing — her writing, my writing — and I loved it. She must have enjoyed it too for when we got up to go at 3:00 she said, "I wish I could stay all afternoon" . . . Yesterday Herbert and I had lunch at Alice Foote MacDougall's "Sevillia" and then went to our first musical here, *A Connecticut Yankee* based on the Mark Twain book.

I'm so happy with today's letter because you and Papa are really beginning to plan to come to see us. I do hope Maude can come to stay with Grammy. Any time after the middle of April ought to be lovely. Cookie arrived last night in a typical whirlwind, entirely unexpected except that I have developed the habit of always expecting her. We rushed off to see *Show Boat* which I had seen before but loved again. When you come I'll go a third time. Seems to me I'd thrill to Libby Holman singing "My Bill" every night for at least a year. Remember how I went to *Rose Marie* in Washington two nights in succession? When I really like anything on the stage I'd rather see it again than to see anything else . . . I think 500 words an hour is tremendous, for somebody who has had a typewriter only a few weeks. *I* still have to scribble my letters while you type *yours*! Herbert says you don't make any of the mistakes beginners are supposed to make. I'll be engaging you for my typist yet. It surely would be fine to get my business back in the family now that Herbert can't do it. Imagine you saying that writing with a pen makes you impatient!

On April 13 Eric wired: CAN YOU LET ME HAVE REVISE OF FIRST LETTER BY MONDAY.

I replied the same day:

Here is your June letter. I had it just ready to be typed when along came your wire, click went the keys and off it goes to Boston. As you see, it is new. I couldn't make up my mind to turn a September letter into a June one just by changing the dates. I want the fun of using summer topics. I've nearly finished July and August and will have them on your desk very soon. Then I'll do what alteration September needs (since it is no longer introductory) and return the original October and November. How far ahead of the issues would you ordinarily like me to write? . . . I have your April issue. I couldn't bear to read another story illustrated by a cryptogram, nor did I read the baseball yarns (no doubt *they're* good) and I gave Miss Fix-It a stony stare which she didn't mind at all, I suppose because she couldn't, having her disposition. The page on plays I heartily commend, and the other articles are fine. Rear Admiral Sims has all but dissuaded me from a foolhardy idea I had of our going to Europe this summer.

The foolhardy idea had begun germinating when it became clear that Herbert would complete his course requirements that college year, and was offered a research assistantship with Dr. Gates for 1929–30 while writing his doctoral dissertation. Thus we were assured of his fifty dollars a week to add to my sure twenty-five dollars a month, he went to his doctor for suggestions as to what he could do to feel better than he did, and was told that medication was keeping his problem under control for the present but for full recovery he must have at least three months of complete relaxation from study and whatever constituted pressure for him. The doctor's advice was to stay outdoors as much as possible all summer. Maybe we could go camping?

We did not want to go camping. We had been camping. We thought about a freighter to Liverpool or Glasgow and spending the summer bicycling all over the British Isles. But I had never learned to ride a bicycle, we doubted that pedaling was good for ulcers, incipient or otherwise, on inquiry we found that even freighter passage had a price tag, and even before I read Rear Admiral Sims's article in the *Companion* Herbert had said he would rather put the money into an old car and spend the summer driving around Maine. I thought that would be ideal but the more we talked about it the lazier and more self-indulgent it seemed. We had already seen a good deal of Maine and could see the rest when we were old, if not before. There was so much we had seen nothing of! If it would be good for Herbert to spend the summer driving around Maine, why wouldn't it be just as good for him to spend it driving to the West Coast, as well as much better for our knowledge of our country? He had a sister living in Stockton, California, where her husband was a biology professor at the College of the Pacific. We could visit her if we got there. We figured what we should be able to buy a car for, how much gasoline we would use, how many nights we would be on the road at no more than two dollars a night in cabins, or private homes, and what we would have left over when college closed at the end of May for our summer's food; we thought we would have just enough.

Eric replied:

The June letter goes to the right spot. I am running an introduction to the series and hope to present you with a proof within a few days. I'd like to have future copy in hand on the dates listed on the attached slip. This will give me time to illustrate and decorate handsomely and present your limpid prose in the style to which it should become accustomed. Prepare yourself. For a little while I shall be forced to flank your copy with Resinol Soap, Rumford Baking Powder, Raise Belgian Hares, Stop Stammering and the like. This small advertising is the curse of many magazines. Just as soon as the G.Y.C. department gets shaken down to its new policy, however, we shall have a new format which should greatly increase the effectiveness of the appearance. I know instinctively that we have the same ideas on presentation . . . Perhaps it is just as well if you don't go abroad this summer. Every other *Companion* contributor is going, and I face the prospect of having to write the summer issues single-handed — Miss Fix-It into the bargain. How would you like that?

I replied:

I am sorry for you. I am. I am. But the day I see your interpretation of Miss Fix-It I shall chortle with unfeeling glee. "Joan's face, tip-tilted, was as lovely as the flowers that grow in gardens with picket fences. 'I am never so happy,' she was saying in her clear, sweet treble, 'as when I am helping others' " . . . The July letter should have reached you today, shouldn't it? But of course I didn't know that. Possibly the over-punctuality of the August, September, and October copy (all four herewith enclosed) will balance it on the editorial scales. Those due August 20 and September 20 may also arrive ahead of time, too, because of the exigencies of vacation. After that, I'll try to be orderly . . . I suppose the shaking down "to the new policy" will be combined with the writing of the summer issues. I *knew* it was easy being an editor . . . I liked getting your letter this morning. You've said quite a bit about liking mine. Maybe you think I don't appreciate yours. But yesterday, coming back on the bus from delivering the galleys of *Cockatoo* (I'd never seen book galleys before those!), I thought, "I'd like to drop a card to Eric and say, 'Would you stop whatever you are doing and write me a letter? Suddenly everybody I know and everybody I see is TOO serious! I can't bear it.' " I did, really . . . Forgive me, but when are checks?

He replied:

Don't be too sorry. I feel much better now that I've read Jan's letters for July to October, inclusive. I have always wanted to have an acceptable October manuscript in the office in April and you have made this dream come true. It is also a help that the letters are so good. Here is the introductory note I wrote to go with the first letter. Never mind the Hazel Grey; she is the mythical secretary of the G.Y.C. Any time you can find me a good new title for this department I shall send you $100,000 in a lump sum and give you 10 percent of the net in perpetuity . . . Many thanks for your comment on my letters. I find it encouraging, never having regarded myself as much of a Clarissa Harlowe. Do you find the open upper decks of buses are particularly conducive to Serious Thinking? I have never had a real idea except while on one of them — and there are none in Boston . . . Checks are usually on the evening and the morning of the first day, as far as the Editorial Department is concerned. The treasury now and then likes to hold them up on the theory, apparently, that some contributor may die unexpectedly and the executors of his estate may lose sight of the obligation. But I think I can promise them to you within two weeks of acceptance — except, unfortunately, on pre-dated manuscripts. For I have not only a budget but an inventory. On these two hang all the law and the profits.

My mother wrote that arrangements were being swiftly completed and that at last she and my father would be with us in a week for a long-anticipated visit.

I wrote her that that was splendid but not to come a minute sooner as one Bates classmate was visiting us for a few days until another arrived for a few days, filling the current week when Maine teachers were on vacation. We had been to the Automat for the first time.

All around the walls there are signs — "Cheese sandwich, 2

nickles"; "Tea, 1 nickle"; "Cake, 2 nickles," and so on. Beside each sign there is a slot and a knob. You put the proper number of nickles into a slot, and pull the knob down. A bell rings, a door pops open, and there is what you want on a shelf. It fascinates me. The place is always crowded with all kinds of people. Some go because it's cheap, and some because it's fun. Ladies in furs at one table, and their black chauffeurs at the next. I have to be dragged away. We'll surely go there when you come.

After the Automat we had seen Ibsen's *The Wild Duck,* — "Much the best of all the marvelous theater we have seen here. Perhaps you wouldn't have liked it. It wasn't pretty but it was powerful and I can't get it out of my mind."

We had been to church at the Cathedral of St. John the Divine ("The service is Episcopal. So grand! Little choirboys in their white surplices, Bishop Manning and other leaders in scarlet and white robes, carrying velvet banners and golden sceptres. We stayed for communion — long and very impressive"), and that evening to a movie on the religious practices of the French in the time of Joan of Arc ("I liked it but the others didn't. I doubt if you would have.") Another day we had had dinner at Alice Foote MacDougall's ("spinach with a marvelous creamed mushroom sauce, and, for dessert, black walnut cake, and tea in a crockery pot") and then seen Katherine Cornell in *The Age of Innocence.* (". . . About wealthy New Yorkers in 1870. What clothes must have cost in those days! Absolute miles of red velvet in one skirt . . . Afterward we went into the Times building for ice cream sodas, and home via subway about 12:30 . . .")

Mother wrote they could not come for yet another week but they would surely be there. She had typed two more stories for me and returned the check I sent her for the first one, saying she did it for practice and for fun; and had Herbert and I gained any weight since Christmas.

I wrote Eric:

I am embarrassed on at least three counts. The first is about what you are going to think when you find enclosed the details of my Past. The second is about having to admit that I am completely baffled by what is apparently the signature of your managing editor who asked for said details; but it is so and that is why I am obliged to present them to you who write an admirable, yes, even a Marlboro hand. The third is that (a) I haven't died and fully intend not to be unexpected about it when I do die, and your treasury may as well know it first as last; (b) I haven't a glimmering of what you may mean by a "pre-dated" manuscript, but (c) you should know that Jan has so far received only one twenty-five dollar check.

I have the May. What can I say? Everything I have said is still true. The articles are splendid. They make the magazine worthwhile and are obviously what have the interest and respect of the editor. Which is fine for the articles. But even the boys' fiction suffers from this favoritism which is perhaps unavoidable. Your girl readers remain your empty-headed, carrot-topped stepchildren and half-grown unexpected country cousins.

After an excellent article on amateur photography a few numbers back, now in G.Y.C. you have a little chat on "taking pictures," like a child's version of an adult book. After E. E. Harriman on camping this month, I hope G.Y.C. isn't about to publish one telling the girls that if they can't afford a camping trip they will be surprised to find how willing Daddy might be to put up a little tent for them in the backyard, if they offer to hold the poles and pegs for him and remember to thank him when he is done . . . Again I assure you, I *do* assure you, girls of the age of your readers are not that different from boys. You don't *need* to keep explaining to them that what they may have heard referred to as the Spirit of Christmas is really their own dear old Santa Claus. Try to make the *Companion* more general. Let everybody read (and profit by) whatever he or she chooses. Don't leave anybody out of anything just because of his or her sex. If you must have prattle for those who can't understand anything else, for heaven's sake have less, and that little not exclusively for girls . . . Enough. Very likely more than enough. After May 25, my address will be South Berwick, Maine, and mail will reach me there eventually if not at once.

I wrote my mother:

> These stories are simply beautiful. I'm so proud of them and Herbert is if anything even more so because he understands better than I do what went into this work. We showed them to the girls and Eleanor said she couldn't imagine her mother learning to type. Herbert said, "Mrs. Hasty didn't appear to have to learn. She seems to do it by intuition." But I *wish* you would take pay for it — just what I would have to pay anybody else.

I said no, we hadn't gained any weight ("How could anyone gain on Herbert's diet?") but I didn't think we had lost, and I was drinking milk for the first time since I was three and had asserted myself by throwing my milk, mug and all, over the stone wall. I had found that by mixing it with malted milk and chocolate syrup I could drink a quart a day. I said we were really intrigued that Papa had been asked to run for selectman on the Democratic ticket but I had been sure he wouldn't for, however he was registered, I was sure he practically always voted Republican even though he wouldn't admit it. I said I kept thinking how lucky it was their radio was working well so that they could hear the Hoover inaugural ("But Mrs. Hoover is no prouder of her Herbert than I am of mine!") and remembering how last spring we had sat out on our stairs at High Street in Fall River to listen to the convention nominating speeches coming in over the Rocklins' radio.

> Yes, *didn't* I look courageous in that little glossy I sent you? I looked something special in every one I sat for that day — brave or noble or patient or distressed; anything but natural. They might have been a registry of moods in a tryout for the movies! On the whole I preferred bravery, and I had to get something quick for Rebecca to use with *Cockatoo*. I do hope the ones I sat for Thursday will yield something better for Macmillan, but the photographer did tell me he didn't think I'd ever get a really satisfactory one because apparently it was not natural for me to look any one way two seconds in succession.

That may have been a compliment but I won't promise you. Anyway, why are you so critical of my pictures? At least I had some taken and sent you one. When I think how much I should appreciate having some of *some* people I know who haven't done a thing about it!

I wrote home that we saw *Street Scene* Thursday and that last night Herbert had gone with Lloyd to *The Front Page* but I had stayed home to read the page proof of *Cockatoo*; and that every time I saw Miss Seaman she passed on more "glowing reports" on *Land Spell*. The children's librarian at the New York Public Library, Anne Carroll Moore, said the characterization was remarkable, and that of Mark Shaw and Jen "masterly." An editor in the adult fiction department at Macmillan said she would like to see the Shaw family in a novel. Somebody else said it was too good for girls ("a point I don't at all agree with") and I was most pleased by the comment of one of Miss Seaman's staff that the style was easy, flowing, natural, sincere, and entirely free of the occasional immature self-consciousness in *Cockatoo*. ("What I want most now in my work is for it to grow up fast.")

We went to a matinee of *Harlem*, about life in the New York Negro community. The only white member of the cast played the part of a detective. It was all about the everyday life of Negroes who live in a large city. Bits were funny but in the main it was very serious and very beautiful.

Herbert has been offered for next year the top scholarship available to Columbia graduate students but had to refuse it because it can be given only to one devoting the year entirely to study, and he would rather do research with Dr. Gates.

Of course I'll go again to *Show Boat* with you — one more time for me to hear Libby Holman sing "My Bill"! And again to the Fred Stone show with Will Rogers because I am sure you and Papa would both enjoy that. And the Automat, and Drake's, and wherever you like. But come quick now!

They came. They really came — to see where and how we lived; to ride the subway, the buses, and the ferries, to go out to the Statue of Liberty and Ellis Island; to go away downtown to Wanamaker's, cross Brooklyn Bridge, walk all day on streets where nearly everyone was eating food from bakeshops where my mother said the bakers obviously used inferior vanilla, and my father bought peanuts so that he and I could do some street-eating too; to see plays I had written them about and to go to the restaurants I liked.

But chiefly they had come to convince us that if we really were going to undertake to drive all the way across the country we must do it in a new car, if only for their sakes. They had been afraid it might occur to us to get some "piece of junk" in New York to come home in, then take our trip in it. This had indeed occurred to us; we had already made a twenty-five dollar deposit on one. But they said we must admit that neither of us was a mechanic, also that we were completely inexperienced in long-distance driving, and beyond that that it would be far more sensible to put our money into a car which would last for years. We could deny none of this, but pointed out that after the summer we would be back in the city for another year, also that we did not have enough money for a car which would last for years. They advised us to come home by train, choose a good but inexpensive new car with low gas consumption, buy it of a dealer we knew and could trust, pay for it with what we would have to pay for a secondhand one plus a loan from my father which we need not repay until we could spare the money, and leave it in the barn in the fall, ready for use whenever we wanted to use it.

So it was (a phrase frequently found in some of the favorite books of my childhood) that after two weeks at home, with new snapshots of Grammy, my parents, Harold, Jennie, and little Richard in my purse, we drove out into the lane in a small but new green Plymouth roadster. The top was down and we intended to leave it that way. Behind our seat was the rumble seat, and that space was our luggage carrier and kitchen, holding among our suitcases a small oilstove, a big bag of potatoes, and many glass jars of stewed chicken one of my district schoolmates had put up for us. We would buy bread, crackers, milk, and fruit both canned and fresh along the way.

Youth had just taken "Coxing the Crew" (presumably the Kansans had had no more experience in varsity shells than I); Miss McFarland was publishing "Blanket Blood" (another name for "Indian blood" of which some flows in me and of which I have always been proud); Mr. Chappell had asked for a serial as early in the fall as I could get it to him; the first "Letter from Jan" was in the June *Companion* and I had been paid for the second, with three more written and accepted. Now there would be no more writing, no more studying, no more research for six weeks or more!

Our first stop was in Rowe, Massachusetts, with Herbert's parents. They had a new wide piazza running the whole length of their house and most of the evenings we were there it was crowded with Herbert's brothers and sisters and their families, all giving us messages to take to Alice in California. It was the first time we had had our own transportation to the Berkshire hills, and now we were just passing through . . .

From then on we were all by ourselves. All by ourselves south to Pennsylvania and West Virginia, through the Blue Ridge Mountains, west to St. Louis and into Kansas, stopping to cook our noon dinners along the way, sometimes having breakfasts and suppers of fruit, bread, and milk under a tree (when we could find a tree) and sometimes buying them near the roadside cabins and private homes where we spent the nights and washed our dishes and kettles in bathroom handbowls.

We had appointments with Mr. Crawford in Topeka and with the Unity people in Kansas City, and in both places were advised to drive great distances every day from there to the West Coast in order to reach excellent hotels and recommended restaurants each night. We wrote down the names of these hotels and restaurants but we never saw the inside of any of them.

Then on by ourselves again to the Rockies, south from Denver to Colorado Springs, La Junta, Santa Fe, Highway 66 and the Mojave Desert where the only trees were Joshua trees.

From the day we turned west we saw no pavement except in cities and towns until we left Denver. From Denver to Colorado Springs the road was better than any city street because it was new. Before and after that our route took us from the main thoroughfare of one city to the main thoroughfare of the next, at first over winding graveled roads, then over dusty roads which were perfectly straight until they suddenly turned at sharp right or left angles (because the farms had come first and had been laid out foursquare) with no warning, and finally over the hard-packed, washboard roads of the desert. As we rode, I was usually the passenger and rarely let the map out of my hand until we reached 66. After that there was only the one road to follow and we knew by the sun which way was west.

From Albuquerque to Gallup, from Gallup to the Painted Desert — and there we stopped, suddenly. Too suddenly. As we bumped along in blistering afternoon heat, the car swerved to the right, went off the road, turned on my side in a bank of sand, thrust in its nose, and turned over on Herbert's side.

With only the round knob of the gearshift of our completely new, completely reliable roadster between us, I asked him curiously, "What happened?"

"Steering mechanism gave way. We'd better get out of here quick. May catch fire. You'll have to go first. Is the door jammed?"

It wasn't, but just try to open any car door while it is facing the sky and you are lying on a fellow passenger and a hard round knob. By the time I had it open and was climbing out with Herbert as my springboard we were quite confident there was to be no fire. He followed me with comparative ease and we tried to seem nonchalant about the fact that in this length of time, with no human habitation in sight though one could see in all directions for many miles, we had been surrounded on both sides of 66 by a dozen or more of my blood brothers on horseback.

Herbert tried to be neighborly.

He made a gesture toward the car we had climbed out of and said, "Steering gear gave way."

They sat motionless on their horses, with folded arms, and continued to stare at us. All had long, thick black braids and some wore headdresses. We tried not to stare back, and leaned against the top of our car or walked up and down beside it in the blazing sun until a car came along and stopped.

The man who was driving leaned out and said, "Maine! You're sure a long ways from home. We're from Oklahoma."

Herbert said, "Then I suppose you don't know any more than we do how far we are from a garage. Or even a telephone?"

"No idea. But you can ride along with us until we get to one or the other if you want to."

We had a quick discussion. There seemed nothing else to do. The only question was whether both of us should go, or one stay with the car. Should I ride alone with strangers to we knew not where (by my map Holbrook was ahead about forty-five miles, but perhaps it had no garage), or should I stay alone on guard, or should we both go, leaving the car in the care of the Indians? We decided on the latter course and it was a wise decision. The next building we saw, kindness of our fellow travelers, was some fifteen miles from the Wreck of the Roadster and was a grocery store. Who bought its groceries I have never known. Nobody was there but the grocer and a very old and magnificent Indian in full regalia who sat and stared at us. The grocer said there was a garage in Holbrook and, yes, we might use his telephone. Herbert called the garage, asked them to send a tow truck, we thanked the grocer, paid the toll, bought two cold bottles of root beer, and went outside to flag down a car traveling east. One responded, and when we reached our wreck again it was untouched, though our audience had vanished. Perhaps it was the Indian supper hour. Or perhaps my blood brothers were not interested in cars, only in foolish people who risked their lives in them.

While daylight lasted several passing cars stopped. Everybody looked at our license plate and observed that we were far from home. An Easterner said he only hoped there was anybody out here who could fix a car smashed up that bad. A Holbrook resident said we were right lucky it happened that near to Holbrook; Tommy was mighty handy with cars. Before driving on he told us to watch out for rattlesnakes and gila monsters; this was the worst time of year for them; the snakes weren't so bad because at least they gave some warning, but a gila monster might drop on you any time.

It grew dark. We had no lights. The few cars which passed did not stop, may not have seen us. But finally lights came toward us which proved to be those of a tow truck. It stopped, and Tommy (or one of his crew) hopped out, said cheerfully, "Well, ain't you in a helluva nice mess! A long ways from home, too, I see." After a good deal of rattling, cranking, backing and filling he had the roadster out of the sand and tilted on its rear wheels; we climbed into it and off we went. That is how we reached Holbrook, Arizona, on a July night in 1929.

Within an hour after the car was garaged we had eaten, found a cabin, carried our suitcases to it, taken showers, and were asleep.

The next morning early Herbert was back at the garage. When he returned to the cabin, several hours later, he said the accident had been caused by the loss of a cotter pin in the steering shaft, probably shaken loose on the rough roads, and the repairs would take several days since parts had to be ordered from Los Angeles and would cost about a hundred dollars, beyond the expense of our stay in Holbrook for perhaps a week.

I told him not to worry. I had just written the November "Letter from Jan" and would write December that afternoon. After that I would write a short story every day until we left Holbrook. This would more than cover the accident. He said yes, but not this week. I had thought of that, too, and reminded him of the gold pieces which had come to me from Aunt Vinnie. In my next telephone call home I would ask my father to take them to the bank and wire their face value to us in Stockton. I was quite sure there were more than a hundred dollars' worth. This would make up for the cost here, or nearly, and give us what we had to have for the return trip. He expressed doubt that Aunt Vinnie would approve of my using her gold pieces to pay for car repairs, but I knew she would; that is, she would have approved of our seizing any opportunity we saw for self-improvement, and certainly of my getting home if I had been away.

Our one-room cabin was at the far end of a bushy yard beyond the house of the people who owned it. The two cabins beside it were unoccupied while we were there. On the back porch of the house tonic bottles cruised the waters of a tub in which a small iceberg floated. The nights were cold, so we slept very well, but by 10:00 A.M. every day the temperature reached 100 degrees and kept on climbing. After the Jan letters I wrote five short stories, Herbert typed them, and we mailed them. Our one indulgence was crossing the yard from time to time to leave a nickle on a tray for each bottle we fished out of the tub. Grape flavor was the most refreshing. I always reached for my bottle with both hands and then patted the blessed cold over my face as I returned to the cabin, while listening for rattlesnakes and watching for gila monsters on all sides.

With the two new Jan's Letters I wrote Eric:

> Out in the Mojave Desert we forget dates and act automatically. But when we overturn and later proceed in a crippled condition, having wired home for money, we do hope to find checks when we reach New England again, and the more the merrier! I hear the waters of Maine calling me, and I think more highly of water all the time. We shall be turning east before long and may be reached at South Berwick until mid-September, soon after which time we hope to see you at 613 West 121st Street in New York.

On the sixth day we left Holbrook about noon for Flagstaff, where a sign pointing right showed us the way to the Grand Canyon. From the first this had been one of our objectives. We followed a narrow, rutted road, exactly one car wide, for some sixty miles and reached the stupendous oasis just at sunset.

I wrote home that night (as I did every night except when I telephoned, which was every third night), saying, "You would love this, Mama, but it's too magnificent for me. I'd rather sit on the riverbank beside a muskrat hole among the skunk cabbage. We didn't see another car, either coming or going, all the way up here, and I just hope we don't see one on the way back in the morning. There's NO ROOM for it!

We drove through the Petrified Forest yesterday, and it is certainly petrified. So am I, just about. We are as brown as if the gypsies had stained us with walnut juice. The top has never been up yet!"

Back to Flagstaff and on through Ash Fork, Dinosaur City, Valentine, Hackberry, Walapai, and Berry (usually nothing more than a gas station *with cold drinks*, and sometimes only a name on my map) to Kingman and eventually Needles, California. Along hundreds of miles of sand, sagebrush, and occasional tortured Joshua trees, friendly natives had been advising us, "When you get to the desert, better take it at night. Daytime temperature is at least 115 degrees, may be a lot higher. You Easterners don't stand it very well. If you think it's hot here — " The first time we heard this, we asked, "Where is the desert?" and were told, "Needles to Barstow." But that was in California, and surely main routes in California were paved, if not with gold, then with something hard and smooth! Anyway, if we had not seen desert yet, we must see desert before we went home.

We slept in Needles and left at daybreak for Barstow. Highway 66 continued to be a rugged washboard and we rode it all day with the Old Dad Mountains, the Marble Mountains, the Clipper Mountains of the Devil's Playground on our right, and Cadiz Lake (dry), Bristol Lake (dry), Lavic Lake (dry), Troy Lake (dry) and dozens of other lakes (dry) on our left.

After a night in Barstow we headed as straight as we could for the Pacific Ocean, reached it in midafternoon and plunged in. It was wet, it was salty, but it was not the Atlantic.

From Long Beach we were two days on the way to Stockton through Bakersfield, Fresno, Merced, Modesto . . .

When we came to Alice's it was nightfall and growing cool, as all the nights had been since we reached the Rockies. Yet I studied her and her husband closely, striving to understand how two who had grown up in the green Berkshire hills could be at home and bring up their children in the San Fernando Valley. I thought only some readjustment they had made in Cleveland, Ohio, while Elwood taught at Western Reserve, could explain it. But a check from my father for $150 was waiting for us. We would soon be starting home. So we picked figs in the Stanford backyard, put everything we had with us through Alice's washing machine, lay luxuriously in deck chairs on her terrace, spent a day in San Francisco, and I learned to enjoy beginning meals with a green salad though sorry for Herbert who could only watch the rest of us while waiting for his mashed potatoes and roast lamb or poached eggs. He ate no chicken while in California, having come coast-to-coast on it and being about to do it again in the opposite direction. But he was so much better! In fact, he was feeling fine and so was I, though Alice's scales showed that he had lost fifteen pounds in three weeks, and I ten.

Leaving Stockton determined not to retrace a mile of our outward journey, we started east through the Calaveras Big Trees to Angels Camp and on to Ebbet's Pass. At dusk of the first day we had negotiated many miles of a deeply rutted road dug out of the sides of mountains, so narrow that cars could pass only at scattered turnouts and with no barricades to obstruct the view or the fall into the canyon far below. We so seriously doubted the wisdom of continuing in the dark that we stopped at the first cabin we came to and asked a man who was drawing water from his well if he could put us up for the night. He gave us a long look, nodded, and motioned for us to come in. There were two rooms in his cabin. One was his kitchen, where his pot of coffee was on the woodstove. The other was a bedroom with a double bed and little else. The bed was very clean but smelled musty when I opened it up, as if it had been waiting some time since last freshly made. There was a china pitcher filled with water and we washed in a matching handbowl. When we went out for our suitcases our host was sitting at the kitchen table, his back to us, eating his supper. We cooked ours in the rumble seat. When we came back, he was nowhere in sight. In the morning when we were ready to leave he was in the yard. Herbert thanked him for his hospitality, asked what the charge was, and he raised one finger. Herbert gave him a dollar, thanked him again, and we left. We never heard his voice. I have always wondered where he slept that night — and other ink-black nights on that mountainside, before and after.

It was apparently the season for the changing of pastures. As the road gradually widened and became dusty we frequently had to stop on meeting a flock of hundreds of sheep accompanied by one small dark boy. Or we came up behind one of these flocks and could proceed only at sheep-speed until they followed their leader into new feeding grounds. This had also happened in New Mexico. The atmosphere was Biblical.

North to Reno, Lovelock, Winnemucca in arid Nevada and east through Elko to Wells where we spent the night and left at daybreak to span our last desert, the Great Salt Lake. We had crossed the West on endless washboards placed end to end. Now we crossed it on what seemed the railroad ties (which my father called sleepers) of an abandoned railroad. The heat of the day was close to unbearable. Speed was impossible. On all sides the scene was more desolate than any we could ever have conjured up in imagination. The sun set behind us. Dark came on and brought the cool, but it was what we called at home "pitch dark." We had no streetlights, no lighted windows, no moon. There were stars but such small ones so far away that they did not belong to us. We had scarcely seen any kind of vehicle throughout the day. Now we occasionally welcomed the lights of a truck traveling east or west at the approved time for travel, or of a heavy passenger car on its way, presumably, to the next really good hotel. But we had no sooner welcomed them than they had gone, moving at a speed which, if used by our roadster, would, we were sure, have scattered cotter pins and other essential gear in all directions; and leaving us in dark more pitchy than ever.

It was nearly midnight when we saw ahead a small circle of faint lights which did not move at all. I did not have to turn on the flashlight and look at the map to know what they were. They were the lights of Grantsville, much farther away than they appeared. It was close to an hour before we reached them and the road grew, if anything, rougher with every revolution of the wheels, but it was a lovely hour. The lamp was burning for us, though the wick was turned low . . . The merry-go-round was still running, though from this distance it seemed to stand still . . . We felt a hard, smooth surface beneath us and darkened houses became our companions. At the first row of roadside cabins we pulled in. As I was falling to sleep the lights of Grantsville danced in my head, better than any vision of sugarplums, and any night since when I have needed them I have been able to bring them back.

The next morning we floated in the Great Salt Lake, walked the heavenly — broad and white — streets of Brigham Young's city, and sat in the blessed shade of the Mormon Tabernacle grounds before beginning the climb into the mountains from which Brigham Young had looked west and said, "This is the place."

Northeast to Wyoming — Rock Springs, Rawlins, Laramie, Cheyenne; east across Nebraska and Iowa; north across a corner of Illinois to Milwaukee where we put the roadster on an overnight ferry and went to bed. There was a violent storm that night and when I was jostled awake I remembered a girl in the Fall River stock company singing, "Oh, why did I leave Wisconsin-a? Why did I leave it at all?" But the morning was bright and we drove off through Michigan to Detroit where we crossed into Canada and rode contentedly among the broad, intensely green fields and roomy brick houses north of Lakes Erie and Ontario and the St. Lawrence River.

We were three nights away from home, according to schedule, when on getting out of the car in the driveway of the roomy brick house in which we were to sleep, I found I did not have my handbag. We supposed I had left it on the seat of the booth of the little cafe where we had had supper, but we could not be certain; anyway, it was too far back to return to, even if we could find the cafe again, on the chance that the bag was there.

Now we had only Herbert's share of our money. We ate no more in cafes but supplemented our much diminished food supply with purchases at grocery stores. And we lengthened our days so that we were out only one more night. That was in St. Johnsbury, Vermont, where a householder had two rooms available — an airy one on the second floor with double bed at two dollars and a very small one on the third floor, with a cot, for seventy-five cents. We chose the cot. When we walked into the kitchen at home in the middle of the following evening, I said, "Look how much money we've come back with!"

Herbert tossed his empty billfold on the table and cleared his pocket of change. We had exactly nine cents and some crumpled one-cent stamps.

"The gas tank shows empty, too!" I crowed triumphantly. "And we haven't eaten since noon. But we never put up the top! Not once!"

"Well, you made it," my father said, equally triumphant. "And you're back!"

"Thank the Lord," said my mother. "There's food in the cellarway. Help yourself."

When we had eaten, we asked for the mail. My mother said the Larkin desk in the sitting room was piled with it. We went in and pawed it over, recognizing from their bulk several rejected stories. These were pushed aside. Finding out why *Harper's* had sent back this and the *Saturday Evening Post* that could wait until tomorrow. At the moment we were most interested in the letter from *Youth's Companion* (which must contain a check for the three Jan's Letters Eric had accepted in April, and perhaps also his acceptance of the two I had written in Holbrook), a thin one from the *High Road*, and two thin ones from the *Classmate*. Being interested in them in that order, we opened them in reverse order.

Mr. Chappell of *High Road* was asking whatever became of that serial he had asked me for in May. Also he was going to have to return the short story I had sent him, now that he had got around to read it. "I think it would go straight over the heads of ninety percent of our readers. Besides, Howard can't be developed in eleven pages. He is a man about whom a million little facts should be known. An ideal character for a novel but a poor one for a short story."

Mr. Moore of *Classmate* had written (1) "We like 'Erica Is No Lamb' but it is too long for us. Can you cut it to 4000 words?" and (2) "We have decided your revision of 'The Randall Ringer' is satisfactory and are putting it through for payment."

But right *now* we had only nine cents and a few stamps!

I tore into Eric's envelope and, instead of a check, two Jan's Letters fell out.

My first thought was, "Oh, I took it to be a long letter! He must want some revision. Well, all right — but where is the check for those he has accepted?"

His letter was still in the envelope. I pulled it out and read it.

The rejection of these manuscripts does not imply any lack of literary merit. It implies a blooming lot more. It not only implies but declares that *The Youth's Companion* has this day been sold by The Atlantic Monthly Company to the Sprague Publishing Company, which will, effective with the October issue, merge *The Companion* with its present magazine, *The American Boy*.

Under these circumstances, all girls' activities in *The Companion* come to an immediate and automatic halt. That is why, with deep regret, I must send back the Letters from Jan.

I am leaving *The Companion* office tomorrow and after a brief vacation I shall land up in New York. Was that invitation to tea conditioned by my official position? . . .

Please forgive the inadequacy of this letter — written on a difficult day. If there is any question I can answer for you, I shall be only too glad to do so, if you will address me at my home, 856 Massachusetts Avenue, Cambridge. Mr. Donald B. Snyder, publisher, is acting as mortician for *The Companion*, and business details can very handily be addressed to him.

And just when we were beginning to have a real magazine with a real (or do you still not think so) girls' department!

The next morning, which was August 12, I wrote Mr. Donald Snyder:

On return from vacation, I find a letter from Mr. Hodgins, former editor of *The Companion*, telling me that the magazine has merged with *The American Boy*, and will use no more material for girls. I am, of course, more than sorry, as everybody is.

Three of my series of 'Letters from Jan' have appeared in the June, July, and August numbers of *The Companion*. The September and October letters were accepted on April 25. For those two and the August one I have not yet been paid. The sum agreed upon when Mr. Hodgins asked me to do the series was $25 a letter, making the amount due me at the present time $75. I should be pleased to have this matter attended to as promptly as possible.

I also wrote that morning to Eric, following receipt of that day's mail:

Of course I am sorry — more than sorry. I liked being Jan, but even more than that I liked *The Companion* and what it was doing and going to do and its lovely, funny old offices which were a place to go with a variety of opinions and ideas. I feel much more as if my house had burned down than there is any sense in my feeling — and if I do, how must you! That you are to be in New York, and somewhat more welcome without the official position than with it, is the only thought I care to think in connection with *The Companion* just now.

I have sent Mr. Snyder, informally, my little bill. Would there be, do you think, anything that I could do in the way of continuing the letters elsewhere? I should not have thought of it except for a letter just now from Miss Seaman of Macmillan's who wrote: "I wonder whether you have heard of the sale of *The Youth's Companion* to *The American Boy*? I wonder what this does to your delightful feature. Yesterday Helen Ferris and I agreed it was a very capable and interesting one and we hoped it would not have to be discarded, or that they would at least place it elsewhere." Will you be so good as to write me what might be done about it? So many things I meant to say that aren't yet said.

I shall be at 509 West 121st Street by the first of October at latest. Please don't fail to give me a ring and come up and talk. I should be disappointed.

My stamps were now exhausted. That afternoon I began a serial for Mr. Chappell which I called "The Seventh Wave."

On August 13 Mr. Snyder wrote me:

Thank you for your letter of August 12th containing your account of our unsettled commitments on *The Youth's Companion*. Fortunately, our records agree throughout, and all that is left for me to do is to find the cash to square the account. As you can imagine, the financial situation on the *Companion* was extremely involved at the time of the recent sale, and I am accordingly able to take care of accounts payable only so far and as rapidly as outstanding accounts receivable come in to me. However, I wish to assure you that your vouchers, which total only $75.00, will be taken care of at the very first opportunity.

Only seventy-five dollars . . . A good neighbor's house had burned down, I could never go there again, and my neighbor had gone away.

Rebecca wrote (enclosing a letter from a girl in Chapel Hill who was enthusiastic in her approval of the first "Cockatoo" serial) saying the second would begin running in September, she was buying as much of *Land Spell* from the *Portal* as she could use, and how soon would I have a new story for her. Mr. Moore's check for "The Randall Ringer" came and we had stamps so on August 27 I sent Rebecca a letter:

I'm sorry not to have answered your note much sooner. I wanted to do a story for you to go with my reply, but the amount of writing I've been able to tuck into this strange, wonderful, devastating summer is shockingly small. Mr. Chappell's serial is not yet finished. Won't you tell me if there is any special issue you need a story for? Only make it far enough ahead so that I can have the serial done first.

We also mailed a shortened version of "Erica Is No Lamb" to Mr. Moore who "put through payment" for it promptly, and I rushed this to Herbert who had gone back to New York on Labor Day to begin his work for Dr. Gates, trusting that lightning had not struck twice and his "sure" fifty dollars a week vanished without a trace. The research assistantship held firm, and Herbert's doctor told him his health was now much improved, bearing out the wisdom of spending the summer outdoors, and that he should come through this college year well if he kept to his diet and continued his medication. But his first salary check would not come until the end of the month. I stayed on at home, board free, finishing "The Seventh Wave," also writing Mr. Chappell frequently that he would soon get it and under the same cover insisting that he had promised me five dollars for a poem I had sent him the first of the summer while the check I had recently received for it was for only four dollars. A dollar was a dollar. I refrained from adding that even five dollars would not take me to New York, much less feed me for a few days after I got there.

He wrote me his apology, added the dollar, and said in a postscript, "Really, I am going to be embarrassed if you don't send that serial in the course of the next few days. I have been counting on it and am just about at the end of my rope."

Payment came for the last words of the deceased Jan who had been far too young and vibrant to die, and I finished the serial my mother had been typing as I went along, put the roadster in the barn, went back to New York on September 20, and mailed the serial the following day. On September 30 Mr. Chappell wrote, asking, "What did I offer you for the serial which came in last week and which I have not yet had an opportunity to examine? I hope I wasn't too extravagant."

On October second I wrote him:

> If I am not mistaken, you offered me $300 for a serial, and I think I am not mistaken for I distinctly remember saying that the sum would clean a dress a hundred times. Not that one dress would endure so much. That being the case, one can distribute such an amount over many dresses. All, however, cost $3.00 a turn — at least in New York — which I consider an insult and an outrage, because not everything has pleats and sometimes there is only one small spot or streak and — yes, the amount was surely $300.00. Are you convinced? . . . I, too, hope you weren't too extravagant.

The audacity of this girl! She did not own "many" dresses. She could remove her own "small spots." She was in pursuit of car payments, paper, envelopes, stamps, and theater and railway ticket money.

For me, the summer had been strange. That fall, it seemed to me, was strange for everyone. I wrote one editor that I was aware of "a not unpleasant sense of impending disaster." Not unpleasant, I suppose, because everything was exciting, even the prospect of disaster.

Cockatoo was published before the end of September, dedicated to my parents, and we mailed a copy to them, to Herbert's parents, and to Rebecca Caudill at the *Torchbearer*; but I was disappointed in its advertising, which stressed its plot. Rebecca replied, "May I be frank and say Miss Seaman did not give you a square deal on the binding and paper? It is not at all worthy of the story. And I agree with you about the advertising. The book deserves better. I hope you did go to Anne Carroll Moore as you threatened. Anyway, I congratulate both you and the *Torchbearer* that neither of us had any part in *Blue Ribbon Stories* recently published. If you haven't seen a copy by all means find one and see what you escaped!" I comforted myself with the conviction that the same advertising could hardly be given to *Land Spell* when it came out as it had by comparison very little plot. And, resolved to tell girls of the '30s what a world war did to the life of a girl who watched and felt it in her own hometown in Maine, I began writing a book which had no plot at all.

John Dos Passos married a Maine girl that year. Rudy Vallee came out of Westbrook and rode to fame with the Maine Stein Song. Robert Hutchins was named President of the University of Chicago at the age of thirty. Professor Rogers of the Massachusetts Institute of Technology was quoted nationally as having said in a talk to the alumni, "You cannot go on the assumption that you are as good as the rest of folks. You should take the attitude that you are a damned sight better." (It was Professor Rogers of whom I had written from Fall River to Professor Mitchell of Bowdoin, "I think he is a Babbitt, modified oddly by his academic associations.")

Eric Hodgins telephoned and came up for tea, stooping a little to get through our door and lowering his big frame into the scoop-bottom chair. His eyes looked haunted. He was now in the business office of *McCall's Magazine*, this young man who after graduation from the institution where Professor Rogers taught had tried in vain to rescue the *Youth's Companion* and bring it back to life. We sat and looked wryly at each other.

He spread his hands and said, "Where do we begin?"

I said, "Where we left off. I just read that your Professor Rogers says everybody should take the attitude that he is a damned sight better than anybody else. At least, if he graduated from M.I.T. And you did. He says Harvard never apologizes, never argues, never listens to criticism, but goes on calmly putting on her front. Where's your front?"

He said, "Oh, I've got one all right. But I didn't think I'd need it today."

I said, "Good. Just so you know where it is —"

We talked over the last days of the *Companion*. I asked him about his present work and he told me there was nothing to say of it. I asked if I could direct a short story to him for possible publication in *McCall's* and he said no, it would have to go to the editorial department and that, wherever else I might publish, it quite surely would never be in *McCall's*. He thought I should "get together" with *Household Magazine* on a girls' page. I showed him *Cockatoo* and the clipped advertisements for it and he shook his head, saying, "I know how you feel but they are trying to sell the book and you haven't proven to anybody that girls will read stories about anything but mysteries and treasure hunts." I reminded him that Macmillan was soon to publish *Land Spell* which had no treasure hunts. He said, "Ah, but it has a mystery, so *that's* what they will publicize." I snarled that now I was writing a girls' book which had neither mystery nor treasure hunt but was all about a girl who had both a head and a heart and used them. He spread his hands again, and sighed, "My dear, I can only say I wish it well." He said he had, in collaboration with Alexander Magoun, written a history of aviation, called *Sky High*, which would be out soon; "but I don't know who will read it." A few weeks later he sent me a copy, inscribed "From a co-member of the Authors Indignation League."

His book was dedicated, "To the memory of those persistent gentlemen who, since the recorded history of flight began, were always quick to assert that It Could Not Be Done — in the hope that this story of courage and sacrifice may make them turn, now and then, uneasily in their graves."

It was autumn, 1929. By now Douglas Fairbanks, Jr., had married Joan Crawford, Jeanne Eagels had died (I had seen her in *Rain* in Providence), Libby Holman was Moanin' Low in *The Little Show* and reminding everyone of Helen Morgan, people whistled "Singing in the Rain" on the streets, the old Waldorf-Astoria was being torn down to make room for the Empire State Building, Babe Ruth was still top man in baseball, Bill Tilden in tennis, Bobby Jones in golf, there was much debate about whether the Prohibition Amendment would ever be repealed but few took the affirmative and we who had no speakeasy cards assumed that every closed door led to one; the great German dirigible, the Graf Zeppelin, had circled the world.

By then Herbert was deep in his research and his doctoral dissertation (one of the requirements was that the dissertation must be printed for placement in the university library and this would cost us from four hundred dollars to nine hundred dollars, depending on its length) and we had added the Mendenhall brothers, Jim, Tom, and Paul, and their sister Ethelwyn, to our circle of friends among Columbia graduate students which previously had included the Max Brunstetters from Pennsylvania and the Frank Dilleys from Ohio, two couples who with their small children were our neighbors in Bancroft Hall. We went to cocktail parties, though we neither drank nor smoked, but our favorite recreation was the theater and the opera. We saw the Lunts in *Caprice*, Eva Le Gallienne in *Peter Pan*, Leslie Howard and Margalo Gillmore in *Berkeley Square*, Noel Coward's *Bitter Sweet*, and Clayton, Jackson, and Durante in Florenz Ziegfeld's *Show Girl;* we heard Galli-Curci, Ezio Pinza, Lili Pons, John McCormack, Lawrence Tibbett, all from the third balcony at fifty cents a seat, first come first seated.

We also read the New York *Times*. It was left at our door every morning. We bought it for the sports pages, and for the reviews of books and plays, but we read the news. Toward the end of October its black headlines told us that there was panic in Wall Street, that everyone wanted to sell stock and no one wanted to buy, that the big bankers were meeting, that the bankers would support prices, that nothing could stop the avalanche, that speculators were committing suicide, that $30 billion had simply disappeared. Not spent either wisely or foolishly. Just vanished. In the little courtyard of Bancroft Hall young wives of graduate students, watching their children at play, hugged their sweaters around them against the crisp wind, and said to each other, "As Frank says, we didn't know how lucky we were not to be rich," or "As I told Max, let's hope we never find out how it feels to be down to our last yacht, or our last Cadillac."

Surely prices of necessities would drop. The whistlers on the street began piping, "Happy Days Are Here Again."

I was writing home:

Isn't it *nice* that the wholesale house in Portland is sold out of *Cockatoo*? I've written Alma Savage of Boston Macmillan that Hobb's Variety in South Berwick can't get copies. Maybe they will supply Mr. Hobbs direct . . . And mother, about my table. I'm pleased papa is painting it, but don't send it to me until we see how I get on as I am. I'd love to keep it there, if I can, as I'll always be needing a place to work when I'm home any length of time. Herbert doesn't need his desk here as he does all his work at the office, so I'm to have it. It just fits between the window and the radiator, and I can put my feet up the way I like to on a rod at the foot of the bed . . . We went downtown last night to see *Porgy*, the Negro play that ran a year here a couple of years ago, now back for a limited engagement. I was so afraid it would be gone again before I got here. But it is still running, and perfectly marvellous. . . . I'd love to hear your new record. As it is, I depend for my daytime music on the orchestra rehearsals across the street. They are very good and practically constant . . . I'm enclosing a bit of the material I used for covering my largest sofa pillow. Isn't it gorgeous? If I thought it would wash I'd send you some for a new couch cover for the kitchen. Wouldn't it go well with your colors? . . . We don't see why there should be such a delay in getting new pistons for the roadster. It isn't going to do Papa much good if he doesn't get the use of it soon . . . Last night I cleaned our chandelier and Herbert put up the ecru scrim curtains and fixtures for the living room overdrapes. I'm sewing on the overdrapes but they aren't done yet. Here is a scrap so you'll know we'll have fall foliage with us all winter . . . Wednesday night we saw *The Commodore Marries*, based on *The Adventures of Peregrine Pickle* by Smollett. Walter Huston (he of *The Barker*) was the commodore. He is wonderful and the play very good. I read *Peregrine* just before . . . Today I had a letter from Bertha Mahony, editor of *The Horn Book*, asking if I will do an article for the February issue which goes to press on January 10! I certainly will!!! And the title of it will be "The Strange Case of the Intelligent Girl" . . . You *should* see the apartment now. You really and truly SHOULD. We got a handsome floor lamp for

$5.00 from a couple in the house who are leaving and selling things in preference to moving; they paid $15.00 for it last year; and we got for ninety cents an electric plate that I can have on the table and use like a toaster. And guess what! Bancroft apartments now have refrigerators! Mine is a tiny one but neatly enameled and sets under the shelf on top of which are the gas plates. How I love it! At last I can keep food! At last I can have salads (for me; of course Herbert can't eat them)! At last we have most of our meals in! And tomorrow I'm having some friends to tea; one of them is Hildegarde Swift who has just published a charming book for small children called *Little Blacknose*. The night after that Jim Mendenhall is coming for dinner, and we've invited Lloyd Hathaway and his fiancee for Sunday . . . Herbert's work is going very well. Right now he is sitting in our scoop-bottom chair reading German. No, we don't *need* two comfortable chairs. When one of us sits in it the other enjoys thinking how comfortable the occupant is. While I finished my sewing and mending he read Julia Peterkin's *Scarlet Sister Mary*. I think you would like it for though Si May-e had nine children by as many fathers, she was sweet and clean and bright and tender; you just have to keep in mind that she was living by her rules, not ours . . . *Land Spell* is ready for the printer and I'm to take it to Miss Seaman Thursday and stay for tea with her. That will be nice. Besides work on that and on "The Truly Brave" I've sent "Subway Easter" to Rebecca and written to Cookie, Ruth, Herbert's mother, and Fred McCreary. Herbert's father fell off a load of apples he was hauling last week, and hurt his back, but is better. Mother C. said it was lucky it didn't happen before they got to Brattleboro Fair! Did you go to Rochester Fair this year? You haven't mentioned it.

Like the whistlers on the street we had no inkling yet of how far out the ripples reach when a bundle of $30 billion in paper money has dropped into a great body of water.

Miss Mochrie, new editor of *The American Girl*, took a two-part story of mine, called "Tenpenny Girl," and, over a lunch at which I first tasted an avocado, I talked with her about possible serialization of "The Truly Brave." She said she would like to see it when it was done, but she could use only five or at most six sections of no more than four thousand words each. I wrote Rebecca, "But my story will have twelve chapters, one for each month of the year, and each will be at least 5000 words. I am writing just what I want to write, this time, and I have never felt so satisfied before. If it doesn't serialize, it doesn't serialize." She advised me to send it when finished to Wilma McFarland of the *Portal*, and tell her "if she buys it, I'll buy it of her."

I wrote feverishly, between long stretches at the public library where I studied and took notes of files of 1918 newspapers, until we went home for Christmas, and finished the manuscript soon after we returned to New York. Before February was out I had sent a copy to Miss McFarland and another to Miss Seaman.

On March 6 Miss McFarland replied:

> The reason that we have been so very long in reporting on your story, "The Truly Brave," is that it has been read all up and down the line. We liked the style so well that we wanted to consider it very seriously before returning it, but the consensus of opinion is that it is really an adult story about young folks and in order to be appreciated thoroughly must be read by someone who went through the experiences of the war . . . Why don't you *try* an adult market at least? I should like to see it done.

I sent the manuscript to women's magazines, received it back with letters saying, "It is good but it is not *Good Housekeeping*," and "This is from too youthful a point of view for us," and "Personally, I am very enthusiastic about this but the editorial consensus is against it." I sent it to young people's story papers saying, "I wrote this for girls but their editors say it is too mature for them. I am aware I have dealt with characteristics and problems which many writers for girls seem to think it best to ignore. Would your readers be interested in reading what it was like to be fifteen years old in a world at war?" And it came back with the word that young people's story papers were for those of college age.

Miss Seaman became Mrs. Bechtel. We were invited to her housewarming in the spacious and handsome Bechtel apartment in one of the first condominium buildings in the city, and I met Elizabeth Coatsworth there, also Lynd Ward and his wife, May McNeer, among other Macmillan writers of juvenile books. We saw and were tremendously impressed by *Journey's End*, a play based on the novel *All Quiet on the Western Front*, and I came out of the theater reconvinced that enough could never be said about the effect of war on the human spirit. We went with Lloyd to a party in the bleak and bare apartment of one of his friends who was a White Russian émigré; his father had been a general in the Czar's army; his pale, beautiful young wife said their greatest tragedy was that they could never have children, being convinced that they had no right to bring them into such an ugly world. We dined with a Bates classmate who was married to an artist with strongly Communist views and who claimed to be helping to plan a Communist revolution here. We thought he had a great flair for the dramatic. We went to a party at the Mendenhalls where, I wrote my mother, "we arrived between 10:00 and 11:00, but most people did not get there until midnight — no end of all kinds of psychologists, dancers, a Russian actress, a woman stockbroker from Wall Street, a man who has done sleight-of-hand tricks for the boy King of Roumania, a bevy of Columbia undergraduates, and a lot of people who didn't say who they were or what they did"; at three to four o'clock in the morning we were riding through Central Park in horse-drawn cabs, and the downtown streets were as busy, the subway on which we came home as crowded, as at midday.

I continued to try to perfect my favorite short stories, "The John Crag Lot" and "So Clyde Was Born," but Edith Walton of the *Forum* wrote me of the former, "This story is a solid, competent piece of work. However, my feeling is that you have not made John Crag a sufficiently vivid character . . . The negotiations for the woodlot seem rather long drawn out"; and W. F. Bigelow of *Good Housekeeping* wrote of the latter story, "It is one of the most interesting we have recently come across in our general mail, but it is not quite our type."

And Mrs. Bechtel telephoned me from her office at Macmillan one rainy morning to say the readers' reports were in on *The Truly Brave* and there was general agreement that it would not have a wide enough sale to justify publication. It was necessary now to be very sure the Company did not lose money. She added brightly that she continued to have high hopes for *Land Spell*, they would be getting galley proof to me soon, and did I have any ideas for the jacket.

I sent her an envelope filled with pictures my mother had taken with her Brownie 2A camera of The House and its yard, the riverbank, the turn of the road over Warren's Bridge, and said I hoped the artist would base his designs on them as they were of the part of Maine in which the story was laid. When I sent back the galleys, I dedicated the book to Herbert's three twelve-year-old nieces, and I asked that, on the page following that which carried the dedication, this be inscribed:

". . . a certain parcel of land situated in South Berwick, Maine, and bounded northerly and easterly by the highway, southerly by land of Charles Nowell and by land of Oliver Boston, and westerly by White's Marsh Brook, and containing thirty acres more or less . . ."

This was a quote from my grandfather's deed to our home place.

In April Rebecca Caudill resigned as editor of *The Torch-*

bearer and went abroad. In April Wilma McFarland of *The Portal* returned my short story, "Maudie Tom, Jockey" saying, "This is another case of an adult story about young folks rather than a story for young folks" . . . It was becoming apparent that there were no outlets in the juvenile field for what I wanted to say to and about young girls and the feelings and thoughts I knew they had. The sensitive and intelligent young, apparently, could be communicated with, in print, if at all, only through books and magazines directed primarily at adults; and in nearly four years I seemed to have made very small advances upon the adult market. Was this, I wondered, because I had been following the wrong path, put too much of my time and effort into a field which did not allow me freedom, gave me an opportunity to publish only when I said a great deal of what I did not think worth saying and very little of what I wanted to say?

By April Bancroft Hall was acutely aware that few colleges and universities were enlarging their faculties or replacing professors or instructors who died or resigned. For most graduate students the two or three years spent in work toward doctoral degrees, especially for those who had families, had required extreme sacrifices and built up staggering debts. The Frank Dilleys and a few others who were on leave from college positions to which they could return were openly envied. Those who could hope, at best, only to go back to what they had made this effort and investment to leave behind, consulted agencies and were shocked to learn that there were few professional openings anywhere and many applicants whose credentials equaled their own for the type of service involved.

I thought, "We could go home. We can always go home." But what Herbert wanted to do, what he was prepared to do, could not be done at home, and he would rest nowhere until he was doing it. Beside that, we were too independent to accept support from anyone, even from those we loved most.

The loan for the car had troubled us though we were faithfully sending each month the payment which would make it entirely ours at the end of May.

Herbert tried to conceal his anxiety from me, but it showed; he lost weight and did not eat or sleep well.

I thought, "He needs another summer outdoors. As soon as he has his degree, and has finished his work for Dr. Gates, we'll go home, take the car, and find some little shack in the woods where he can walk and fish and I can write, while we wait for something to turn up. Surely I can earn enough for a shack in the woods, and at least bread and milk?"

Then Dr. and Mrs. Gates invited us to dinner in their penthouse on the roof of Bancroft and told us that Dean Melvin E. Haggerty of the University of Minnesota would be in New York in a few days, interviewing candidates for an assistant professorship in educational psychology; and that he had recommended Herbert. The interviews were held and when Dean Haggerty had returned to Minnesota he wrote offering Herbert the position. It was not in Herbert's area of specialization, the salary was three thousand dollars (scarcely more than his had been at Durfee High School), and we did not want to go so far from New England. But this was no time to quibble. He accepted the offer. We would be in Minneapolis in September.

But Herbert's health did not improve. We were concerned as to whether another summer outdoors would be enough to make him ready for his first year of university teaching and research. He mentioned this concern to Dr. Gates who advised him strongly to consult with Dr. Hugh Auchincloss before he left New York.

He lost no time in doing so, and at the end of three days of examinations and tests came home with the astonishing report that if he had ever had an ulcer, actual or incipient, x-rays showed no trace of it now, and the problem was dietary deficiency. He needed red meat and all kinds of fruit and vegetables, raw as well as cooked. Though we could not afford it we celebrated by going out for a broiled steak, and as soon as the corner grocery opened the next morning I was there to buy the makings of a big tossed salad for our lunch. What we had been spending on medication could now be added to our food budget. We thought we had an idea of what it feels like to be released from prison.

After my "Maudie Tom, Jockey" had been returned by every juvenile magazine with which I had had previous contact, *St. Nicholas* took it (and it was much later to be selected for inclusion in several anthologies, including Henry Steele Commager's *St. Nicholas Stories*, school readers, and the *Reader's Digest*'s *Great Stories for Young People*). I was pleased but not halted in my rapidly growing belief that I must find my way out of the juvenile field if what I wanted most to say was going to be heard. At Eric's urging I was discussing with Antrim Crawford in Topeka, Kansas, a possible monthly page of straight talk to girls in his *Household Magazine.* I was writing Edwin Chappell of *The High Road* that I could do another serial for his "college age" whenever he wanted it. But I was also writing new and re-revising old short stories to send to established and "little" literary magazines, and carrying on spirited correspondences with their editors, particularly with John T. Frederick who, in addition to being the editor of *Midland*, was a professor of English at Northwestern University. And I mailed two short stories about the Shaw family of *Land Spell* to Wilma McFarland, saying I should like to do twelve of them, one for each month of the year, but that as the family was now a few years older than in *Land Spell* they might be too old for the *Portal.*

I was also saying goodbye to New York.

We sat on benches on Morningside Heights for hours, by day and by night, with what we felt was all Manhattan spread out below. We walked for hours in Riverside Park along the bank of the Hudson, watching the ships tied up at dock, the ferries and the riverboats moving with their own proud majesty up and down the river in spring sunshine, in rain, in fog, and in the dark; and every night in bed I listened to their warning whistles, telling myself sleepily, "I must remember this sound . . . I must put it where I can keep it and call it back when I am not near any body of water large enough for craft with whistles. I've heard them on Buzzard's Bay, in Long Island Sound, and on the Hudson. And at home, when there is a seaturn, we hear the foghorns from the lighthouses and lightships along the coast . . . People still awake when I am sleeping. People taking care of people . . ."

I rode downtown on the top deck of buses, though the fare was ten cents, familiar with every block, every turn, but with my head spinning as if I had never seen it before; and back on the subway for five cents, reeling happily as I clung to a strap, studying the faces, listening to the voices and accents around me, feeling the pressure of the bodies next to mine reeling as I reeled, and loving the rush through the dark with the sudden glare of each station we reached and then the headlong rush into another dark tunnel. Or I went down by subway and back on the top deck, to see and feel it all from the opposite direction. People look different, sound different, feel different to the touch when they are going out into the world than when they are coming home, whatever home may be.

I walked the streets of Greenwich Village, trying to absorb something of what other young writers and artists of the time gained or sought to gain from living there. I roamed the Garment District and Macy's basement, and then walked slowly, as sedately and confidently as I could, through Saks-Fifth Avenue. It seemed to me that the life, the vigor, and yes, the joy I found was mostly below Forty-second Street, cheek to cheek with all the reasonable despair. I thought that if I could choose I would prefer being in pursuit of my next bowl of soup to a desperate search for an apparently nonexistent exact match or perfect compliment in one piece of apparel to some other piece of apparel for which I had spent a small fortune last week.

I went for the last time between the marble pillars of the Macmillan Company, for the last time to each of my favorite restaurants (Mary Elizabeth's, Drake's, Alice Foote Macdougall's, King's College Inn), and lunch counters with the friends who had often joined me there; and the night after Columbia Commencement, with another Bancroft couple, we put the two Ph.D.'s in our pockets, left the dancing in the Quadrangle, and rode on a bus top to Washington Square. From there we walked to The Pirate's Den where we had been once before and to which I had always wanted to go back. It was as salty as before, but since we had so little but Ph.D's in our pockets we could order only sandwiches. When the waiter asked what we would have to drink we said, "Nothing, thanks." It was a blow when the checks came to find that each man owed $1.50 beyond the price of the sandwiches. When they asked for an explanation they were told the water brought to us was seventy-five cents a glass. They said if they had known this they would have sent the water back; and the waiter shrugged. We had not sent it back, had we? We had drunk it with our sandwiches.

This experience helped me a little, but not much, a few days later, when after our frenzy of packing, crating, and shipping, my train pulled out of Grand Central Station, and I was leaving not only New York but Herbert behind. New York I might never see again, and though Herbert would follow me to Maine in a few weeks, as soon as he had completed his work for Dr. Gates, a few weeks was a long time.

But by the time the train reached Connecticut I was feeling fine. I was going home and I put far back in my mind the knowledge that I was going early because once the summer was over I could not foresee when I would be there again. I was going home to do dishes with my mother, check old stone walls and trace boundary lines with my father, wash Grammy's hair, sing in the swingchairs after supper, listen to the whippoorwills, and start a serial for Edwin Chappell.

My father met me at Salmon Falls station. Coming down the iron steps of the coach, I saw him by the baggage truck talking with the baggage master, his hat as always tipped a little rakishly over the twinkle I knew was there, the high color in his cheeks visible even from a distance, his shoulders braced back, his feet well apart and his weight on his heels, and holding his cigar exactly as George Burns held his. The curtain was going up again on what would always be for me more absorbing than any play. I ran toward him, he strode toward me and took my bag. When the bag was in the back seat of the Willys-Knight we hugged and kissed before I got in beside him.

On the ride home he talked and I half listened, with my hand on his knee. I was looking at the Salmon Falls mills, the Salmon Falls River, the point of South Berwick which ran down to the bank of the river, the town hall where our grammar school graduation had been held, the little stores in the old brick block, the church spires, Academy Street, the great elms along Portland Street, the Soldiers Monument, Powder House Hill, two village cemeteries, Old Swamps, the Junction bridge over the Newichewannock (nobody had wanted to print my "Legends of Newichewannock"), Goodwin's Hill, Witchtrot Road, Nason's pump, the district schoolhouse, Nason's hill, White Marsh Bridge . . .

But I heard what he said as we turned into our lane.

He said, "Your grandmother isn't very well."

"Grammy?"

"She's been losing strength lately. She fell when your mother was helping her into her room one night last week.

We had quite a time getting her onto the bed and she hasn't been able to get up since. Dr. Ross thinks she may have broken her hip."

"Why, I've heard from Mama since then and she didn't say —"

"She thought just as well not to worry you about it until you got here."

My mother met me at the door.

We held each other close for a minute and I asked, "How's Grammy?"

She said, "She's waiting to see you."

I went into her room and bent over the bed to kiss her. Her double bed nearly filled the small room with its single window and she looked tiny and pale in it.

I asked how she felt and she said, "Well, there, I fell down and here I am. I don't s'pose I got my never-get-over-it."

I laughed, said of course she hadn't, and asked if she had pain.

She moved her head as if irritated and said, "Not much if I'm left alone. Only when they try to move me . . . Well, how are you? I expect you had a great time when Herbert got that degree he was after."

I sat down and described the Commencement. Then I told her about paying seventy-five cents for a glass of water and she said that was the most ridiculous thing she ever heard in her life. She said she pitied anybody who had to live in New York on her pension, and I said if any Civil War widows were trying they probably had too much sense to go to the Pirate's Den, and she said, "I should hope to the Lord! And I hope you would again."

But when I went back to the kitchen my mother told me the doctor was quite sure Grammy's hip was broken and had said it was no use putting her through going to the hospital to find out because at her age nothing could be done about it if she had. She would never walk again, if it was broken. It took two people to move her now and she screamed in agony when they had to. Dr. Ross had left medicine to ease the pain but said her heart would not stand its use long. My mother said she could hardly bring herself either to give her the pills or not to give them to her, nobody had had much sleep for ten days and nights, and she was about ready to ask Lizzie Higgins if she could come to stay for a while; everybody said Lizzie had a real knack in the sickroom.

I asked if Lizzie had a telephone.

My mother said she did not think so; anyway, it would be better to go to her house because Grammy heard telephone conversations.

"You don't think Grammy would want Lizzie?"

"It would frighten her to hear what Lizzie has to be told, and might worry her to think of an outsider coming into the house. If Lizzie comes, I'm sure she'll like her. Everybody does."

That night we sent my father to bed and I, staying up with my mother, was close to excruciating pain for the first time and learned how long a night can be. But Grammy said, "It's easier now Gladie's come"; and sometimes, "Let Gladie *start* me, Frank." I thought this might hurt my mother and whispered to her when she was back on the sitting room couch and I on the chair beside it, "She thinks that only because I'm a change, Mama." And my mother whispered back, "No. It's because you're calmer. I feel so bad to touch her that I shake all over. I'm as thankful as she is that you're here."

I did my final growing up in those next few weeks. It was I who gave Grammy the pills that eased her pain, kept her more and more asleep, and shortened her life. I went for Lizzie and brought her home, and after that my mother could go to bed at night, though she slept little. Lizzie was invaluable. She helped everywhere and kept the strength in my arms, the resolve in my heart to give Grammy peace at whatever cost. Only my voice did not break when I read to Grammy from the worn Bible she could no longer lift or see, only my hand did not spill the half-filled spoons of tea, thin soup, warm orange juice which soon became the only nourishment she could take.

Gradually she slipped into a coma. Lizzie sat beside her and I kept going in to look at her, to touch her cheek with my finger, just as my mother did at other times. Once in silent tears I asked Lizzie, "What else can we do for her?" And Lizzie put her arms around me, let me cry against her, and said, "Nothing more. She don't need us now. She's safe and comfortable. She's in God's hands and knows it." Dr. Ross came, bent over her, said, "How do you feel, Louise?" but she did not answer. He came out of her room and said to my mother, "Don't grieve, Frankie. She's been through a lot. She helped me deliver all Lula's babies and Lula always had a hard time. She saw Lula go, after the last one, and her own two husbands long before that. She's a little woman but strong and proud and saintly. She has earned her rest."

Grammy had used her first pension money to buy a lot in the village cemetery nearest to us, put it in perpetual care, and have the earthly remains of her parents moved there from a corner of the long-uncut field behind the ruins of the old Brooks house. Later she had had a stone set, with the name BROOKS on the front in large letters, and on the back, in smaller script, "James Brooks, 1823–1900; Catherine Joy, his wife, 1826–1905; S. Louise Emery, 1851–." Herbert came for the funeral service in the parlor, and all her other grandchildren with their wives or husbands, and before the coffin lid was closed we covered her with a blanket of the pansies she had loved. Then, though married early to Ephraim Dow who had died two years later of tuberculosis contracted in southern swamps and been buried in the shadow of the White Mountains, and later married to Jack Emery who was drowned in Round Pond and buried in his family's little graveyard in a corner of an Emery field, she went to lie under the name of BROOKS, beside her father and her mother; and we added the date, 1930, after her name on the stone.

Some time the next week I showed Herbert a letter which had come — I did not know when — from Edwin Chappell of the *High Road*. It said:

> I am sorry I haven't written you sooner about the serial. Of course, I shall be delighted to see it, and I trust you felt that you know me well enough to go ahead in the preparation of it. Send it in as soon as you can, because my resignation here takes effect the first of September and I'd like to have a chance to pass on it before I leave.

Eric Hodgins was no longer an editor, I did not know what had become of Rebecca Caudill, and Edwin Chappell's resignation would take effect the first of September. If I had indeed grown up at last it was only just in time.

I had also had a letter from Wilma McFarland written, as it happened, on my twenty-fifth birthday, regarding my two stories with *Land Spell* characters. It said:

> I like them tremendously. I can't tell you how very much I liked them. I think you have the making of a beautiful book if you do more and gather them together later . . . My youngsters would love them and be simply charmed to have more Shaw family stories, but *Classmate* readers would get more than this out of them. I feel like a martyr but I have offered them to Mr. Moore who has enthusiastically accepted them. Now can you outline further for us your idea for the series? He says if there is enough variety he may have room for all twelve, certainly for six or eight. They will have a deep appeal not only for our college age group but for the many adult readers of the *Classmate*.

And Antrim Crawford had reached the point of accepting material suited to an August page for girls in the *Household*.

He would call it "Around the Family Table," had paid me fifty dollars for it, and wanted me to rush him copy for the three following months, to allow time for any necessary revision.

In our preliminary discussions of the course such a page should follow, I had again become involved in a struggle to write on topics which seemed interesting and significant to me and which were identical with those I believed American high school girls felt a deep concern about. One of these topics was current literature. I had sent him from New York several reviews I had written of both "teen-age" and adult books which might be in their public libraries and which I felt either were or were not worth their reading. He had replied:

> Yours is good literary criticism, but it is not so very different from what appears in *The Saturday Review* and that periodical, if I am not mistaken, has not been able to build a circulation of as much as fifty thousand. You cannot appeal this way to all the girls in a million and a half families. It is probably all right to make some comment on books occasionally, though I am not enthusiastic about it for this page . . . I don't want to interfere unduly but the members of my local staff and I are pretty familiar with the types of reader that our magazine reaches, and I am anxious that your page develop a strong appeal in its first few months.

I had responded by including just one review in my first "Table Talk" and at the end of the page by inquiring what topics the girls themselves would most like to discuss.

It was now near the middle of July.

I wrote Edwin Chappell:

> I am appalled that you are leaving the *High Road*. Do tell me where you are to be. I should be very sorry to lose touch with you entirely. I can't tell you how warmly I feel toward the purchaser of my first story, nor how much I have enjoyed our resultant sketchy acquaintance . . . I had not started the serial

until your letter came, but it is now under weigh with the title "Lotusland" and should reach you before your resignation takes effect.

My parents went for a week's visit to my brother and his wife and little Richard in their summer cottage at Bow Lake in New Hampshire and, alone in the Hasty house, I wrote and Herbert studied in preparation for his fall courses. They came home, a little bewildered to find themselves now the oldest generation, and more bewildered by being for the first time in their married lives in an uncrowded house, without responsibility for anyone's welfare except their own, without financial worries since what my grandfather had so contentedly accumulated, at whatever sacrifice to himself and others, was now theirs, and thus with the freedom to do whatever they wanted to do and to go wherever they wanted to go if they could think what and where that was.

We all stayed up late over High-Low-Jack and whist. Usually I played the piano for my mother to sing just before we went to bed around midnight. It was no longer necessary to be quiet in consideration of those who were sleeping, for no one was asleep who would waken. By day they called on friends, or took picnic lunches and drove over country roads remembering who had lived along them when they were young and who had built all the crumbling stone walls, or went to the beach for lobsters; and as often as we could we went with them.

By mid-August I had finished and Herbert and my mother had typed "Lotusland," two "Table Talks," and an outline for the series of Shaw family stories. We sent them off and went to Rowe, Massachusetts for a week's visit to Herbert's parents and his six sisters, all of whom either still lived or now summered in that or neighboring towns.

When we came back, letters from the Southern Methodists and the Northern Methodists were waiting for us.

Edwin Chappell wrote:

> Here is your check for $225.00. I am sorry I cannot make it more. I think this is the last check I shall send out as editor of the story papers, and it seems quite appropriate it should go to you who sent me your first story and whose progress has been so marked since that time . . . I am sorry you are going to Minnesota, for I wouldn't be at all surprised if New York would be my resting place this coming winter. But you won't stay away forever, will you? . . . I've neglected to tell you that Miss Caudill is in Chicago. I understand she is working for a trade journal. Maybe you will see her when you get up there.

Wilma McFarland wrote that Mr. Moore was certainly expecting to use as many of the proposed series as he could, hoped to receive the third story by the middle or last of September, "though sooner would be very nice." And she added, "Is there any bayberry in your town? And is there a local florist who sells it and sends it out by express? If so, do let me have his address."

Bayberry grows on rocky points along the seacoast, and my town had no seacoast; neither had it a florist. But my parents had rented a cottage at York for the first week of September, and bought themselves their first bathing suits.

I wrote Wilma:

> I'm a little perturbed about the matter of getting the March "Land Spell" story to you by the middle or last of September, as you ask. You see, the next ten days are the last of the rather brief vacation I've allowed myself, and then we start driving through to Minneapolis where we are to live this year. I had planned to do the March story the very first thing after arriving, and could get it to you early in October if that would do. If it positively wouldn't, let me know right away, and I'll try to jamb it in somehow. But I had made such a good resolution to do nothing until we get there! Nothing, that is, beside altering clothes, packing, and improving my swimming. Oh, yes, one more thing I'm surely going to do! — go bayberrying! A box will be off to you soon.

When we came back from the week at the beach where

none of us had ever stayed so long before, my six author's copies of *Land Spell* had been delivered and together we admired them. Not only did the jacket bear a picture of The House looking exactly as it did and always had, with the Bellflower apple tree in front and the row of maples my father as a boy had planted beside the driveway, but to introduce every other chapter the artist, William Siegel, had done what appeared to be a woodcut suggested by the Brownie snapshots my mother had taken.

I wrote in Herbert's copy, "For Herbert, who loves the same 'parcel of land' I do, and who remembers what is buried under the white birch by the brook." And in my parents' copy: "For my mother and father, and that certain 'parcel of land' we know best. September 14, 1930."

Finally, on a Sunday afternoon, we went to the home of Dr. and Mrs. Nutter for the wedding of their daughter, Ruth, my Academy and college classmate and college roommate. Girls who had been with us in the Academy and those who had been our closest friends in Bates dormitories stood together behind her and the man she was marrying, whom none of us knew. We listened to the words and felt the distance widen between girlhood and us. Ruth was the second of us all to marry. I remembered that she had written after being my bridesmaid, "When you left, everyone looked a little lost and I felt really awful . . . Even when I came home I couldn't make it seem possible that things would never be the same again. The first night here I heard someone moving in bed and thought vaguely, 'That's Gladys' and it came over me so suddenly that it wasn't and never would be that I came wide awake with a start. It's a strange feeling to have your roommate disappear from the face of the earth, leaving Mrs. Carroll in her place . . ." Now it was Ruth's wedding ending. Dr. and Mrs. Nutter moved up to kiss their daughter, and Mrs. Nutter said, "May we join you and your husband to greet your guests, Mrs. Smith?"

V

To Minneapolis

In New York that fall bathtub gin parties were popular, and weekend cruises beyond the twelve-mile limit where the Prohibition Amendment lost whatever punch it had. Lindbergh was inaugurating air mail to the Canal Zone, and Costes and Bellonte were flying *The Question Mark* westward from Paris to Long Island. "Prosperity is just around the corner" had become a cliché, while on the corners unemployed men were trying to sell at five cents each the apples they had bought wholesale from the International Apple Shippers Association. Many of those who bought of them had no other lunch.

And in Washington President Hoover fought to sustain American confidence in "rugged individualism," struggled with problems of the Treasury, his Farm Board, tax reduction, tariff bills, pension plans, and received discouraging reports on the London Arms Conference.

But we were not in New York, nor in Washington.

Hauling west all we could take with us on the four wheels of our very own topless roadster, with two hundred dollars in cash and travelers checks, on our way to a three-thousand-dollar-a-year salary from which debts to educational institutions must be paid, we felt personally carefree, singularly blessed, and talked as we went of what people like us should be able to do to make the world a better place for all to live in. We were young, eager, happy, grateful, felt we were really looking the world in the eye at last, and still undismayed. We talked of how soon we could have a baby.

In the tourist homes of northern New York, Ohio, Indiana, wherever we had a room for the night, the voices of Amos and Andy came through thin partitions or up the stairwell from the radio in the family living room; and by the same means we heard of Bobby Jones's triumphs in golf, Max Schmeling's defeat of Jack Sharkey, and new records made in tree-sitting and marathon-dancing. On the street men were whistling "Body and Soul." Moving picture theaters were showing Jean Harlow in *Hell's Angels.* And every little way along every road into or out of even the smallest towns there were spanking new miniature golf courses, always brilliantly lighted in the evenings and always crowded with people merrily knocking little balls through little holes and over little bridges in tiny, mock-Japanese gardens.

We marveled at what constituted recreation for so many. Ours, as we traveled on, was watching everything in sight, overhearing all we could, looking in the card files of every public library we came to for the titles of last year's *Cockatoo* and the new *Land Spell*, sending postcards each night, calling home every other night; and talking to each other.

From the time we crossed the boundary into Minnesota — one of the shrinking number of states in which we had never been before — I was watching for the Mississippi River and it seemed that we would never get to where we could see it. When we did we were about to cross it, having left behind St. Paul which had encouraged me by its resemblance to Boston, and enter Minneapolis which looked to me like a metropolis which had sprung up around the flour mills in the past ten years. The university buildings were on our right as we approached the Mississippi and we stared at them rather than the river since it was from eagerness for our first glimpse of the campus that we had not stopped in St. Paul to look for lodgings for the night, though it was already dusk. But we could see no campus, only buildings. We supposed the open campus must be somewhere in the center, a spacious courtyard dwarfing that of Columbia's Quadrangle. We would look for it in the morning. Now we must find a place to wash, eat, and sleep. We looked on all sides for faculty homes, but saw no private residential areas at all.

The haven we found, after driving straight ahead along a street flanked by small stores and other neighborhood businesses, called itself a hotel but was more a large rooming house, and it remained our haven for three weeks, while we took our meals, together or separately, wherever cooked food we could afford was being served.

I telephoned home that night, giving my mother an address to which to write and to forward mail, and the next morning I wrote her a long letter. I had ridden with Herbert to the westernmost shadow of the university buildings where he parked the roadster on the grass among the bushes at the edge of the Mississippi so that the river would keep me company and, hopefully, help to orient me to the Land of Lakes while he searched for the College of Education and whatever would be his nook in the vast complex behind me. I wrote my mother that I had been speechless from admiration of the courage and even enthusiasm with which he had set off on this quest; that I hardly dared even look behind me, and was almost as reluctant to face the distant view before me — one high tower with the name Foshay on it, and everywhere else as far as I could see buildings jammed against one another, many of them one-story, none I thought more than four stories high, and most of them shabby though not from age; and that when I looked up from my letter I tried to keep my gaze on the river flowing at the bottom of the deep gorge it had made through sandstone walls, a much narrower river at that point than at St. Louis where I had last sat and looked at it. I had loved that river ever since Aunt Vinnie had taught me to spell its name (Mis-sis-si-ppi) but I had yet to learn to love Minneapolis and the state where this proud and storied river had its source.

Herbert came back and drove me around among the university buildings, showed me the windows of his office in

Burton Hall; but there was nothing which looked to me like a campus.

From then until his classes began we searched for a furnished apartment we could rent. Later, while he taught, I searched alone. Though the number of apartments for rent seemed endless, most of these were unfurnished. Of those which were furnished, some were dilapidated with dilapidated furnishings, where we did not feel we could, with proper respect, do the entertaining expected of a faculty couple, and the rest were brand new, in buildings of mock-Spanish design, with Spanish names, and the furnishings were heavy, ornate, overstuffed — Spanish and Italian styles out of Grand Rapids — which horrified me. I could not understand Spanish architecture and copies of southern European furniture in Minnesota. Maybe not English, maybe not early American; but why not Scandinavian, why not German? *Why* Spanish and Italian?

The answer I was given when I asked was that this was what most people wanted.

Meanwhile, our copies of the September issue of *Household* had come, and Mr. Crawford was inundating me with forwarded, unread letters from girls all over the country.

I wrote him:

> Out of about 150 communications, between 70 and 80 have asked particularly for more about books. Only one topic has surpassed books in frequency of mention — boys, of course. Clothes, sewing, etiquette, complexions are far behind. Am I warranted in saying I-told-you-so to you and your staff, or haven't I sufficient data yet? . . . I am enclosing carbons of the letters I have so far written in reply. It has not been necessary, I am glad to say, to answer all that came.

Shortly thereafter I received a bundle of stamps from the *Household*, and a note saying, "You will need these in connection with the large amount of mail you are receiving. It is a grand response."

Two weeks after the October issue went into the mail I wrote Mr. Crawford that I was long out of stamps, could he also supply me with *Household* stationery for my replies, and for that matter would his budget allow his covering the cost of my dictating these replies to a stenographer for typing. I had just handwritten the 266th letter in a fortnight, and was paying a college girl to type them. "I am honestly trying to be very selective in those I answer," I pleaded; and mailed him carbons of the whole 266. I was also awarding prizes for and publishing the best letters received from the girls, and reported that this time first prize had gone to Peggy Pars of Williamsport, Pennsylvania, second to Mabel Lee of Winslow, Washington, and third to Edna Burns of Towner, North Dakota.

He wrote:

> I hardly know what to say regarding the letters. To begin with, this is of course a very bad year financially, and we don't want to make unnecessary expenditures. For that reason it should never be announced that you will answer letters. On the other hand, what you write to these girls is splendid, and we might be considered obligated to answer questions. Would an addition of $25 a month compensate you for the additional cost — we, of course, to furnish stationery and postage? This is not pay for your work, I realize; there is no adequate pay for the service that you are giving.

And I replied:

> Fine! Just what I hoped for! And I have found a girl who is working her way through the university who can take shorthand. We do about twenty-five letters in an afternoon. Yesterday among the letters was one from a certain troubled girl seeking help. Today there was one from her mother who knew Miriam had written to me but didn't know what she had said. Of all the examples of bad parenthood I have ever seen, this was the worst. How I should like for at least a million women to see those letters side by side — Miriam's and her mother's — with

my comments! Don't worry. I know "Around the Family Table" is not the place for it! ! ! . . . Is it beautiful now in Kansas? I can't believe this exhilarating weather! There is no brilliant foliage, but the turning leaves have the same heady, fallish fragrance as in Maine.

By then we had found an apartment. The building was new; it was Spanish and its name El Capitan (in Viking country); but it was furnished — to the extent that it became furnished — in an atypical way by an atypical arrangement.

We had answered an advertisement for a furnished apartment there, but when we arrived to see it were told it had just been rented; there was one unfurnished apartment in the El Capitan which we might see if we wished. Since we were near it we looked at it — a big living room with polished hardwood floor, stucco walls, an electric "fireplace," and a long, narrow "studio" window on either side of the "chimney"; a small "dinette" with one "studio" window facing in the same direction as those in the living room and separated on the opposite side by a counter from the "kitchenette" which had no window; a tiled bath without a window; a small bedroom with a rollaway bed in the only clothes closet, and with a small window facing in the same direction as the "studio" windows — toward a brick wall no more than ten feet distant. We thanked the manager for showing it to us, but said we really had to have a furnished apartment as we had lately come from the East without furniture. The manager asked where Herbert worked and then said no doubt we would be desirable tenants and the apartment could be furnished for us but in that case the rent would be twenty-five dollars a month more. I asked how it would be furnished and she said like the one next door which was just like it; no one was at home there now and, having a master key, she could show it to us. When we had seen it we thanked her again, said we would consider it, and went back to our room.

What we considered were the possibilities of avoiding paying twenty-five dollars a month for living with furnishings we did not like. First we went to furniture stores asking how much we could buy to be paid for in monthly installments of twenty-five dollars. Several questions were asked us and then we were told with varying degrees of politeness that inasmuch as we seemed to own nothing but a much-traveled roadster, had no savings and only a very modest checking account, and had never established credit through charge accounts anywhere we had lived, we could not qualify for any installment plan.

About a week after our first visit to the El Capitan we went back. The unfurnished apartment was still vacant. We asked the manager how much she was allowed for the furnishing of an apartment and she said five hundred dollars. We then proposed that she let us make the selection on the understanding that we would pay her twenty-five dollars a month toward it until it was ours, and that if we should leave the El Capitan before that was accomplished we would at that time pay the remainder in full and take the furnishings with us. She looked doubtful, said she would take this up with the owner. She telephoned me the next morning and asked when we could meet her at a certain furniture store, saying the owner had instructed her to find out what our selections were likely to be. The time set was a half hour after the close of Herbert's last class that afternoon.

Our selections were a machine-hooked rug of a size suitable for the living room, a Duncan Phyfe sofa, a rosewood spinet desk and matching chair, a wing chair, block linen draperies for the living room, four small folding chairs, and a lamp. The price of these totaled just under five hundred dollars.

The manager smiled at the total and said, "And still no bedroom or dinette furniture."

I said we would sleep on the rollaway bed, thus acquiring

closet space for our clothes, and keep the rest of our things in our trunk; also that we would eat at the kitchenette counter until our card table could be sent to us, along with some lamps and a favorite scoop bottom chair we already had. We did not mind bare floors; the hooked rug was a concession to appearances and for the foot-comfort of dignitaries from the university; deans primarily; we were not expecting the president, at least not this year.

I said all this so ecstatically and with such a display of girlish innocence that Herbert had to fight an urge to wander away to where people would assume he had come in alone to look at linoleum. But the manager, while shaking her head, was smiling sympathetically, perhaps thinking wistfully, "*How long ago was I that young?*"

"I don't believe the owner will ever agree to it. If anything happens that you can't pay for it, he will certainly be stuck. What you like is not practical. Nobody else would want it. And everybody else would want bedroom and dinette furniture. But I'll tell him. I'm only the manager. All I can do is tell him."

But there was a long, cold, Depression winter ahead, and Herbert *was* on the university faculty. The next day the manager telephoned that a contract was being drawn up. If we could sign it that night, the furniture would be delivered tomorrow and we could move in whenever we wished. When we went to sign the contract, I had bought sheets and a blanket, and we had checked out of the "hotel"; we slept on the rollaway that night, and I was there to tell the delivery men where to put the furniture. Even after the lamp came it was so dark one could hardly see, but this was easier to bear because I did not want to look at the stucco walls, the studio windows, or the electric fireplace. The effort to distinguish the outlines of our rug, our sofa, our wing chair and our desk was well rewarded.

I wrote my mother:

Oh, we were *so* pleased with the letter that came yesterday. It really sounds as if you and Papa *will* come out! It came at noon and before night we had been downtown for timetables. Herbert is making out a suggested itinerary for you this minute, almost as excited as I am. No, I won't do anything about an apartment for you until you say so, but tell Papa the sooner he makes up his mind the better. I want to be sure you have a nice place very close to us . . . We're both fine, and want you SO MUCH . . . P.S. Herbert says to tell you not to wait until the Falls freeze over. He says can't you hump yourselves and get here for Thanksgiving. I'm *sure* he isn't thinking *only* of what you would cook!

In November, for Children's Book Week, many newspapers and most family magazines gave a special section to children's books, and Macmillan sent on to me all references to *Land Spell.* Though a lion's share of the allotted space was devoted to picture books — and rightly so, for "teen-age" books were neither here nor there — *Land Spell* did get more favorable notice than *Cockatoo* had, and more than most other "teen-age stories" at the time. However, only one review fully satisfied me. That one appeared in the New York *Herald Tribune* "Books," was signed by Constance Lindsay Skinner, and said that if I had "risen above the temptation to include" a mystery as to the identity of the plane which crashed in the farm pasture and of its occupants this would have been a very fine book indeed. I wrote her, in care of Macmillan, saying I agreed with her on both counts, was increasingly determined to write such a book, and was completely convinced that when I did it could not be published as a "juvenile."

By then I had written more than half of my promised dozen short stories about the Shaw family a few years after their experiences in *Land Spell*; was enjoying doing my girls' page, receiving an average of three hundred letters a month from my readers there and answering at least half of them, often at great length; was continuing to write and revise adult short stories and discuss them with encouraging editors; and was beginning to learn what it meant to be a professor's wife — the teas, the dinners, the receptions, the clubs, the afternoon calls from faculty wives, the evening calls from couples, and the long committee meetings.

My parents spent Thanksgiving with my brother and his family but we sent them a page from the Minneapolis *Tribune* devoted entirely to MINNEAPOLIS THE CHRISTMAS CITY with a large picture of the snow-piled business district below swinging garlands of colored lights, underlining the printed statement that it was worth traveling miles and miles to see, and they came to us well before the holidays and stayed until spring. They were pleased with the semi-basement apartment we had found for them in the older building beside the El Capitan. They liked it much more than our apartment, and so did we, but we still supposed it was better for us to have the use of a front entrance even if it was Spanish. Their coonskin coats which they had mailed to us when they left Maine arrived soon after they did, and their Christmas gift to me was a black sealskin coat, to Herbert a black sealskin cap. Thus armored we took to the roadster every bright Saturday and Sunday, regardless of the thermometer, and remained with it all day, watching the iceboats on the city lakes — Harriet, Calhoun, Lake of the Isles, Cedar, Nokomis — driving out to Minnetonka, Minnehaha Falls, through St. Paul, to Fort Snelling, to Northfield, downriver to the Indian Mounds; I always in the rumble seat and my mother usually (but sometimes my father) beside me. Herbert, always behind the steering wheel and so protected by windshield and buttoned-down car top, could and did survive without more fur than was in his cap.

It was a beautiful northland winter. I walked miles with my father, took streetcar tours of the Twin Cities with my mother, and on the days when Herbert was at the university and I was writing, my father walked alone, stopping in wherever a door seemed to invite him when he grew cold and making friends everywhere just as he had in Fall River, while my mother set off happily for downtown where she took lessons in knitting, in ceramics, and in painting. They had recovered from their bewilderment in the face of unaccustomed freedom, knew where they wanted to go and what they wanted to do. They had a key to our apartment as we had one to theirs. If it was not too late when we came home in the evening, we ran around to see if their lights were still on; if their lights were off we often found them in our apartment, waiting to hear how good a time we had had. After I had been out for a morning of skating in Loring Park with Marion Engelhardt and Alice Eurich, there was likely to be a warm apple pie on the kitchenette counter when we came in for lunch. The four of us always had dinner together at one apartment or the other, whenever Herbert and I did not go out or have other guests. They came to know and like our closest friends on the faculty but were more interested in casual acquaintances they made who were native Minnesotans; and they preferred informality.

When the time came for them to go home, they shopped for the complete dinner set my mother had never had and always wanted, a rug to replace the worn ingrain carpet in the parlor, and a few other souvenirs to be shipped to Maine, and took with them pictures to show their neighbors and stories to tell which would grow better with each telling. After that we sent them a dozen doughnuts every Tuesday from the Betty Crocker bakeshop on the corner, because my mother thought them more delicious than her own. We missed them sadly, but I knew The House was glad to have them back.

At the end of January 1931 I had sent Mr. Moore of *The*

Classmate, in Cincinnati, the twelfth and final short story in the Shaw family series. Some of the early ones had already appeared in his paper. On March 5 I wrote Wilma McFarland:

> It is some time since I had a pleasant letter from you asking that I keep the *Portal* in mind for short stories. Indeed I have done so, but found no time to work on one. As you may know, I am running a page for girls in the *Household*, a Capper publication in Topeka, Kansas. This, together with the series for Mr. Moore and now a new book I'm starting, fills every free minute. For the next few months I can do nothing but the page, beside the book. By summer I hope to be able to think more constructively about the *Portal*.

She replied:

> I have been feeling so tremendously noble — and sorry for myself — for giving up that series to the *Classmate*. But they are certainly better suited to the older field. I wonder what your new book is and whether it may be for the *Portal* age. If so, do keep me in mind . . . I have very happy memories of Minnesota, having summered at Lake Minnetonka in the old days when it wasn't so civilized.

There is no record of my having answered Wilma McFarland's question as to the book I was writing, but it was not for the *Portal* age exclusively, nor for the *Classmate* age exclusively. It began, "Outside the house it was storming, a busy downfall of flakes that the wind blew lightly across acres of old snow left from December . . ." It was the story of a year in the life of the Shaw family at a time when Jen Shaw was old enough to consider marriage, and I called it *As the Earth Turns*.

And we were moving! Having found exactly the apartment we wanted in a brand-new building which was of what we considered good Midwest construction and style, we had felt we must go there and found, to our grateful surprise, no barriers in our way. The El Capitan now had a waiting list for unfurnished as well as furnished apartments, and its manager had no objection to releasing us from our contract provided we completed payment on our furniture. We consulted the establishment from which it had come and found it willing, even eager (since we now had a savings account, could establish credit, and were sure to continue our connection with the university at least for another year, though with no increase in salary) to draw up a plan by which we would not only make to them the remaining payments on the furniture bought in the fall, but could also on the same terms add to our furnishings a bed and other bedroom pieces necessary now that daylight was to be ours again and reveal just what we had and did not have.

On Easter Sunday night I wrote to my parents in Dover where they were staying with my brother, waiting for snowdrifts to settle so that they could drive over to open The House:

> We are in love with this apartment. I was so happy last night when I was getting dinner that I could have *wept* — and imagine me that happy getting dinner! But setting a table beside a wide open window under which youngsters are passing swinging tennis racquets, and Nicollet Field stretches away before your eyes, dim and green, and the sunset light shines on the wall! I feel again as I did that first year on Hanover Street in Fall River when I hung dish towels on the line after supper; as if I were playing the part of a busy and not too awkward young housewife . . . I am enclosing a diagram of our rooms. Faint crosses indicate closet space and heavy crosses the closet doors. Dotted lines in ink are furniture we have, and those in pencil are pieces we hope to have. Mostly pencilled dots in the corner bedroom which will be my study as soon as we can find a secondhand desk. I simply couldn't bring myself to put the

spinet that far out of sight, so it is in the living room as before, for Herbert's use; he is *naturally* neat, and besides he does very little work at home. I work on the card table in the dinette; it jiggles but I revel in the daylight that streams in. How wonderful it will be when I have a desk in a study where I can have all my stuff strewn around day after day and when I leave it just close the door on it! Soon now, I'm sure.

At Christmas they had given us a birdcage with a pair of parakeets, to satisfy my longing for something small to take care of, and in a previous letter I had sent them a feather from Pitti-Sing's wing.

Now I wrote:

A parakeet feather is no rarity any more; Pitti-Sing, poor creature, now has few left on. It isn't the moulting season but they're doing it anyhow . . . Your new Willys-Knight sounds exciting. You had your first one eight years, didn't you? How the prices of everything are down! But I understand they're rising a little in some lines, so the tide must be turning. We're glad this was our year to buy furniture . . . A funny thing happened lately. We had ordered maple syrup and sugar from Herbert's sister Josie and when it got here the syrup had been taken out of the wooden box in which she had packed it all and which couldn't have been easy to open. What I don't see is why whoever took the syrup didn't take the sugar too.

After the examination period at the end of May, a dream came true. We drove on a Friday to the North Shore of Lake Superior and stayed until Monday at Star of the North Lodge, its only guests that early in the season. Its low, weatherbeaten buildings clung to the shore with dark wilderness surrounding them. The woman who owned and ran it had always lived there and the dining room where we ate was her own. She prepared and served the meals and every crumb, every forkful, was delicious — hot cheese biscuits, lake and brook fish, venison, fricasseed rabbit, quail, duck, and desserts of home-canned fruit and wild berries.

We had a cabin with a hearth on which we built a blazing wood fire as each chill dusk came down, and by day we walked the trails of a forest which seemed truly primeval, with the two Lodge collies romping ahead of us, starting up birds, deer, and small running wildlife to delight our ears and eyes as the birds settled on branches above our heads to stare back at us, and animals, moving warily but slowly, exchanged glances with us as if to say, "Oh, it's you!" and then loped across the trail to get on with their plans for the morning or afternoon. It was a brief "second honeymoon" extended incredibly by our clock having ceased to run. It became in our minds a sequel to the summer we had spent in the shadow of Mount Bigelow in Maine, and we left the Star of the North with the ecstatic feeling of newly married people starting a new life for which all that has gone before has been only an introduction.

By mid-June I had been through winter and spring with the Shaw family and their new neighbors, the Polish Janowskis, and now it was coming summer for them and for me. Herbert would be teaching in the summer session into August, but we had agreed that I would go East by train and stop over in New York for a week. I not only harbored the familiar urge to go back to where I had been; I also wanted to see Constance Skinner and show her what I had been writing. My mother planned to meet me in Albany so that we could go down the Hudson by boat and have the week in New York together.

I wrote her:

> Just four weeks from this minute I'll probably be leaving for the station to take the night train to Chicago, and so four weeks from day after tomorrow morning I'll be appearing in the predawn dark at the door of the Wellington in Albany and asking at the desk for the number of Mrs. Warren V. Hasty's room. Maybe you should write there asking for a room to be

held for you for the night of July 15, to be sure of it, though there would probably be no difficulty. If you *should* happen to have to go to another hotel, just leave word at the Wellington as to where I can find you. Then, a few hours later, it's up the gangplank for us! . . . Today here has been glorious and I haven't even stepped outside. Tomorrow, though, I'm going to play tennis with Marion and then we'll go swimming . . . I had a letter from Nellie Mae who is studying at the University of Michigan this summer and will be in Chicago for five days the last of this month and wonders if I can meet her there. Of course I can't. George's cow is dead, so Mark has had to give him one of his which may mean Lois May will have to come home soon, and Margaret finds she is going to have a baby, so I'm a busy woman. I hope to finish "Summer" before I see Miss Skinner. So glad you really like my title, *As the Earth Turns.*

On June 30 the top headlines on the front page of the Minneapolis *Tribune* (price three cents within the city limits) were 9 DIE IN CITY; MERCURY HITS 102, 14 PROSTRATED; CROPS BURN UP; STOCK IS KILLED. Below that an article by the City Health Commissioner was headed SIT IN FRONT OF FAN, DR. HARRINGTON SAYS; AND DON'T WORRY; LET THE OTHER FELLOW DO THAT — TELLS HOW TO EAT AND DRESS. Elsewhere on the front page a headline read NOW IF THIS DEPRESSION WOULD ONLY HIT MERCURY — CITY SURRENDERS TO OLD SOL — NORMAL LIVING GOES BY BOARDS. The story following this last was broken up by headlines in smaller type — "Jam City Beaches" ("All attendance records at Minneapolis beaches were broken yesterday when 143,000 persons sought relief from broiling heat in the waters of park lakes"); "Park Lake Temperatures Up" ("to 77 degrees . . . may rise 10 or 12 degrees more"); "Deranged by Heat, Girl Sheds Clothes" ("at Fourteenth Street and Stevens Avenue, on her way to work . . . had tossed the last item into the gutter by the time an alarmed police radio squad arrived at the scene"); "Sun Tan Fad Boosts Sale of Olive Oil"; "Creosote

Paving Blocks Explode"; "Icehouse Catches Fire—It Must Be Hot"; "Roads Out of City Jammed, Autoists Drive Through Fences" (Deputy sheriffs called out to protect farmers from further property damage"); "Thousands Hasten to Ice-Cooled Theaters"; "Hundreds Try to Sleep in Autos"; "Men Bathers Keep Trunks, Shed Shirts" ("Men bathers in the continental countries for years have worn just trunks as their beach attire. The custom is spreading to Minneapolis"); "Water Consumption Sets New High Record"; "10 P.M. Law Means Nothing These Days" ("According to the city's laws, bathers are supposed to be out of the lakes at 10 P.M., but police have been lenient"); "Strange Duck Antics Reported by Wardens" ("The ducks, it was reported, stay under water so long to escape the sun that they are assuming fishlike habits") "Lawn Shower Helps Adults Keep Dignity" ("Those who have been too dignified to enjoy the favorite hot weather sport of children—running through the spray from a hose—may now cool off yet maintain their usual aplomb. Just before the heat wave there came on the market a lawn shower bath, consisting of a standard with a spray at the top and an attachment for hooking it up with a lawn hose"); and "Family Eats Dinner on Own Front Lawn" ("A staid family on Lake of the Isles Boulevard threw dignity to the wind last night. Dismissing their corps of servants, they proceeded to arrange a table for dinner on their expensive front lawn. The gray-haired mother and father, with their son, sat stiffly on camp chairs in front of their mansion, with a bottle of catsup prominently displayed on the table, while passing motorists grinned").

I wrote home:

The enclosed clippings will tell you more than I can. We have carried our bedspring and mattress into the study (which is *supposed* to have cross ventilation) and put them on the floor. They serve as a sort of focal point at night but we never stay there long. The worst part for me is not to be able to run outdoors. Did I tell you I got sandals instead of slippers as my birthday present from you? Very open, intended for wear without stockings. They and my pajamas are all I can bear to wear inside, IF I can bear them. This morning I sat and wrote for three hours without a stitch on — but that way you stick to whatever you touch and it hurts! I don't *think* I'm deranged, but I may be . . . Poor Herbert! He is not only teaching university classes (fully clothed) but doing a great deal of research work with children suspected of being intellectually gifted, and he is intensely interested in them . . . I'm at least as interested in my Shaws, but I don't like *sticking* to them or to anything else! Phooey — phooey —

But a week later:

The heat wave has broken. Now the paper says it is traveling east; I do hope it will burn itself out before it gets there. We had our first real night's sleep last night. Tonight we have been making out our budget for the coming year. Since we finished it, I've come upon a model annual budget in a magazine, telling what percentage of one's income should be spent on this and that. It says 24% for rent, ours is 20%; 20% for food, ours is 15%; 17% for clothes, ours is 9%; 15% for running expenses like gas, light, gasoline, and spending money, ours is 12%; 10% for savings, ours is 15%. That's how we keep up our payments on the furniture and reduce the Columbia debt, and how I pay for dictation and typing. Of course we budget only what we are reasonably sure of — which is Herbert's salary and my income from the *Household* page, totalling $4125. If I sell other pieces we add as much as we can to savings, but also use what we need for special indulgences (investments?) like the long weekend on the North Shore and train trip home with week-in-New-York. Luckily the returns from the *Classmate* Shaw stories are holding out to cover that! I haven't taken time for anything but this book since . . . You are going to so many different places with so many different people lately. How I hope it will keep right on after I get there and you will take me along! There is nothing I should love more than long day's trips around the periphery of home, finding old cellar holes and hearing about the people who used to live on them; I realize more every day how much I want to know every detail. When you began these pilgrimages last summer I couldn't take much time to go with you, but this summer I WILL, whatever else goes by the boards. You know for years I didn't believe anything really existed that was more than a mile or two away from home. Tell Papa I want him to be thinking up places to take me and things to tell me about them. I've longed to go again to the old Brown place, for instance. Could we get anywhere near it by car? And I want to go over every Tatnie road and those on the back side of the Hill—*everywhere* we can get to! . . . A week from next Tuesday night I leave for New York, a week from the next morning you leave for New York, and the twain *shall* meet in Albany. I've written King's College Inn to hold a room for us, beginning Thursday night. Is Papa going over to stay with Harold while you're gone?

I boarded the train to put more miles between Herbert and me than there had ever been since our first meeting; had a berth but slept as fitfully as any character of Shakespeare's. The next morning, between trains in Chicago, I telephoned him while he was getting breakfast in the apartment which I could see around him as clearly as if I had been there. I said I just wanted to hear his voice. I said nothing of my premonition that by the time he reached Maine in our roadster I would have the biggest and best news for him that either of us had yet had for the other.

I traveled day coach from Chicago to Albany though I would not arrive there until after two o'clock the next morning. It would have been absurd to take a berth for a night when I would never close my eyes for fear of not waking in time to get off where my sleeping mother would be. At lunch in the dining car I met a young man who told me he was a parachute jumper; this was his profession. After lunch he brought a pile of scrapbooks to my seat and we looked at them and talked about parachute jumping all afternoon, through dinner, and all the long evening. He was still in his early twenties and had jumped into every one of the United States and nearly every country in the western world. I was fascinated. I was also appalled by wondering what a professional parachutist did after he grew too old to jump. I have forgotten his name, but he was a Frenchman. At Albany he went down the coach steps ahead of me, put my bag on the platform, reached up to help me down the steps, and, when I gave him my hand, raised and kissed it. This had never happened to me before. It has never happened since. If he is still alive and reads this, I want him to know that I have not forgotten him, that I am grateful still to him for taking me briefly into a strange new world and making me feel like royalty when I left it.

My mother drowsily unlocked her door to me when I reached the Wellington. The next day we spent on the Hudson. During the week we saw *Green Pastures* and Katherine Cornell in *The Barretts of Wimpole Street*, returning to both in preference to seeing anything else on Broadway. We ate at King's College Inn and at the Automat, Drake's, Mary Elizabeth's, and Alice Foote Macdougall's. We traveled by subway, bus, and ferry boat. We read in the New York *Times* that three officers of the Bank of the United States had been convicted of mismanagement of the bank's funds; under the caption A NEST FOR THE LONE EAGLE that a house in which they could have complete privacy was being built for the Lindberghs and their newborn son, Charles, Jr., in Hopewell, New Jersey; that President Hoover had proposed a moratorium on war reparations and war debts; that Pearl Buck's *The Good Earth* was at the top of the best seller lists; and that Empress Eugenie hats were high style.

Early in the week I had met Constance Skinner for lunch and left my manuscript with her. She was, as I had remembered her from our one previous meeting at Louise Seaman Bechtel's apartment, a towering, dark-complexioned woman with a strong personality, dressed in flowing robes of vivid colors, with necklaces and bracelets in still more vivid, even barbaric hues. She had grown up in the Canadian Northwest, was intensely proud of her Indian blood, and had published several books for girls and an adult novel, all of which drew on her early experiences and impressions. She moved about with difficulty but nevertheless with majesty. Later in the week, by appointment, I went to the apartment where she lived alone with a black cat who looked and prowled like a panther; and we talked for hours. She thought I was off to a good start on my book, but made several suggestions for revision, particularly with regard to beginning closer to a time of change in the life of the Shaw family and introducing gradually its usual routine. She urged me to try to finish it in time to submit it in the Atlantic Monthly Prize Novel contest for which the deadline was the end of the year. Then, at sunset, my mother and I sailed down Long Island Sound on the Boston boat, and the next day were at home.

I had resolved not to look at my book until I was back where the shape of it had been conceived, also not to do any other imaginative writing which might affect the course it was following. Instead I wrote *Household* pages in advance, to clear the coming fall of this duty, answered my readers' letters in longhand, and revised again and sent out short stories which had been rejected many times. A new magazine, to be called *Earth*, accepted one of my favorites, "The John Crag Lot" for its first issue, to be paid for on publication (but with its first issue it went bankrupt and ceased to exist). I sent another old favorite of mine, "So Clyde Was Born" to *Redbook* magazine, with a letter saying, "Dear Sir: — [I did not know the editor's name.] A few summers ago in a little Maine town I came upon a rather young old maid who laughed a great deal and scalloped the hems of her skirts. So I wrote a story about her and about a kind of girl who never does become an old maid. Does this interest you?" It didn't.

Otherwise, until Herbert came, my parents and I spent every day visiting relatives and neighbors in the area, all those still living there and many more of whom our family memory was still bright. After Herbert came, he and I woke mornings in the chamber with one window which I had first shared with Aunt Vinnie, in which she had died, and which then had become mine. It was there I told him what I had known since another morning in Chicago, that we were to be parents. Then the fragrance of bacon cured last fall in my father's smokehouse came up the back stairs and we went down to meet it, to sit around the kitchen table and talk while we ate it along with our cousin's fresh eggs, our neighbor's butter, our own hash-brown potatoes, and cucumbers just off the vine. There were the familiar dishes to wash in the familiar iron sink (the new set of china from Minneapolis was enthroned in the sitting-room cupboard for company use) and returned to familiar shelves. Together the four of us made pilgrimages to old cemeteries, walked in the pasture where a neighbor's cattle now grazed, picked berries, climbed the mountain, went to the beach and went to the beach and went to the beach.

Early in September we spent a week with the Carrolls in the Berkshires, and toward the end of the month left home to start back toward Minnesota. This was the most difficult goodbye I had yet said for my father doubted that they would go west again, though my mother promised me secretly that she would try to come for a few weeks in the spring. Twenty miles from home, we stopped at Hampton Beach and ran once more into the waves.

I wired home the night we reached our apartment on First Avenue South, and wrote the next day:

We made the mileage we expected every single day except the first when we stayed too long at Hampton. It seemed then as if I *couldn't* go on and leave the ocean! I blame myself for seeming upset the night before we left home but you two and the place mean so much to me it hurts to go away; still, that doesn't mean I can't be happy anywhere else, for I can be and am . . . This morning Herbert was off early to the university and I've been busy all day scrubbing and polishing. I love this apartment and everything in it. I *had* worried about our parakeets and the fern, which I told you we left in care of the janitor. On the way up yesterday we talked about what we were looking forward most to seeing and we both said it was the birds. When we drove past the bedroom windows I thought I didn't see the cage, and we hardly dared come in, for fear something had happened to them. But there they were, hopping and blinking, glossy and brilliant as ever, and one of them chirruped inquiringly the instant we stepped in! They are all the more precious now because I read somewhere that a small baby will watch birds play. And the fern has grown to immense proportions; some of the fronds almost reach the floor.

The accumulated mail included a letter from Miss Skinner in reply to that note I sent her as we were leaving New York. In the midst of much gratitude and many expressions of appreciation I must have said something which indicated to her I still had some lack of confidence in my ability to say what I want to say. Her letter was written several weeks ago and sent here. I wonder if it could be I never told her where I was heading. She must have got the address from Macmillan.

She says:

"I wish I had the chance, leisure, and instrumentality to give you a strapping. I've treated your talent with the same regard I give only to arrived and achieved art like Willa Cather's. I don't know anybody else I would urge to go and study and work and rewrite and fill in and fashion until *the* big farm novel emerges. That I feel it *is* big and its possibilities bigger is plainly said by my absorbed interest. But for that interest I shouldn't be losing myself in your literary output for a minute. I've no time for it.

Only something that gripped me could occupy me at all. I'm no impassioned philanthropist about young writers, save to wish heartily most of them would take to something else . . . I've been by way of asking you please to be a Sigrid Undset with that novel, or thereabouts —— —— wish I could get my hands on you! . . ."

She is nice. Too nice. I'd gain more confidence from less extreme comparisons and predictions. But I *will* "study and work and rewrite and fill in and fashion."

Now you must not worry about me. I look forward to every week between now and spring with the greatest eagerness. It's fun being back. In this one day ever so many people have telephoned, the laundryman and the groceryman were good to see, Mr. Mack, the janitor, just beams that I'm so pleased with his care of the birds and plants, the librarian sent me a "welcome" note in the book Herbert picked up for me, and Johnny J came over tonight (Marian is in St. Louis). So think of us as happy, busy, and full of plans, often talking about you and our wonderful summer and the even more wonderful summer we'll have all together next year.

I enclosed a clipping from a Chicago *Tribune* we had picked up in that city. A column headed "Nitrates Start Painting Maine's Forests for Fall" said tourists often wondered why Maine's fall foliage was so brilliant, and a horticultural expert explained it was due both to atmospheric conditions and to rich soil nitrates, a rare combination. The column concluded, "In the same manner as iron, sulphur, lime, and magnesia dye the flowers in Maine with brighter hues than elsewhere, the nitrates give the turning foliage its beauty."

Comforted by scientific proof that Maine's flowers and leaves were indeed brighter than elsewhere and its atmospheric conditions also unique, I began again my effort to demonstrate that its people were no less so.

In New York the editor of *Cosmopolitan* had gone to Moscow to sign up Soviet writers, the *World* had ceased publication, it was next to impossible to get a ticket for *Of Thee I Sing* to see John Wintergreen campaign for the Presidency with Love as his platform, and Rudy Vallee in George White's *Scandals* was singing:

Life is just a bowl of cherries.
Don't make it serious.
Life's too mysterious . . .

I was writing home:

Norma Barsness who is going to do my shorthand and typing this year made a special trip down from Duluth (her classes haven't started yet) this weekend, and I've been dictating almost constantly for two days — only thirty letters left out of a stack of over two hundred . . . Do you think it would be a good idea to cut to crib size those sheets that were Aunt Vinnie's and are too short for our bed? Or wouldn't they wear long enough to be worth the trouble? . . . Wouldn't I have loved to be there for that Harvest Supper! Tell me *everything* about it. The Shaws may go to one this fall . . . Don't try to come out here this winter unless you feel just like it. I know you want to and you know we want you to, but it *is* a hard trip and expensive, and I'm sure if you try you can be comfortable at home. One-pipe heaters are selling for $49.50 here now — last year they were $175 . . . And now that big wooly white dog you got at the Fair! Nothing makes me feel so rich as knowing *anything* is all ready and waiting for this baby; but a big white dog, oh, my! ! ! When would the baby be old enough to have it — while we're home next summer, or not until Christmas? . . . We've bought a little Majestic radio! It cost $42.50 but it has five tubes and tone control and we get everything perfectly over it. Herbert has wanted a radio so long for sports events and especially for the World Series, and we both feel that if I can't get out much in the winter it will be great company for me . . . I was so curious about Northwestern Hospital I couldn't wait any longer to see it and went over this afternoon. The nurse who took me through the maternity ward (whole fifth floor of a new wing) let me look at the babies. There were twenty of them, nearly all awake, and not one of them crying. The nurse taking care of them was so loving. I appreciated that. As it happened, my own Dr. Ehrenberg came along while I was looking into the pink and white nursery and looked with me, as pleased and proud as if he were solely responsible for each one of those happy, healthy, good babies.

The hours and days could only be described as winged.

I've sorted, proofread, signed, folded, and sealed 55 letters this morning, given the apartment a lick and a promise, listened to the Damrosch Music Appreciation Hour (I *knew* how pleased you'd be that we have a radio at last) and now I go for my walk. This is my day for everything but keeping up with the Shaws. I feel absolutely marvelous — running like an expensive clock! . . . The foliage here has the coloring of French bedrooms on the stage — pale yellow with an occasional streak of pink. If one tree on the shore of Lake Minnetonka turns pink, everybody gets excited and the road out there is crowded with people going to see it . . . Miss McFarland of the *Portal* has taken my girls' story "In Threes," and asked me for a serial. I've written her that I can't touch it before Christmas, and have another project which will occupy me beginning in March (! ! !), but if she wants it I will devote January and February to a story for her about "a young girl's awakening to the appeal of boys," saying I have three young nieces at that point and that it seems to me a most lovely and wholesome experience. I've tried to outline the story, as she asked, but you know I'm no good at outlines. Wonder what she'll say!

What she said in early December was:

Frankly I'm a little afraid of it. I would much rather have the less subjective type of thing. *Land Spell* was almost a perfect serial from our standpoint . . . You say that by spring you will be involved in something else. Will that be anything that might be for *Portal* age? . . . I find the check for "In Threes" has somehow been held up, but you will have it now in a few days.

I worked on "Winter Again," the final section of *As the Earth Turns*, and wrote Wilma:

It seems we won't be able to get together, at least on any long piece, for some time. What I am to do in the spring is not for *Portal* age, and the work of these next two months is all I could have promised you . . . We both understand that you liked *Land Spell*, but you have already *had Land Spell* and I couldn't do it over again if I would — and I wouldn't. I quite firmly believe that I have taken pen to the Shaws for the last time. Merry Christmas!

Sheer bravado.

On the same day I wrote Mr. Moore of *Classmate*:

Miss McFarland does not take kindly to the serial outline I offered her, and I am not surprised since it has been my experience that nobody ever likes my outlines though they do quite often like my stories. So I am not offering an idea to you, simply state that I am now free to start work on a serial for the *Classmate*, if you are likely to want it. It will *not* be about any of the Shaws. Do you have any other suggestions which I might consider but need not promise to abide by?

He replied that he did want the serial and a recent questionnaire "has brought in a quite general demand for a love story — not one of the high temperature kind, of course, but a romantic story."

I wrote back promptly:

Are you really serious? You want to print a sure-enough love story? Of course your readers think a lot about love and like to hear about it. Who doesn't? If I had had an inkling you would indulge them so, I should have sent you the enclosed three-part months ago instead of dallying with women's magazines. And my Number One New Year's resolution will be to write you a serial.

He replied with equal promptness:

"Sure I was serious. I like the love story and we will be accepting it if we may pay for it in the new year. What's left of the December budget can't afford it. Now on to the serial (with love motif, too)!

It was Sunday, December 13, when I wrote home:

Big news — and it rolls deliciously off my pen! The book is finished! The very last words of it went to the typist last night, and I think it is good, though I may be wrong. I was afraid I might not be done by Christmas, and see how far ahead I am? Of course I have the proofreading to do as the typed copies come back, but that and the *Household* letters are the ONLY work I shall do before New Year's. I have the page done through April. (April! !) Yesterday's mail brought me almost 150 *Household* letters. They just stream in. It's lucky Mr. Crawford sends them all together in big brown envelopes or our mail carrier would go mad!

All fall my mother and I had been writing each other at great length every other day, the letters filled with questions and answers having to do with what we did every day, what my doctor told me on my periodic visits, instructions for knitting wrapping blankets and for crocheting sacques, comparative prices on baby furniture, the lacquering of Maine maple leaves, and the radio programs we all listened to regularly, including, every Sunday night, "The Three Bakers" and "Seth Parker." (" . . . I heard Hoover's address to the chiefs of police last night and Mrs. Hoover's christening of the new ship of the Pan-American airlines this afternoon. And how I enjoy the Seth Parker hour! I suppose it doesn't mean as much to you but out here it makes me feel I've been lifted on a magic blanket and carried to where I hear those voices — Mother Parker sounds like Aunt Em — and the way they pronounce words and the phrases they use and the old hymns. Did you know that 'Seth Parker' was graduated from Bowdoin the same year I was from Bates — Ted Miller's class? . . .") I had enclosed a page from the rotogravure section of the New York *Herald Tribune* showing the blimps *Los Angeles* and *Akron* (largest lighter-than-air craft in the world) passing at the same time over Manhattan; also President Hoover being enrolled in the Red Cross, King George arriving in London for the national elections, Maude Adams in Cleveland to play Portia in *The Merchant of Venice*, Pope Pius IX on the inauguration of the first telephone service in the Vatican, and Mahatma Gandhi visiting the goats at an English dairy show.

I had written on Thanksgiving day:

> The Annual Dinner for the faculty of our college was a great occasion, Herbert in his tux (oh, for the day we can buy one for his own, since he needs one so often!) and I in my Old Faithful green chiffon. Alice Eurich had a new pale pink chiffon, Grecian style with tiny metal stars all over it, but both Marions wore last year's dresses, like me. Marion E's is black with an ivory lace top and Marion J's is rose taffeta. We sat at the dean's table and Mrs. Haggerty said I was looking so *well*. The dean is eager for Herbert to get his Prose Appreciation Test on the market — says there is now nothing remotely like it (as *we* well know) as an aid to teachers of English in placing a student's level in appreciation of literature and later finding out whether the training he is being given in discrimination is effective. So exciting, as so many things are! . . . By the way, Herbert is using Flozone in his radiator this year instead of alcohol. It costs $6.25 but it can be drained off in the spring and used over again the next fall, and it keeps the radiator safe at *any* temperature and doesn't heat up on warm days as alcohol does. He thinks Papa may want to try it . . . Now will you please take a long breath and describe for me a scene in the kitchen when a newborn baby is being washed and dressed? That is something I never saw and as Jen will so officiate for Ed's baby I want to know the process in as much detail as you can give me.

A week later:

Your last letter came in exactly the nick of time. If you can believe it I had been working hard all morning and part of the afternoon and Ed's baby had just appeared in the kitchen when I saw the mailman coming up the walk. So I left the Shaws, ran down to get your letter (yes, I mostly do forget not to run) and found your wonderful description in it, so I sat right down and finished the scene! Have you seen Eunice with her new baby? I know how pleased you always were to find her out pushing Joyce in her carriage, and how adorable Joyce was. I think we can manage without a carriage. Surely our baby can get his — or her, of course — airing in a crib in this big sunny room with all the windows open until big enough to lie on blankets on the grass. But that bedroom will be too far from ours when we're asleep, so we've found a chaise longue on sale for $13.00 and bought it; I can sit on it now to read with my feet up, as Dr. Ehrenberg recommends; later it will be perfect for nursing the baby (as I am SURELY going to do); AND I know where I can buy for $2.00 what is called a carrying basket which I can tuck between the arms of the chaise longue for the baby to sleep in nights until he outgrows it. I've taken apart one of Auntie's bed pillows and washed the goose feathers to make a pad for it as soon as we get it and know just the size we need . . . Seems as if everybody is having a baby — and they're all sons, come to think of it! I just got an announcement from the Dilleys in Athens, Ohio, of the arrival of Frank, Jr. It delights me to see how fast those couples at Columbia who got their degree with us followed it with a baby at the first possible minute. A year ago when I wrote Geneva about the Brunstetters' little boy she wrote back, "I'm sorry I can't report that there is a new Dilley on the way, but orders just aren't being filled at our house right now." But this fall she wrote that when Ann went back to school after vacation her teacher told Geneva that Ann announced, "We're going to have a secret at our house but we can't tell about it until it's born." And this *is* a secret, for Ruth says I'm the first to know beside her and Lloyd that they, too, are expecting their first baby in May.

The prose appreciation test had been Herbert's top research project since soon after coming to Minnesota. It had begun with the selection of a variety of brief quotations from prose classics in the English language, each of which had its own category—a description of a man, of a woman, of a child, of a landscape, of a mood, of the sky, a section of dialogue, a dramatic confrontation, and many others. Then came a selection in the same categories from an equal number of lesser but respected writers, and finally one from "hack" writers who had a large popular following. My contribution then had been to write the fourth possible choice, the worst examples I could compose without recourse to misspelling, poor punctuation, or flagrantly bad grammar. I never had more fun. The game was to try to write, for instance, a poorer description of spring than the poorest one Herbert could find in any newsstand magazine; one so poor that no one of the hundred judges—nationally known book critics, professors of English, and outstanding preparatory school teachers of English—could fail to rate it fourth, though some high school and even college students actually would. This was not as easy as one might think, but it was a great challenge. I never looked at the first choice (on spring it was from Tolstoi) until I had finished mine.

At the end of November I had written home:

Except for my "health measures" and the minimum of housekeeping, we both work all the time. Herbert is driving on what promises to be the last stages of his test, and I help him evenings. We never sit down to it that we don't think of how you and Papa helped us with the grading last winter and how cosy it was those nights in your apartment at the Latona, after we had run through the cold or a storm from our back door to yours. Herbert is using for the test only about the twelve best from seventy-two sets of four prose selections each, as shown not only by the unanimity of the hundred judges but by their comments. In its experimental forms it has been given to over 4000 high, junior high, and college students. Next month he will standardize it by giving it to at least 4000 more. You can see that just the selecting and mimeographing and then the giving and scoring of so many tests has been quite an undertaking, and you couldn't — nor can I — even imagine the amount of statistical computation he has done to make sure it holds water at every corner. All I know is that this long process establishes the test's *validity* and *reliability* (whatever they are in this context), which is essential, and that all that is now left is to *standardize* it. I just think it is hilarious that every once in a while we come up with a test paper on which some student rates *my* description of spring as better than Tolstoi's! But seems if this never happened the test wouldn't have *reliability* and would have to be thrown out the window! He has to get a nice, neat distribution of scores all the way from 0 to 60, with the big concentration about halfway between; and that's what he is getting. The test should be out early next fall, maybe sooner, in three forms, one for junior high schools, one for senior high schools, and one for colleges. They will of course be of three degrees of difficulty, this to be accomplished by "weighting" each set, placing the easiest first and so on in order, then adding still more difficult ones for senior high at the end of the junior high list, and adding still others for the colleges. The first set is on "A Man." That means that very few have thought I described a man better than Rolvaag. I don't see why, when I tried so hard! I said, "Peter was as handsome a fellow as a girl would hope to meet. He was tall and broad shouldered, with eyes as blue as summer skies, hair black as a raven's wing, lips as red as red roses, teeth white as milk, skin brown as a nut, wonderful hands, long legs, a wonderful nose, the best-looking build, walked like a soldier, and had a wonderful voice. He was a prince among men, that was what Peter was. He was so handsome he ought to have been in the moving pictures. Everybody knew this." . . . I appreciate more than I can tell you what you wrote about Herbert. The day I wrote you as I did I had been thinking how I should feel if anything happened to him, even though I should have so much left, while if he should lose this baby and me at the same time he would have so little. I knew you and Papa would feel as much affection for him as you always have but I did want to be assured you wouldn't hesitate to show it; because even if he seemed very reserved and self-contained, as he probably would, he would really *need* you. Well, this baby is just going to bind us all more closely together than ever.

We had written a great deal about whether or not my parents should come to Minneapolis for the winter, and if not whether my mother should come by herself in March, and more about family life and experiences.

I read many articles on the difficulties and disagreements parents and grandparents have on the training of children and don't see how they would ever come about if people would talk things over as we always do and be as open to suggestions from each other as we always are. . . .

Everybody has been telling me that a baby that is active very early and increasingly is a boy, but Dr. Ehrenberg says no such thing, it means it is a very alert, healthy, active baby who is likely to remain so all his — or her, of course — childhood. So prepare yourselves, Gramma and Grandpa! I tried to get him to say how far or how fast I should walk in an hour but he didn't want to for fear whatever he said might be too much. He said first, "Just walk naturally for an hour or until you get tired, whichever comes first." But I don't get tired; lately I do get bored. He finally said, "Try to walk two miles, but don't push yourself." So last night I got Herbert to measure with the car what point was exactly a mile from here. This morning, after an hour and a half of cleaning up the apartment I got ready, looked at the clock, locked the door, went downstairs and out to the corner Herbert had named, came back facing a strong wind, climbed the stairs, unlocked my door — and I had been gone exactly 35 minutes! So now what am I going to do — start hiking to St. Paul and back? I don't know *where* it would take me a half hour to get to! I wish it would be safe to skate. Dr. E. says it would IF I can promise him I won't fall down. Well, I'm making no promises. There'll be ice next winter. But a section of

Nicollet Field is flooded right outside my window and when I see the crowds spinning along over there I'd be envious except that I couldn't envy a queen. The books I read say a woman should try to forget as much as possible that she is going to have a baby. Yes, try to forget Christmas when it's tomorrow and you're about nine years old!

Now the proofread manuscript of *As the Earth Turns* had gone to the Atlantic Monthly Press, one carbon copy of it to Constance Skinner and another to *Household* in the hope that Mr. Crawford might use it as a serial. My parents had begun a winter visit to my brother and his family in Dover, and The House was closed and cold. My mother and I were writing mostly about Christmas until the end of the year — the first Christmas of my life that we had ever been apart.

You didn't have enough left of your Thanksgiving mincemeat so that you could send me a jar, did you? Herbert said tonight, "I wish we were going to have mince pie for our Christmas dinner." I said cheerily, "Well, I'll see if I can find some mincemeat and make one." After a minute he said, "I wish you knew where you could get some like your mother's." Thus I am applying at the most likely source I know! It is not a bit painful, really very gratifying, for a young wife to hear *her* mother's cooking dinned in her ears all the time . . . Do you realize that by Christmas Even it would be possible — not probable but possible — for this child to be born and live? Dr. E. says it occasionally happens now that a child born at the sixth month is saved. So any time after Christmas Even I can have that hope if I should need it. . . .

Our tree is up! We got a little one like last year's, but this one has been dipped in something which makes it look like any evergreen tree after an ice storm. We have it on the black console table by the door to the dining-space, with its base buried deep in a great drift of cotton snow sprinkled with powdered crystals. The smell is sweet all through the apartment. Only wish it would last all winter! We'll decorate it soon with the ornaments you gave us last year, but tonight we go out to mail the last of our packages. The time is getting short! Yours, the Carrolls', and the Stanfords' went first, being big ones and having so far to go. We put Harold's family's in with yours. Be *sure* to open your carton as soon as you get it for everything inside is gift-wrapped . . . My Mother-to-be letter from *Good Housekeeping* which came today says sympathetically, "I know just how you feel. All you want to do is get into a comfortable chair and stay there." Who, me? I never felt more energetic in my life — until nine o'clock at night, that is. Then I drop asleep wherever I am. But I do have bad dreams! They're usually about something happening to the baby — I can't remember where I left it and am hunting frantically for it, or it has been smothered or crushed. What makes me, do you suppose? *I* think it is because I've come to think of the baby so much as a real person that when I'm asleep I can't understand why I don't have it within my reach . . . Marion Engelhardt was over to borrow my skates this afternoon and had tea with me. I used those little old Austrian china plates you found for me at that auction last spring and she exclaimed over their quality and pattern . . . My Christmas gift from Herbert won't really be a surprise because I *had* to help him choose it to be sure I can get into it all the next three months. It is a black and white crepe dress. I thought I could get through with my one dinner dress but I've already worn it so often and seem to have so many dinner dates ahead that he thinks I should be able to change off, and I suppose dark will be more suitable than the Spanish tile color toward the end. I'll put it on as soon as I get it Christmas Day and he will take a snapshot of me to send you. I love my Hoover dresses, too. A woman told me the other day I'll probably keep on wearing the same dresses while I nurse the baby because they are so easy to adjust. "And when you're through with *that*," she said, "you'll want to roll them into balls and throw them so far you'll never lay eyes on them again!" I can't imagine feeling a bit that way. I'm sure I'll clean or wash and press them and put them tenderly away for next time. Do you get sick of hearing about babies? If you ever do, you'll have to tell me . . . What fun you must have had all going together to the Nubble for a *December picnic*! I don't believe I've ever seen the ocean in the winter and I *must.* It seems a long time since I've been home even in October or November. Herbert and I have been talking about taking the fall instead of the summer quarter for vacation some year when the baby is no longer a baby but not yet old enough for school (we don't intend to send him until he is seven); here professors have their choice of quarters, you know. Then maybe I could come early in August and Herbert the last part and we would all be home through Thanksgiving. Would you like that as well as summer? Later, when Somebody is six, perhaps, we can take the winter quarter to come, because we very much want Somebody to know what every season is like at home. Or maybe we'll leave him — or her, of course — with you while we go abroad some spring, and you will take him — or her, of course — hunting ivory pips, mayflowers, violets, and strawberries in proper sequence, and let him — or her, of course — help furrow and plant and clean house and all. Because this is going to be your baby, too, you know. Your responsibilities aren't going to be over when you finish knitting that lavender blanket! . . . Much as I've always loved Christmas, every sight and sound and smell of it this year makes lumps in my throat. I miss dreadfully having you and Papa with me, but Christmas itself is so beautiful I'm filled with what I can only describe as ecstasy. Every person I see, everywhere I look makes such an impression on me! And just the physical sensations of lying down when I'm tired, getting up when I'm rested, tying a ribbon, or adjusting a curtain make me deliciously warm inside — like champagne, I guess. I feel so alive all over and through and through. I want it to last. I want to be just like this when I have the baby where I can see and hear and touch it . . . I wish you could see the halls of our apartment house this week, all decorated with green branches and red bells, and a big wreath hung at every apartment door. It means all the more because the owner who did it is Jewish. But it happens that none of his tenants are, and he does everything possible to make us feel our homes are our own . . . So many cards have come from people we used to know well but hardly ever see now — people who were at Bates with us, and in Fall River, and in New

York — and nearly all have news written on them. That's the kind I like best. Aunt Lou enclosed some sweet geranium leaves with hers and I've put them in the baby's drawer.

Christmas night.

You must have smiled when I wrote about pretty soon packing my suitcase. If I had already packed it, I certainly should have to repack it now! Do you suppose I'll ever be able to act to the manor born in pink silk, wide ivory lace, and pink and blue ribbons when I never had such things before in my life, even when I was married? Truly I never saw anything of the kind so lovely as those two gowns and the bed jacket. It just doesn't seem yet as if they can be for *me* — but let anybody try getting them away from me now! The handkerchiefs, too, are most welcome as my supply was low as usual until this morning. I've laid out the six prettiest to go in the suitcase, also a string of blue beads Ruth sent me . . . but delighted as I was with my presents, Herbert was fully as much so with his from you. When he got to your box he had already opened the one that had in it the three shirts I had given him and while he was glad to have them I think he was a bit disappointed they were all plain white. But when he saw yours with the raised leaf and tiny blue figure he was delighted. I know it will long be a prime favorite, like the one you gave him last year with the narrow yellow stripe. Then when he opened Papa's box and saw that smoking jacket! He looked at it and then at me, and it was so clear he had *never* expected to own one (the same way I looked when I saw those silk things, no doubt)! He tried it right on and it fits like a glove. We don't see how you knew so well just what size to get, even to the sleeve length. He has worn it all day and has it on now . . . Now I have to say good-night and write you about the rest of our Christmas in my Sunday letter; but I didn't want to wait another minute before trying to tell you how happy you two have made our day even though you couldn't be with us, which would have been the best present of all. I know you're glad we called you last night, even though we couldn't get through until so late and the reception was poor. Wasn't it good to talk together? . . . Much love, and a Happy New Year to you both and all at home.

In January, 1932, President Hoover named a woman to the U.S. delegation to the League of Nations general disarmament conference to be held at Geneva the following month. Chancellor Brüning of Germany asked Adolf Hitler and his Brown Shirts to agree to an extension of President von Hindenburg's term of office and was refused. Japanese troops were landing at Shanghai in an effort to force the Chinese to call off their boycott of Japanese goods, and in Tokyo a bomb was thrown at the carriage of Emperor Hirohito.

Professor Albert Einstein arrived in California by steamer from Germany through the Panama Canal, having avoided crossing the United States by rail lest he encounter either rabble or newshawks. Greta Garbo was appearing on the screen as Mata Hari, a Parisian dancer who had been executed for espionage during the War, and Edward G. Robinson in *Little Caesar* and *Smart Money*. William Faulkner's *Idyll in the Desert* was published, and *Swiss Family Manhattan* by Christopher Morley who said in it, "The Americans fall into mass hysterias on small provocation; they continually suppose themselves on the verge either of calamity or of salvation; everything is exaggerated to a panacea or a menace, so much so that I could not tell, reading the advertising, which was believed the greater peril to the republic: Russian communism or sore gums."

In three years nearly ninety thousand business enterprises had failed. We now had some twelve million unemployed; at least a million of these were minors, many of whom were on constant, aimless migration by whatever means of travel they could find. Morton Downey was singing, "Wrap up your troubles in dreams," and the Paul Whiteman jazz band was playing, "It Happened in Monterey." There was, as there had always been, no government provision on any level for the jobless except the poorhouses, now everywhere overcrowded with long-time residents of the immediate area. *Brother, can you spare a dime?* A dime, perhaps. But who could spare a dollar? Every philanthropic organization — the churches, the Salvation Army, the Red Cross, the Service Clubs, the Legion, the Veterans of Foreign Wars — was in earnest pursuit of every dollar, every hour, every useful article any individual could and would contribute, guaranteeing that it would be wisely used. But the need was of such monstrous size that it could not be encompassed, and what was given to charity seemed often to be taken away from those who, already deprived, were struggling mightily to earn it. Stay away from a restaurant, eating bread and milk at home or fasting, and the restaurant closed. Buy little at the grocery store and the store closed. Do your own housework and you employed no household help.

We read that only one family in five had as much income as we did. There could be no assurance that ours would continue at this level. Deep cuts were already being made in university budgets. Familiar periodicals were disappearing from newsstands. Publishing houses were among the failing businesses. But there was always The House for us, and nobody in my family was in need at the moment. In Herbert's large family there were already homes where fear was rising and justified, even among people who had never had or expected luxury. We felt as we always had that this was our prime responsibility, after providing for ourselves what seemed to us necessities. We discussed what we could do beyond that, and it seemed to depend mostly on my continuing to write and to publish. We hoped that if *As the Earth Turns* came out and was read, it would help people to see that it was possible to live richly on very little money; but only where an individual's basic needs, physical, spiritual, and psychological, could be met under those conditions. I changed the title of my *Household* page to "At the Crossroads" and emphasized on it and in my letters that my readers there were now making or about to make important decisions which would affect not only the course of their own lives but also that of their country and the world. Payment for my shorthand and typing was helping one ambitious girl through college.

What else?

I had bought our Christmas cards at our apartment door. Now I bought a box of birthday cards. And the little muffled-up woman who sold them to me asked if I had any cleaning she could do by the hour. She said she had been a maid at one of the houses on Lake of the Isles until the summer before, one of a household staff of seven and the last to be let go. She had hoped to be called back, but the family she had worked for had hired no one since, and she had found no other place. I told her I would like to have her come for two hours the next afternoon, if she could.

That night Herbert and I talked long and decided that we would have her come as much time as would be paid for by what I could write while she was there. I was already at work on a serial for Mr. Moore of *Classmate*. The day she came I left that to start a short story for him called "Daughter of Elizabeth." Before the end of the month I had finished it during the hours she cleaned, sewed, and baked for me, and Mr. Moore paid one hundred dollars for it which covered her wages and left me something ahead for February. In his letter of acceptance he had asked if he could have "some time before April" a short story suited to a coming agricultural issue of his story paper. If I could do it this might take us into March.

When she was not there, I worked on his serial which I called "Last Port."

On February 6 I wrote him:

Here is the serial. Will you please like it? Will you please accept it? And, having granted these two favors, will you please try to wangle my pay for it at the very earliest possible minute? Not that I lack bread, but I do lack a number of things I could put to good use very soon, and writing a book followed by a serial has had a sad effect on my income since summer. You've been so good about hurrying payment to me at times in the past that I venture to ask again. See what trouble a reputation for kindness can get one into? . . . The story you say you want for the agricultural issue is exactly the kind I like to do, and shall be my next job.

And I was writing home that, as I could no longer button the fur coat they had given me and had no other warm one, I had bought a black one with Persian lamb collar marked down from $55.00 to $29.50 because "no one seemed to want a black coat in a size as small as 14"; "We miss many fine things on radio because it is the policy of the newspapers here to give no free advertising to the radio stations, so they just say there will be 'music, 8:00', and we never know whether it is a hotel dance orchestra or Lawrence Tibbett . . . You say my Christmas nightgowns won't stand careless washing. Well, they shan't *get* careless washing. Unless I'm sure Mrs. M. will do them as well as I could, I'll do them myself." We were very concerned about Herbert's favorite sister, Josie, who was going into the hospital for emergency surgery just as her daughter and a daughter-in-law were momentarily expecting babies, and her son (husband of the daughter-in-law who was expecting her first) had fallen while loading logs and one of them had rolled on his head and he had been no more than semiconscious for a week. Because of what Mrs. M. could do ahead, mornings, to help me, I was completing all my entertaining obligations, had had the dean and his wife to dinner before they left for the South, and the acting dean's wife and three children to tea, and had invited the Engelhardts to dinner next week, the

Eurichs the following week. "It's wonderful to be able to leave the dishes, for dinner guests seem to enjoy themselves and stay until 11:00 or maybe 12:00 and after that much trying to sit properly and keep up my share of the conversation until what seems to me SO LATE, just stacking seems quite enough"; and "I must tell you about a dream I had last night. I'm having good ones now. Night before last I dreamed all night long about doing things for the baby and how sweet and funny it was. But last night was so vivid! I thought a special faculty meeting had been called at the university and I was supposed to go too, and when we got there we found it was to urge Herbert not to go East this summer. After a lot of speeches Dr. Pike rose and said, '*Mrs.* Carroll is the one we should address these remarks to. It is *her* influence that takes her husband away." And then he made a very impassioned speech, ending with these words shouted so loud I can hear them yet:—'*This woman would rather go to hell from South Berwick, Maine, than to heaven from anywhere else!*' . . . I had a *Household* letter lately from a girl who addressed me as 'Dear Hasty,' saying she loved my middle name and asking if it was given me at birth or if I earned it by my actions! . . . Yes, yes, Miss Skinner did get the ms. of my book, but wrote just a note saying she couldn't even take it out of the box until after February first as that was the deadline for her to deliver a ms. of her own to the publisher. The minute I hear from her again I'll tell you what she said."

A little later Constance wrote that she was on her way to bed after being up all night with *As the Earth Turns.* She said, "I suppose your book has flaws but I'll let others find them if they can. What *I* feel is a big, slow, inevitable rhythm — your earth in her seasons — which reduces persons to atoms and less, indeed, if they try to move out of step. The conception is poetry and lifts to the plane of poetry all the minutiae of daily life in that family of unpoetic individuals. I *hear* the rhythm, the symphony, of the earth turning. There is, to my sense, great beauty in it. I am impressed by the way realism, endless actualities, are used to project a big poetic conception, making even the drabbest event and person part of a beautiful design. In places — Mark's reception of the news of Ralph's death, Mrs. Shaw's storm about Lois May's cow — it grips deep and hurts, hurts a lot. It has a saga quality. The dialogue *is* life. You have a very special gift for speech. I can't go into further details at present."

About the same time Mr. Crawford returned the book manuscript I had sent him, saying he saw no serial possibilities in it, but "The novel is original, free from the typical, and that is rare in a book with such a setting. The atmosphere of North New England is beautifully presented, and the characters most clearly drawn. The title, a really fine one, just fits the book, which I am sure will delight many people."

I wrote home, "With reactions like these, do you suppose the book can go unpublished? But of course it can. Anything can happen. Anyway, no doubt I'll have to send it to one place after another for a long time before I find a resting place for it, if I ever do. I hope I needn't, but we can't hope for all our projects to turn out well, and the baby is so much the most important . . ."

Before February was out I had written the agricultural short story, "Smart as a Whip" for Mr. Moore, and an article for *Household* on "Is This Your Daughter?" in which I only joined together, without specific comment, quotes from my letters from *Household* girls which revealed nothing of their identity but told a great deal about girls which their mothers ought to know.

I wrote home:

We plan to start an After-High-School Fund in the baby's name just as soon as it has a name. Not a College Fund because we don't know that this child will want to go to college. This is just to help in whatever direction does appeal . . . Really cold here now. The mercury didn't get above twelve degrees below zero yesterday. Yes, I did take my walk. Can't keep this child in! . . . Tonight Herbert is out and I entertained myself by taking all the baby's clothes out of tissues to look at them before putting them away again. The very prettiest things are from you. If this baby doesn't love you it will be a queer baby, and it is not going to be a queer baby . . . Did I tell you one of the blue blankets I bought got a faded streak across it when I washed it? I took it back to the store and showed it to the saleslady I got it from and when she looked at it, she said, "Oh, that's a shame. But we can't be responsible. Only one thing could have caused that — the baby wet it!" When I made it clear how unlikely this explanation was, she said she would send it back to the manufacturer.

Japan, having overrun Manchuria in September, had occupied Shanghai and a U.S. transport ship carrying the 31st Regiment and six hundred Marines was steaming out of port for the protection of U.S. citizens there; the cruiser Houston and six destroyers left Manila for Shanghai. In Germany Adolf Hitler was nominated, among others, to run against eighty-four-year-old von Hindenburg for the Presidency. Yehudi Menuhin, who with his violin had been a concert sensation at the age of eleven, was now fifteen and had a driver's license, having passed the driving test on San Francisco's Market Street. Unquestionably a musical genius but refusing to be called a prodigy, he carried this license in his pocket during recitals and asked for strawberry ice cream sodas after his programs.

I was buying stationery at thirty-five cents a box from a girl who could neither hear nor speak, and writing on it that a market which had delivered meat and groceries to us had now become cash-and-carry so that any food we needed which I didn't bring home from my walks we had to drive out for as soon as Herbert came. The Benjamins were our last dinner guests of the winter, and my final gesture of hospitality was having Marion Engelhardt and Alice Eurich to spend the afternoon and partake of a tea so substantial they could stay into the evening without the need of dinner. "We had chilled fruit salad, hot biscuits, toasted cheese crackers, cupcakes, and three big pots of tea. Marion said she had never seen me look as pretty as I did today. Take that for what it is worth, but it is what she said!"

But mostly my mother and I were writing about whether she and my father would come out together to be with us in March, or he would stay with Harold while she came alone, or it would be best all around if neither of them came. My father decided for us all that there was no point in his making the effort to travel so far for such a short time. Then he and I worried over many closely written pages about whether she could safely make the trip alone, she and I over whether he could get along without her, and they about whether I could get along without her. He said he would be fine, she said she would be fine, I said I would be fine; but nobody really believed any of it. The fact none of us could fully accept and certainly could not ignore was that what we all four wanted was to be at home together at what we all considered the most important time of my life; but I had left home and could not be there.

Sometimes it seems as if I can't wait another six months, especially when I realize that it has been only a little over four months — well, nearly five — since we came away. I never hear a train whistle in the night that I don't wish with Uncle Columby that "I was aboard of it a-goin'" home. Minnesota is beautiful and Minneapolis exciting and all our friends here are so good to me. Still I feel as if I were on a strange planet, and remember the light on the back stairs door at supper time, the fences between the fields and pasture, going down the lane to the mailbox, the sound of Papa's and Henry's voices in the yard, the road through York Woods to the beach, opening the gate to cross the tracks when we go to the pond, Cora's lamp at night, dust whirling on Jim's hill, lying in the hammock on the piazza, peas in the white ironstone dish on the kitchen table, a blueberry pie cooling on the tank of the stove, and — everything I see there, hear there, smell there, feel there.

Then it was March, and on the morning of its second day, the country awoke to the news that the evening before, the twenty-month-old son of Charles and Anne Morrow Lindbergh had been kidnapped from his crib in the new Lindbergh home in Hopewell, New Jersey; from "The Eagle's Nest." A half hour after he was known to be missing no car crossed New Jersey's borders unchallenged, and by morning a gigantic posse was combing the whole eastern seaboard from Baltimore to Boston. No event before or since has ever caused such intense personal anguish throughout the nation. The death of one we do not know but nevertheless have admired, trusted, loved, casts a pall of sadness that inevitably lifts as the hours pass; the violent death of such a one adds to sadness a sense of shock which lasts at its height for no more than days. Death comes to all. But uncertainty as to the condition of a nationally adored baby in unfriendly hands is a horror which never ends as long as there is a ray of hope to cling to. Charles Lindbergh was the only democratically crowned prince the world has ever had, he was seen as Everyman at his best. Everywoman's son, grandson, brother. The daughter of Dwight Morrow was his princess whose wedding bouquet he had picked in her father's garden, who had been with him in a plane accident and flown with him again in the same plane a few hours later while he had the use of only one arm, who had, since the birth of Charles Augustus, Jr., been his co-pilot on a flight to the Orient and written a beautiful book about the experience, and who was now expecting their second child. Charles Augustus was also our son, our grandson, our beloved brother's little boy.

The story had top headlines for many days, was on the front page for many weeks. The baby had had a cold. His mother broadcast on radio prescriptions for his medication. Nurse Gow . . . the President of Mexico . . . the ransom demand for $50,000 . . . the effort to pay it . . . Jafsie . . . the underworld . . . applejack distillers . . . Evelyn Walsh McLean and Gaston B. Means . . . the "boad" off Gay Head on Martha's Vineyard . . .

The Depression was for a time seen in a new perspective. Everyone felt fortunate that he did not have fifty thousand dollars, he was not famous, and so no baby had ever been kidnapped from a crib in his house. By comparison, other troubles were easily borne. But *this* was unbearable, this child increasingly belonged to all, and there was no comfort anywhere.

My mother wrote that she was coming at once, and I no longer had heart for trying to dissuade her. She left Boston one evening on the *Minute Man*, reached the La Salle Street Station in Chicago late the next afternoon, took a taxi to board the *Zephyr*, and arrived at seven thirty the next morning at the Great Northern in Minneapolis where Herbert met her and brought her home before going to his first class. I had written her that it was too cold that early for anyone to climb into the rumble seat and there was not room for four in the driver's seat. She and I had breakfast together beside the window overlooking the glittering snow and ice of Nicollet Field.

That night we put in a call to Dover, New Hampshire, to tell my father of my mother's safe arrival in Minnesota. But my brother told us he had gone over home after taking her to the station, saying he might be back by dark and might not, depending on whether he could get The House warm enough to sleep in. He had not returned, and his telephone had not been reconnected so they could not reach him directly, but

Harold had called our nearest neighbor that night and she said she could see his light. He said he would check every night until my father came back. Probably the telephone would be in in a few days.

My mother said, "I knew well enough he would go over there, but why couldn't he sleep at Harold's while I'm gone?"

I knew why and I think she did. Without her, no matter how kind Harold and Jennie were to him, The House was his closest family and he needed it. I could see him going up the steps, unlocking the door, going down the shedstairs for wood and kindling, bringing kerosene from the shedroom, opening the drafts in the kitchen stove, building a fire, watching it a few minutes, half closing the drafts, and going out to clear a passageway to what had once been his paint shop and now was his garage. By the time the car was under cover, the kitchen was warm. He could take off his coat when he went back into The House, lay out on the sinkroom counter the groceries he had brought, open a can of beans, and stir up his drop biscuits. A little later he had lit the lamp and was eating by it at the kitchen table, with the door ajar into the passageway to what had been my grandfather's bedroom to let the heat of the wood fire warm the bed and take the winter dampness out of the patchwork quilts. He was where he wanted to be. The House was glad to have him. And Cora and Dorothy were saying, "Good to see Verd's lamp." Tomorrow Dorothy would bring him some hot doughnuts and Cora would run out, if he passed, to give him a pie.

On March 8 I wrote Mr. Moore:

> I have your letter in comment on the short story and the serial and have hastened to make the revision of "Smart as a Whip" at once as you requested.
>
> The changes you want in "Last Port" are on the whole not difficult and I shall be glad to see what I can do about them soon.

Very likely I did, in the interest of drama, make the atmosphere surrounding the Farrars almost too dark. I am sure I can alter it enough so that readers will feel the sacrifice of the children is only temporary, but a considerable sacrifice all the same . . . I believe my tax scheme is sound, and am supported in this belief by a long-time and present resident of Maine who is now visiting me . . . I doubt I can enliven the action of the first few chapters very much. I needed some tranquillity at the outset to draw my characters. I don't want to seem cocky, but don't you think you are justified in allowing rather more characterization and less plot in my stories than in some others? However, I'll carry out your suggestions insofar as I possibly can . . . Could you see your way clear to making a payment on this serial now and telling me what the balance will be when the revision is completed? As I wrote you, I am in need of money, and since your consideration of the story up to this point has taken quite a while, I should be glad of a check . . . I'll do the biography thing next.

On March 14 Albert Einstein, about to leave Los Angeles for Germany on the Hamburg-American *San Francisco*, and asked by the press, "Aren't you finding it easier to talk to reporters?" replied, "There is a German proverb which says that anyone can get used to being hanged," and added that he was on his way to the dining salon for "a German meal cooked as only Germans know how to cook it."

On that same date Mr. Moore was writing in Nashville, "Just couldn't see you trying to make Last Port without rations these cold depression days," and enclosing payment in full for both the short story and the serial on which I was still working.

A few days later I came up from the mailbox to tell my mother, "All set now to buy nursery furniture when we are ready for it. And the next time we go out I'm going to buy a new toothbrush to go to the hospital with me."

We went out every day which was not stormy. My mother walked with me, rode the streetcars with me, shopped with me. When we stayed in, we sewed together, talking or listening to radio, or she cooked while I worked on the revision of the serial or dictated letters. On Sunday afternoon we squeezed into the roadster seat beside Herbert for the short drive to Lake Calhoun to watch the iceboating. Mild temperatures had caused so much water on the ice that a wave followed every boat as it flew past us. We talked of the iceboat Harold had built when he was a boy and the rides he gave us on White's Marshes. In the evenings I read the whole manuscript of *As the Earth Turns* aloud. By now Herbert had memorized the first page and had it in his mental file along with Milton, many speeches from Shakespeare, and the whole of *The Ancient Mariner*. But there was no word from the Atlantic Monthly Press.

On March 20 the serial was finished and with so much revision that I sent it for complete retyping, together with a letter to be left undated until I assigned a date to it:

> I have developed the idea of horsebreeding instead of the orchard. More dramatic and pictorial . . . The last chapter you will find almost entirely rewritten. I thought it quite fun to have the old boy brought in to face his upstanding young nephew . . . Thanks again for the promptness of your check, and do let me know whenever you need something for a special time and place.

Four days later, just before dawn, the roadster was taking Herbert and me through the dark and icy Minneapolis streets to Northwestern Hospital. About seven thirty that night we heard our child's first cry and Herbert was beside me when the nurse brought the child to where I could see him; Dr. Ehrenberg, ruddy, beaming, glistening with perspiration, said, "Here you are! A fine little boy!"

As I left the delivery room, Herbert went to get my mother. I was hardly back in my bed when they came in together. He was laughing because she was crying. She said this had been the longest day of her life and this was the happiest minute she had ever had. I said she must stop crying because I wanted to have a telephone brought in so that we could call my father.

While Herbert was at the desk arranging for that, my mother asked, "Do you know what you are going to call the baby?"

I said, "By his name! We've always known what his name was, if it was a boy. But I'm not going to tell quite yet."

While we waited for the telephone they went to the nursery window and saw Baby Carroll asleep in his white bassinet.

When the telephone rang at The House my father had gone to bed, but he answered.

"Hello?"

"Hello. Papa?"

"Why—that you, Gladie?"

"Yes. I called to tell you you have another grandson!"

"I *have?* Well, how are *you?*"

"Fine. We're all fine. He was born about an hour ago. And his name is Warren Hasty Carroll."

". . .Well! He'd better be rugged, if he's got to live that down."

"It's the best name we could think of to give him. And he *is* rugged. He weighs over eight pounds. We'll bring him home next summer."

"Good. Come as soon as you can."

"We will. You want to speak to Mama? She's right here."

"Yes. And you'd better get some sleep."

"I'll try, but I'm pretty excited."

"I can tell you are."

"Good-night, Papa."

"Good-night."

I thought I could hear a chunk settle in the kitchen stove, even see the circle of lamplight . . .

The next morning at five o'clock I was wakened by the

bird-like sound of many babies being wheeled along the hall. I thought, "Is one of them ours? Will they bring me ours?" It was, and they did, and we were alone together for the first time.

During the next few days I proofread the new copy of "Last Port" and Herbert mailed it to the *Classmate* with my letter dated March 30. My mother was with me every afternoon, and Herbert every evening. We sealed announcement cards into small envelopes already addressed and stamped, for him to mail. Friends came bringing flowers and looked at Warren through the nursery window. The nurses on the maternity floor were young, gay, and sweet and seemed to me like the sisters I had never had. They were surprised when I began to walk about. They had thought I was tall! I surely felt queenly. This place was a throne room for mothers and babies. Nobody spoke there of the Lindbergh child, but everyone was thinking of him; every day the papers featured the continuing fruitless negotiations for the return of this little boy whose absence from his crib had been discovered while its sheets were still warm. Every four hours when our son was brought to me it was a new miracle to have him in my arms, and I was racked with joy for myself and agony for the Lindberghs; each time he was taken away, sleeping, I followed him with my eyes as far as I could, trying to hold him, praying for him and for all babies everywhere that they encounter nothing but tenderness; and began waiting for him to come again.

Into a world in which we had been confident good was slowly overcoming evil, an ugly root had suddenly put up poisonous shoots. Something inexplicable, sinister, even diabolical was abroad. Where any human being could bring himself to hurt, or endanger, or frighten a sleeping baby! . . . It had become the habit in America to fear only Gangland, and at first people had said, "It's that gang from Detroit or

Chicago, or one in New Jersey"; but even Gangland leader Al Capone from his cell in Cook County said, "This is the most outrageous thing I ever heard of," and offered a $100,000 reward for the safe return of the Lindberghs' child; the Lindberghs issued a statement to the nation's press, saying, "We fully authorize 'Salvy' Spitale and Irving Bitz to act as our go-betweens . . ." Suddenly we did not know which way to look for humanity, could only search our own hearts and try anxiously to penetrate those of others. It seemed that there was nothing except his own child anyone would not risk in an attempt to return their firstborn to Charles and Anne Morrow Lindbergh, yet somewhere among us there was one . . . or more . . .

Before we left the hospital, papers brought the news that the Atlantic Monthly contest had been won by Ann Bridge's *Peking Picnic.* But I had harbored little hope of *As the Earth Turns* winning an award. I was only trying to get it published. Though I had had no word from Atlantic beyond one line saying the manuscript had been received, I was encouraged by its not having been returned and did let myself hope that it was undergoing consideration.

On April 6 Herbert came for us and took us home and my mother met us at the door of the apartment. They had bought the crib I had been looking at longingly for so many months, and it now stood where my desk had been. My study had become the nursery, with baby scales on the little old drop-leaf table we had brought from home and painted yellow, like the crib and a small rocker also from home. The room was large for such a small person and so few furnishings, but we were glad of its spaciousness, its light and air. The studio couch was there for my mother to sleep on at night. At present it would be a nursery only by day. The white basket with the goose-feather pad on the chaise longue in our room would be Renny's sleeping place when it was dark.

My mother stayed ten days longer, taking care of us all and teaching me all she could. Instead of growing tired, she seemed younger every day. Her raven's wing hair was turning white at her temples and thickening as it turned. Her eyes, large, lustrous, purple, charmed me as they always had. I said, "When we have our little girl, I hope her eyes will be just like yours." She said, "I'm glad Renny's are brown like Herbert's." And I was, too.

Two days after she went home, *As the Earth Turns* came back from the Atlantic with a letter:

> It is fair to tell you that your novel was one of three from which our prize-winner was selected . . . *As the Earth Turns* made friends for itself in this office by virtue of the firm and vigorous characters you have created. Your knowledge of the seasons and your Virgilian sympathy with things of the soil were, of course, elements in your favor, but what really made your book stand out were people like Jen and Mark Shaw. In the expansive years such as '28 and '29 I think we should have wished to publish this book, even though with some uncertainty as to its ultimate sale. But at the present time, with business still on the ebb, and with such book buying as there is highly selective, the question of its publication appears, frankly, in a much more dubious light. I say this, thinking not solely of the extrinsic difficulty of launching a work by a new writer, but also because I have some apprehension in regard to the "innerds" of your novel itself. In the first place, the fine details and close observation are not supported in due proportion by the march of your events. The central thread of your narrative is at times so tenuous that I wonder if it is sufficient to sustain the reader's interest . . . I think you owe it to your reader to tell a story which will have some high points of catharsis, or some elements of stress and strain which will stir the emotions and quicken our sympathy for your characters . . . If you wish to discuss this further, please do not hesitate to write me.

Instead I forwarded Constance Skinner a copy of this letter, said the manuscript was now free to be sent to Macmillan, and asked her if she would suggest the name of an editor to whom to send it. Instead she put under her arm the copy she had and marched it between the marble pillars, demanded to see a vice-president, told him here was a book he would be a fool not to publish, and left it on his desk. Every few weeks after that she either dropped in or telephoned the Macmillan editorial offices to "wake them up over there" and "to give them a piece of my mind."

I had no idea what effect this approach and persistence was likely to have on a publishing house, but my book was now out of my hands. Herbert's prose appreciation tests were in print, and he was giving talks on their use to teachers and educational administrators. I was preoccupied with nursing and bathing our baby, playing with him, rocking him to sleep, and listening for him to wake up. While he slept I did the housework, laughed over the astonished responses from my story paper editors to our announcement cards, and dictated, proofread, mailed *Household* letters. Mrs. M. and her husband had moved into our building as its caretakers; since she had a washing machine and I didn't she took our laundry to do for me. By the end of April we had bought a baby carriage and found a college girl who would come to sit by it for two hours five afternoons a week. Each day I gave her the key to the basement door so that she could bring the carriage to the entrance. By the time she got it there I was waiting for her with Renny, just fed and growing sleepy. I tucked him into the carriage, pushed it around the corner to a sunny corner where the wind did not reach, and adjusted the hood while she opened a canvas lawn chair and spread out her books. Then I left them there. When he woke, she pushed him back around the corner and rang my bell. I ran down to bring him up while she put away the carriage and chair.

I did not dare to leave him unwatched, unlistened to, for a

moment. The Lindberghs had paid their son's ransom, but there was still no response from his kidnappers after two months.

I wrote my mother:

I wish our Marion Finney had come while you were here, so you could know how sweet and dependable she is. Last night Herbert and I left Renny with her for the first time. We went to see *Arrowsmith* and it was marvelous, the best photography we have seen. He was already tucked in when she got here, but I telephoned as soon as we got to the theater and she said she hadn't heard a sound from him and had tiptoed in and seen him fast asleep. We got back at 9:45, to find Marion reading in the wing chair with the door ajar into his room, which was just the right temperature and he was just beginning to stir with that ten o'clock feeding in mind . . . He is still angelic. His smiles grow more expansive every day as well as more frequent; we don't know what to *make* of him! He takes twenty drops of orange juice a day now, and sends you and Papa a smile and a gurgle each. When I tell people he turns over on his bath table they say I must have it on a side hill. You wait! I'll have them all in the bathroom some morning soon to see for themselves! . . . You already have an icebox? AND Papa has bought a bassinet? It almost sounds as if he wants us to come home. Well, it won't be long now! . . . Mrs. Chase, widow of our Greek professor at Bates, has been in town, came up for lunch with me, and told me Bobbie Howe, '24, who married a Universalist minister, lives over near Lake Harriet. I talked with Bobbie tonight, (her name is Rice now) and she says the Rices will be over some evening very soon.

On May 12 I wrote her:

You know what an effort it has been for me to get up in the morning ever since I was a child, even at eight o'clock or later. But do I ever hustle out of bed with glee at six o'clock these mornings! Why? Because our son is going to smile at me! Wonderful as his smiles are the rest of the day they are never with *quite* such sheer delight as the first thing in the morning. I'm never in bed at night before eleven and usually it is nearer twelve, but I guess I don't need as much sleep as I used to for I am always wide awake at six, so happy that it is time to go and see if Renny may be awake. If he isn't I sneak away and wait — as I am doing now. When I hear his first wiggle I run in again, and the way he looks up with mild interest that suddenly breaks into that wide, bright, ecstatic smile and flings up his arms and kicks up his heels almost to his chin is what I'd rather see than any play, or any scenery, or any painting, or anything else I know . . . I feel as if I'm not keeping you up with all the things he does at five weeks and I want to. Yesterday morning when I was giving him his orange juice, he took the spoon away from me and waved it a long time, looking at me mischievously, exactly as if saying, "This is fun! Try to get it back! Just you try!" . . . Ruth expects her baby next month, you know. I've written her absolute reams, telling her what it was and is for me. I used to hate it when people (anyone but you) tried to tell me, but I hope she will like what I've told her . . . Now I hear him and must run! If I wait too long he will begin to shout. That's right — *shout!* Hardly ever any fussing or tears any more. What he knows he wants he shouts for in peremptory tones and then when I get there he doesn't smile but looks at me as if to say, "Well, took you long enough!" That's your grandson speaking.

The next morning the newspaper headlines were LINDBERGH CHILD FOUND DEAD.

The first heat wave of the year had reached the Twin Cities. The papers said the mercury had soared above ninety-five degrees and two had been prostrated in the Minneapolis Loop, three had died in Iowa; it was ninety-nine degrees in various cities in the Dakotas.

That was the month President Paul Doumer of France, who had lost four of his five sons in the war, was assassinated by one who said he was Dr. Paul Gorgulov, the President of the National Fascist Party of Russia; in Tokyo Baron Dr. Takuma Dan, one of four Japanese peers created by the Emperor at his coronation ceremonies, was shot by a youth of twenty-one. One by one, leaders working for peace in their various countries around the world were falling. In Shanghai a Korean bomb blew up a grandstand, seriously injuring Japanese ministers, consuls, generals, admirals.

The Farmers and Merchants State Bank of the little town of Walters in Faribault County, Minnesota, closed. Lack of earning power and desirability of liquidation were given as the reasons. Charles M. Schwab of Bethlehem Steel said in New York, "I'm afraid, every man is afraid. I don't know, we don't know, whether the values we now have are going to be real next month or not." The president of Hoover's Reconstruction Finance Corporation, Charles G. Dawes, had to resign and rush to Chicago so that the corporation could authorize $90,000,000 to save his bank, caught in a Chicago bank panic. Rumors of imminent collapse were everywhere. Only astrologers and fortune-tellers were prospering.

But to the great majority of Americans, May, 1932, was the month Charles Augustus Lindbergh, Jr., was found dead in a shallow grave within a few miles of his parents' home. The news reached his father by radio, in the dark waters off Cape May, New Jersey, where he was still trying to make contact with the child's abductors. A few days later burial took place in Englewood, the home of Mrs. Lindbergh's widowed mother, Mrs. Dwight W. Morrow.

At the end of that month Constance Skinner wrote me:

> Your manuscript still awaits definite answer. Two readers are very impressed. If it doesn't go through it will be only because of hard times, retrenchments, etc. It may have to wait until next year. The first step was quickly gained, — they know you are a writer. I'm delighted with the interest Mr. Latham, vice-president of the company, shows; he is a person of literary discernment.

I wrote home that the governor had just proposed that the next two weeks pay of all state employees be withheld indefinitely, and this would mean the loss of over a hundred and fifty dollars to us, but we had been aware of this possibility and were prepared for it; if after that Herbert was paid as usual we could still come home at the end of July, after the summer session. Also, I had "sliced" a "Love Story of Jen Shaw" out of *As the Earth Turns* and we were mailing it to Mr. Moore as a possible serial. "We can't believe he will take it — wouldn't it be miraculous? — but we think there is a chance. Even though it has no plot, it *is* a "wholesome love story" and it *is* about the Shaws . . . That nice Mary Everly of Clearfield, Iowa, (what a charming name for an Iowa town!) wrote Mr. Moore in a letter he had copied for me, "I have read with deep interest Mrs. Carroll's sketch of her life, "I Remember," and have located South Berwick on the map not far from the salt seacoast. Her life needs nothing wildly exciting to make it absorbingly interesting. May many of her readers one day see her whole life story in book form . . . Perhaps by then she will be back in South Berwick, where her heart seems to be all the time" . . . Herbert had too busy a birthday (his thirty-fifth) to celebrate much, but while he went to a meeting in the afternoon he left Renny and me in the Lake Harriet gardens to get the sun surrounded by an acre of lilacs. Renny lay in his basket for three hours, without sleeping more than twenty minutes, and hardly even moving — just looking, looking, looking up through the leaves and fragrant blossoms which surrounded him. I think he thought he was in Paradise and I could easily imagine that I was. I had a book with me but couldn't read, I was so happy . . ."

In June I wrote home:

Herbert is still getting his paycheck. It now seems more likely that there will be a percentage cut in salaries, instead, which seems perfectly fair to us. Poor Mrs. M.'s husband started a house painting job this morning and the ladder let him down so he had a bad fall and beside that ran a piece of iron into his hand.

She is worried about him and about his having to lose a job he was going to get $35 for. She was crying when she came up for the baby's laundry, and said she didn't know what she would do if we shouldn't come back to this apartment after vacation. I told her we surely would, and would pay her to look after it and the birds and plants while we are away, and when we come back she and I would try our partnership again — my paying her whatever I could earn during the time she took over here for me. This really seemed to cheer her up. Now I just hope I can figure out how to do it. I wouldn't leave Renny with *anybody* but Herbert or Marion. Or you, of course; but you won't be here. I'll leave him with you sometimes this summer. I'll feed him and go right off with Herbert to the beach and not come back until his next feeding time! He *wants* some time alone with his grandparents . . . If we *have* to send our children from home to the village school by bus (and I *know* how everybody must hate that, as I would), we can be thankful they are taking our own teacher as its principal! Maybe the town decided on this consolidation just so they could all share our Lois! . . . Last night we talked again as we often do about our trip to Washington and wondered if some day we would go somewhere like that with Renny and all have as good a time as we four did then. We remembered sitting around in your hotel room there, each trying to decide what spot in the whole world we wanted most to see, and Papa was the only one who had no difficulty deciding. He said, "*This* is where I always wanted most to go — Washington, D.C."

In Munich Herr Hitler, bringing suit for "libel and perjury," shouted, "I won't be insulted! I will no longer answer these Jew lawyers! *I* am the party, do you understand? *I* am the party!" and his Brown Shirts filled the courtroom with a chant of "Germany awake! Awake! Awake!" and the next week savage rioting put nearly a thousand Germans in jail, cost a dozen lives; Amelia Earhart, first woman to fly solo across the Atlantic, set her ship down in a farm field in North

Ireland; a friend wrote us that sirloin steak was fifteen cents a pound in California, and that was about all she had to be thankful for financially at the time, for faculty salaries had been cut so much that she was trying to sell her home on "faculty row" but nobody on the faculty had money to buy it; French's, the Twin Cities' best shop for fine antiques, imported items, and decorator pieces had closed and their remainders were on sale in Donaldson's department store. In four weeks we would be boarding a through train for Boston.

Herbert gave me *The Collected Poems of Elinor Wylie* for my twenty-eighth birthday and I quoted from it to my mother:

> *As I went out by Prettymarsh*
> *I saw the mayflower under the leaves*
> *Life (I said) is rough and harsh*
> *And fretted by a hundred griefs:*
> *Yet were it more than I could face,*
> *Who have faced out a hundred dooms,*
> *Had I been born in any place*
> *Where this small flower never blooms.*

I've had a beautiful birthday — the nicest ever. Maybe I should feel old but I don't. Herbert took me to dinner in air-cooled Ivy's, and if you had seen us tearing up Nicollet Avenue in our old roadster with the top down, he bareheaded and I in a white crocheted cap and my white dress with the tangerine cape, I don't believe you would have thought us ancient . . . It worries me that Harold can't take a vacation this year. He must need one . . . Now we're going to listen to Seth Parker. He will make me feel as if I had just stepped into your kitchen, which is all the day needs to make it perfect. Don't you love it when he sings the oldest hymns alone with his guitar? Like Grammy's beloved "The Lily of the Valley" last week, and "That Old-Time Religion"? Only he didn't sing the latter alone, and every time he said, "It's gooden 'nough for me," his company was singing "good e-nough" like city people. I only wish I could find a church which still has "that old time religion" just like Elder Knight's. I've been looking for it and lonely for it so long!

Herbert did some figuring and came to the conclusion that my mother and I had now been writing to each other an average of every other day for ten months out of each of eleven consecutive years. That made three thousand letters exchanged or, by careful estimate, about two million words. Thus each of us in the course of a year wrote an average length book. Eleven years, twenty-two books.

Quite a library. But I don't know of any other library that could have taken the place of this one for us, do you? . . . By the way, you really shouldn't complain of late frosts. What if you lived in 'hopper country? Our newspapers talk of little else but the scourge of 'hoppers. Here's a clipping about them for Papa . . . I get so impatient to be home. I ought to enjoy it this year even more than ever before for I have never been so happy. Sometimes I doubt if I shall ever again be quite the same person physically that I was before I had Renny but it doesn't matter much. When he lies crowing on the bath table or splashes gleefully in the tub or jumps up and down on my arm as he looks at himself in the mirror, it makes no difference to me what my back is doing. He is just beginning to love to be frolicked with and I can stand bent over him anticing, or toss him in the air as long as I think is good for him, and just not *care* whether my back is splitting or not, I'm having such a good time! I've had very few hours to myself since he came, and I'm always up early and get to bed late, but this one thing I glory in — I've never missed a minute of Renny. I think I am a sensible mother, but whenever he has been awake I've been with him or near enough to watch him, and whenever the longing has come to me to see him asleep I've left everything to go and stand or sit by him as long as I wanted to, and every instant of it has been pure joy, whether I was playing with him, doing for him, or just looking at him . . . Here is our schedule! Leave Minneapolis, Sat., July

23, 10:35 P.M. Arrive Chicago Sun., 9:05 A.M.; leave Chicago 10:00 A.M. Arrive Boston, Mon., 10:35 A.M.; leave Boston 11:30 A.M.; arrive Dover 1:23 P.M. . . I guess I haven't dared to let myself realize it before — but it seems so long since I saw Papa that it almost scares me; even since the middle of April when I last saw you is a long time, and anyway seeing either of you here isn't the same as seeing you at home . . . No word yet from Macmillan, but Mr. Moore of *Classmate* will use "The Love Story of Jen Shaw" early next spring. I gather from Constance that is well before the book could be published now — if it ever does become a book. I haven't heard when Mr. Moore will pay for "Jen," but we're all set financially, as far as we can know, at least until we get back here in the fall.

We had been at home about ten days when we found in the mailbox beside The Lane a letter for me from the Macmillan Company, one from Constance Skinner, and one from the *Classmate*.

The Macmillan envelope was quite fat, and the reason for that was twofold: — (1) the size and weight of Macmillan official stationery, suited to bear the official headquarters address, the names of the officers of the Board (George P. Brett, Chairman, George P. Brett, Jr., President, two vice-presidents, Richard M. Brett, Treasurer, the secretary, and the heads of eight editorial departments) and the locations of all its branch offices (Chicago, Boston, Atlanta, Dallas, San Francisco, London, Bombay, Madras, Calcutta, Melbourne, Toronto, Shanghai, and Manila) plus a communication of some sort; and (2) the number of these sheets, which was three.

None of these was signed by any of the personages whose names appeared, handsomely engraved, on the heading. All three were signed by A. J. Putnam, Assistant to the President.

On the top sheet, dated August 1, 1932, he wrote:

I just learned from Miss Skinner that you are not in Minneapolis but at South Berwick and I am, therefore, sending you herewith a copy of my letter sent to you at the former address last week.

The second sheet, dated July 29, was the herewith copy.

It is with a great deal of pleasure that I am writing you to offer you a contract for the publication of your novel, *As the Earth Turns*. We have had the book under consideration for some time and all of us have read it. I am sure that I need not express to you our very definite appreciation for the quality of the book since an offer for publication itself in times like the present will speak for itself.

With your permission I shall have a contract drawn up at once providing for a royalty payment to you of 10% on the first 5000 copies sold and 15% thereafter with an advance of $250 on publication.

I have written Miss Skinner today telling her of our offer to you as I know she has been very anxious indeed to know of our decision.

The third and last sheet was a copy of his letter to Constance:

You will be interested to hear that we are today writing Mrs. Carroll with an offer for the publication of her novel. Mr. Latham, as you perhaps know, is absent on vacation but, because of your interest in the book, I am not waiting until his return to pass along the news to you.

We have taken a long time in considering the book and have had many readings on it. There is much of my own reaction to it which I could give you but you have already expressed much of my feeling in your report. The public taste is indeed a weathervane, and how much of a reception this book will receive is, of course, impossible to say. I do feel strongly, however, that Mrs. Carroll has the restraint of a genuine artist and an unusual faculty for portraying characters in three dimensions. I read the book several weeks ago but the Shaw family is still as vivid to me as though I had been brought up as their neighbor on an adjoining farm.

May I thank you most cordially on behalf of us all for your interest and enthusiasm for this book?

We sat on the porch steps with these letters, Herbert reading over my shoulder.

At the end of the third he said, "Then they *are* going to publish it."

I said, "I gather . . . But what unbounded courage it seems to take!"

I had no feeling whatever of achievement or excitement, only of vague bewilderment as I stared at the strange names. Of all the cities named on these sheets I had seen only Boston, New York, Chicago, and San Francisco (one hot day with the Stanfords, and at lunch tossed salad was the first course). Of all the people mentioned I knew only Constance.

Herbert asked, "What does Constance say?"

Constance enclosed the letter she had received from A. J. Putnam and said he was right that nobody knew nowadays who would want to buy any book or for that matter who would have anything to buy it with even if he did want to, but at least we could be pretty sure now that *As the Earth Turns* would be published, though certainly not before next spring and maybe not before next fall. Meantime, how was the baby, and had I started another book? She hoped so, heartily, because it was of the utmost importance that I not pin all my hopes on any one piece of writing. She said if I was a one-book author she would be sorry she had ever bothered with me.

I had not started another book. But I would.

We opened the letter from Mr. Moore who said "The Love Story of Jen Shaw" would begin in the December 31 issue of *Classmate*; and since "Daughter of Elizabeth" would follow immediately after the last installment of the love story, would it be all right if he used a nom de plume for "Daughter," for a change? If I did not object to this, what nom de plume would I suggest?

I told Herbert, "I think I'd like to be Brett Calcutta."

We went into the kitchen and told my mother Macmillan was going to give me a contract for *As the Earth Turns*, and showed her the letters.

She dried her hands and sat down at the table to read them, smiling.

When she finished she said, "Well, that's nice, dear. I hope you'll dedicate this one to Herbert."

I said I certainly should.

That night I wrote Mr. A. J. Putnam that I would be happy to receive the contract.

On August 15, Mr. J. R. de la Torre Bueno, Jr., Editorial Department, the Macmillan Company, was writing me:

> As Mr. Putnam is away from the city now, I am sending you herewith the contract for the publication of your novel, *As the Earth Turns*. If you will be good enough to sign this, we will send you a copy signed by an officer of this company for your records.
>
> According to our present plans, we shall schedule the book for publication next spring.

I returned the contract to Mr. Putnam with this comment:

> I think the next *two* novels are too many for me to promise before we have had any dealings together. May we wait until I have seen what the Company does with this before I sign up so many? I promise the second cheerfully, and if you are good to my stuff you will get them all, of course. I have made that alteration in the contract as sent to me and hope you won't mind.

On August 28, Mr. H. S. Latham was writing me on the Macmillan stationery which carried his name twice in the heading, as one of the two vice-presidents and an editor of the trade department:

Your letter of August 26th addressed to Mr. Putman was handed to me as Putman is at present away on his vacation . . . Although I was absent on vacation when our proposal of publication for your book was put before you, I had a good deal to do with it myself. I thoroughly admire the story and am very happy indeed that we have taken on the responsibility of publishing it. I have felt very grateful to Constance Skinner, an old and valued friend, for bringing your script to me in the first place.

I am sorry you have not sufficient confidence in us to feel entirely justified in signing the contract as it is, with its option on the next two novels. As I haven't any particular doubt or anxiety about the outcome of our association, however, I am content to accept the alteration, and am sending you herewith a duplicate of the contract with our signature.

You ask about the date of publication. That has not been definitely settled as yet . . . We shall put the book in hand in the late fall, and schedule it as seems best when our list is being made up for the spring season . . . Again my pleasure that you are with us, Cordially yours.

I replied:

I was much pleased that you found time to write to me and happy that you have a good opinion of my book. I understood from Miss Skinner that you were the one person to whom she was eager to submit the manuscript and who could be depended upon to appreciate what I was trying to do . . . I suppose I should have been content with the acceptance but I confess I wanted a word from you . . . May I tell you that I have some reservations about publicity for the book? I much prefer that no mention be made of my work in the juvenile field and that personal details be omitted as far as possible. Can the jacket concentrate on the book itself, perhaps quoting from Miss Skinner's report to you? I trust you have found what I tried to put there — the rhythm of the rotating earth and the effect of this inexorable movement on the life-style of people who live by the sun — but many may not sense it without help at the outset . . . Of course all this is in your province, not mine . . . After

September 20 my address will be 3948 First Avenue South, Minneapolis, Minnesota.

In the meantime we were completely absorbed in home and family.

I had announced on arrival that our baby would go to visit nobody, so everybody came to visit him. Harold, Jennie, and Dick came as many weekends as they could stay away from their lake cottage. Aunts and cousins came mornings to spend the day. Uncle Than and other neighbors stopped by afternoons and waited for him to wake up from his nap on the porch where he was always late in getting to sleep because of his joy in watching the motion of maple leaves and syringa bushes. But when he was awake he graciously entertained by showing how he could almost creep, how hard he could shake things, how loud he could shout, how much cereal and mashed banana he could gobble, and that he could drink from a cup. Toward the end of our stay his grandfather thought it safe to begin to boast that he had never yet heard him cry.

We had no carriage for him that summer, so he rode all over the farm on somebody's shoulders, sat in all the memory-filled corners of yard, field, and pasture on somebody's knee, lay in sunny and shady places on a blanket someone had spread, kicking, rolling, shouting, trying to stand on his head, trying to creep. He was at least as content alone with either or both his grandparents as alone with us. He liked best to have all four within sight, and usually we were; then it did not matter how many other people also were. His close second choice was to be — or to feel — all by himself with his leaves, flowers, and wild birds. He talked to them softly a great deal, and we felt they understood his language.

But then we had to go away. As our train chugged in and we said goodbye on the platform of Salmon Falls Depot, my father looked just as he had the night I was married — beaming through unashamed tears — but my mother could not speak and tried to hide her face. We said, "Maybe you will come out this winter." But none of us really believed they could. Unless they did, we would not be together again for nearly a year.

It was cold for September. There had already been frosts. Renny had grown so much and become so active he needed a coat to keep him warm, but we did not have one for him. His sacques were now too small to go over his sweaters so we put the sacques under the sweaters. All across New York State, Ohio, Illinois and halfway up into Minnesota we were covering him with small blankets which never stayed in place on one side while we tucked them in on the other, unless he was asleep. He was too long for his carrying basket. It now carried only his belongings, and I carried it. His father carried him.

It was good to get back into our apartment and wire home word of our safe arrival.

A week later I wrote that I had been "more or less in bed" with a cold, and that day had been out with Renny for the first time.

Marion came and took him out yesterday, but she can't be with us much this year as she has afternoon classes. She suggested we try her sister Donna who is just out of high school. Donna is here this afternoon and I'm delighted with her. She is a dear and has Marion's quiet, capable, dependable ways. One of them will come every afternoon, at least as long as good weather lasts, to take him out 2:00–5:00. Thus that will be writing time . . . The first night on the train we had the wrong berth reservations and had to change after I had Renny all ready for bed. We carried him like that through several coaches and everybody smiled at him, from other children to painted ladies in imitation ermine and old men with beetling brows and ugly jaws. I had him in my berth both nights. Or rather, I made what use I could of the edge of his. I decided then and there that the babies who used to sleep with their parents, all warm and cuddly — as you said — weren't like my baby. I've slept in an upper with Herbert and had lots more room! I find mine usually sleeps on his side with his head and heels flung back and his stomach thrust out. If he touched me he gave a great snort and flopped over to lie on his back with both arms and both legs spread as far to each side as they could reach. Sma-ll wonder I nearly froze to death and got a cold! But *he* didn't! . . . Have I said enough about our baby? He looms so large in our lives that we hardly notice anything else even if it does happen!

Miss Susan S. Prink of the manufacturing department at Macmillan sent me a sample of the type being considered for the printing of *As the Earths Turns* and asked my opinion of it.

I replied:

I showed it to the owner of a lending library here, thinking her opinion more useful than mine. My eyesight is good, and I can read anything if I want to enough. But she said her experience had been that it was unwise to stock a book which had such small type and such narrow space between the lines, unless it had had outstanding reviews and even then such a book was less readily borrowed and often did not pay for itself. She disliked particularly the close crowding of one word upon another and would prefer taller letters.

Would it be desirable to use off-white paper instead of this stark white? . . .

By the way, I haven't mentioned to anyone that I should like this book dedicated "To H.A.C." Please take care of that for me.

Miss Susan S. Prink replied:

Your suggestion as to a larger sized type has been accepted. I am quite sure the page will be satisfactory. The manuscript, however, is quite long and we must keep it within a specified number of pages in order to price it fairly. We shall be glad to include a dedication and shall incorporate it in your manuscript . . . P.S. We shall use a buff-shaded paper for the book.

I wrote home:

Renny has a tooth. It popped through on his sixth month birthday and now shows every time he smiles and tinkles against whatever he puts in his mouth. We have a playpen for him now — took the table from under the French windows at the end of the living room and put the pen in its place, where the sun streams in all morning. He travels all over it, pounding his pad, chasing his ball, and shouting his eager, excited crow. Half the time he is too busy to pay us any mind whatever . . . Herbert's classes are crowded and his prose appreciation tests will be out next week. The current *Journal of Educational Psychology* features his article on them, and the dean told him this morning that everyone is excited about it and he thinks it is a research classic. Nice welcome back to the job!

Toward the end of October Mr. Fritz Lund, Macmillan art director, wrote me:

Mr. Latham has suggested that I communicate with you regarding the jacket for *As the Earth Turns*. I am therefore enclosing the sketch which has met with our approval.

I replied:

I like the coloring and the idea. I don't like the birds. As drawn, they don't mean anything. And the man at the plow should be smaller — less as if he dominated the earth. There is a feeling of his being carried along with its movement which delights me, and there is a lovely significance in the shadow across the furrows.

I wrote home:

Renny has *another* tooth! He also has a brushed wool set

(sweater, leggings, cap, mittens) and a snuggle rug all to match his eyes — golden-brown. He now says "d-d-d-d" and "b-b-b-b" and "t-t-t-t," making *such* faces to get them out! As I was about to go into Dr. Ehrenberg's office yesterday for my cold shot, the doctor who shares his office, Dr. Solhaug, came in and the nurse, who was holding Renny, asked, "What do you think of this chap?" Dr. Solhaug said, "Oh, he's a pippin. He eats carrots." Over my shoulder I said, "No, he doesn't. Not yet." And Dr. Solhaug responded, "Well, you do then. He never got that physique out of a bottle." Hah — he's never even *seen* a bottle! . . . I wish I dared start another book but I'm afraid we can't afford to gamble again this soon. Herbert's salary has been cut 4% for the rest of this year and it seems to be generally accepted that it will be a 20% cut beginning New Year's. Some say no educational institutions in the state can reopen after Christmas. Banks are failing all around us and those that haven't failed are ransacked by bandits. We're hanging on and practicing nonchalant facial expressions. Renny remains completely unconcerned.

A few days later I wrote home:

We went out looking at houses advertised for rent yesterday afternoon. Every one we saw was either five rooms or ten, and either had a lawn as big as the back field or none at all. Very disappointing. It was a relief to get back to this apartment. But we can't keep Renny here much after this year; he will need a yard to play in, and we want something less expensive than this if possible. Potatoes are fifteen cents a bushel. The farmers are paying no taxes; they can't; and they are organized to hold back anyone who tries to drive a truckload of produce into the Twin Cities — have nail-studded planks laid across the roads. Real estate values in the city have dropped 50% in the past year; still few can afford to buy and those who can't sell can't pay the taxes. And taxes are what pay teachers' salaries! One of the houses we looked at yesterday cost $30,000 to build six years ago and the owner was begging us to buy it for $12,000. Not that we could consider it for a minute, but it shows what is happening . . . Don't think we are worrying. We aren't. It's no use . . . It is interesting to figure how we could get along on a much smaller income if we have to. The only possibility which worries me at all is that Herbert may feel he has to teach both sessions next summer and in that case we couldn't come home. But next summer is still far off — and I feel two ways about *that*, as I'm sure you know! I loved hearing about your ride up over Hedgehog Rocks with the leaves in full color. Some day I'll be there in October again . . . Renny is eating several different cereals now, and ever so many different kinds of strained vegetables and fruits . . . What fun that you had a pie social at the parsonage! How soon do you begin having Sunday school? I can't tell you how much it means to me to think of the church being open again. Though when I do, Elder Knight always seems to be speaking from the pulpit or shaking hands at the door . . . I have written an article at least partly about Renny and shall try it first at *Household*. The title is "Still We Have Babies" . . . Herbert is speaking on his test at three different sessions of the State Teachers' Convention in St. Paul tomorrow, and he and Al Eurich are about to collaborate on a textbook in educational psychology. One of the professors showed Herbert a report yesterday on how a California university spent $10,000 trying to build a test on prose appreciation and had to give it up. Herbert spent almost exactly $200 on his (largely because he did most of the work himself) and it's done and on the market! If only there *are* any markets! . . . We saw Lunt and Fontanne in *Reunion in Vienna* last night. And on the way to the theater we registered to vote. That will be two for Mr. Hoover. We are convinced he will get us out of this Slough of Despond. We are also doubtful we — or the country — could survive four more years of Franklin Roosevelt's slippery charm wriggling all over every newspaper and every news magazine.

We may also have been influenced by Christopher Morley's report in the *Saturday Review of Literature* of an interview with President Hoover. It described his reading tastes, saying he "sank his shafts deep into Balzac, Brontë, Cooper, Dickens, Dumas, George Eliot, Bret Harte, Hawthorne, Howells, Kipling, Meredith, Scott, Stevenson, Thackeray, Mark Twain," and that of late American novelists he preferred Booth Tarkington, Edith Wharton, and Willa Cather.

But in November a man was arrested in Beloit, Wisconsin, for pulling up spikes out of Chicago and Northwestern tracks over which the Hoover campaign train, with the President aboard, was soon to pass, and when the President reached St. Paul he was booed by street crowds between the station and his hotel. White House secret service men had never before known this or anything like it to happen to a President. And on Election Day Roosevelt carried all but six states of the Union. Three of these six were Maine, New Hampshire, and Vermont.

That November Comrade Nadezhada Alliluieva, young wife of Dictator Josef Stalin, died mysteriously in Moscow, and her body in a red coffin was placed on a red hearse to be drawn by six spirited black horses with red streamers around their legs to her grave in the Convent of New Virgins. Eugene Ormandy was engaged as conductor of the Minneapolis Symphony. On radio the Song Sleuth was tracing the ancestry of currently popular songs, finding that "I'm Always Chasing Rainbows" came from Chopin, and "Yes, We Have No Bananas" was a medley of Handel, "My Bonnie," "Aunt Dinah's Quilting Party," "I Dreamt I Dwelt in Marble Halls," and others. Balloon races were much enjoyed all over the world, by both participants and onlookers; but in the United States — and only there — country people occasionally yielded to a curious desire to shoot down the balloons. *The Princess Marries the Page*, a play written by Edna St. Vincent Millay for campus production when she was a senior at Vassar in 1917, turned up among her old papers and was published and hailed as "a little masterpiece." Likewise Barrie's "Farewell Miss Julie Logan," his first story in nearly thirty years. And Dr. Albert Einstein accepted an appointment with the Institute for Advanced Study at Princeton to work there from October 1 to April 15 for the rest of his active life, reserving only his summers when he wished to continue sailing as before his little boat on Berlin's Wannsee. An attempt was under way to raise funds for a survey of the results of school instruction throughout Minnesota in which Herbert's prose appreciation test would be used, but fund raising was a discouraging occupation.

I was reading long pages of galley proof on *As the Earth Turns* to be returned to Miss Susan Prink by the end of the month, writing *Household* pages and dictating letters, and writing home.

Yesterday was the first in nearly eight months that my personal presence has not been required by Renny at any of his three meals — only at my bedtime now, and that for no more than the next few weeks. So Herbert and I had our first full day off as parents. We left at 10:30 when Donna came, came back a little after 5:00. We did nothing exciting. It was enough excitement to be out by ourselves all day. A lovely day, too, as to weather. True Indian summer. We drove through St. Paul and out toward Stillwater, then back to the university near which we had a chicken dinner at a teashop; afterwards we drove along the river and parked among the trees and read the paper and talked the rest of the afternoon . . . I'm so thankful for every warm day when I look at those metal and tar paper shacks right at the river's edge which people put up last summer and are still in because they have nowhere else to go. How can they possibly get through a Minnesota winter there? And if they do, what will happen in spring floodtime? . . . We went to dinner at the Hilperts' last night. He is a professor in the art department. Most of the conversation was about the election. Everyone is very much pleased that we have a Farm-Labor governor and that Roosevelt won by a landslide if at all. He certainly has a mandate to do something. I wore my black velvet . . . Renny is so cute now. I think he's a budding scientist. He shakes his spoon gravely — no sound. Then his cup — no sound. Bangs them together — Eureka! Sound! But he doesn't smile at it. He looks gravely at the spoon, shakes it — no sound. Now the cup, shakes it — no sound. Cup and spoon together — yes, sir, that's *certainly* how you get the sound! And we say he harks back to his great-grandfather Hasty about not wanting to waste anything. If we ever spill anything on the high chair tray, he has to go after it then and there like a squirrel pouncing on a nut. Of course it is really just part and parcel of his new determination to provide for himself. I am no longer allowed to help him hold his cup while drinking. If I try he scolds, shakes his head, and pushes my hand away. He lets me offer spoonfuls of food at the beginning of a meal when he is ravenous but as soon as he can put up with a little inefficiency he insists on feeding himself and unless I let him he refuses to eat at all, won't even look at the old spoon, just grabs his own precious zwieback and munches away, staring into the distance as if to say, "Oh, very well. The whole matter is of minor importance," knowing, I suppose, that this will bring me round! . . . You know I've always said I should do all I could to make my children independent and the earlier the better — but it doesn't look as if this would be much of a job with him! And how he loves his father! At night when it is time for Herbert to come he will do absolutely nothing but watch the outside door and at every step in the hall he becomes completely motionless until it either stops or goes by. If it stops and Herbert comes in, he squeals and jumps and beams and shouts and can't make up his mind whether to hold up his arms or climb right out of the pen . . . I so wish you could see him when I put an extra blanket over him, either at night or during a nap. He opens his eyes without stirring, stares blankly for an instant, smiles, says "Coo-oo-oo" very softly and shuts his eyes, sound asleep. I don't believe he really wakes at all at those times; he must think it is a dream. If I didn't have so much else to do I'd probably wear us both out just marveling at him . . . Mr. Crawford has accepted "Still We Have Babies." The Macmillan people don't know yet when the book will be published. They say probably in March. For Renny's first birthday?

We had Renny's First Thanksgiving, and soon after that Renny's First Christmas.

Now it was 1933.

In December my parents had closed The House and taken

an apartment in Dover, near my brother and his family, and my father was attending court sessions so regularly that Dover police called him The Sheriff.

Until just before Christmas my few continuing contacts with the Macmillan Company had been with Miss Prink, about the galleys, and with Margaret Conklin of the editorial department, about the jacket. But one day, among the greeting cards, I had found two letters postmarked New York, neither from the Macmillan Company.

One was my first from Annie Laurie Williams, an authors' agent for motion picture rights and Constance Skinner's close friend whom, with Macmillan approval and my permission, Constance had some time before asked to seek placement of these rights.

She wrote:

> I have been trying to get something definite to tell you before writing you about your book . . . Now I have had a reading of the story at RKO where the reader praised it as a fine piece of literature saying it should get the Pulitzer Prize but added, "So far nothing this big has been attempted by the picture companies" . . . Even though it is not what we call a natural for pictures, I am going to devote the next several months to trying to prevail upon some director with imagination to see the possibility of transferring the Shaw family to the screen. For days now I have lived with your people . . . Each and every character in your book stands out as perfectly as if in a fine painting. I can not only see Minnie Foote's clock; I can actually hear it tick.

The other letter was from an authors' agent of whom I had never heard before. She said that among her clients were Ellen Glasgow, Sinclair Lewis, Warwick Deeping, Katherine Brush, Kay Boyle and "others of international reputation," that it was seldom she felt justified in adding to this list but it would "be an honor indeed" to represent me. She had just lunched with Mr. Latham who was "so filled with enthusiasm for this first novel" that she had taken it home and found it "as fine, as distinguished, as unusual a novel as I have read in a long time . . . almost epic in its quality and extraordinary character delineation." If I had not made arrangements for its publication in England, might she take a copy with her when she sailed on the *Champlain* next Wednesday? And in view of the little time remaining, would I wire her if she might act for me?

Instead, I wired Mr. Latham asking in effect, "What about this? What have you done? What am I supposed to do?"

His wire in reply recommended soothingly that I refer to Macmillan all inquiries as to various rights to my material, and inform inquirers that this was my policy and practice. I forwarded to him the letter about which I had wired him, along with one from another agent which had by then come in, and retired contentedly to Christmas preparations.

On December 22 he wrote me that he was sailing next week for England where London Macmillan's was already considering an English edition of *As the Earth Turns.* If they did not take it he would, while there, offer it to other English publishers.

He added:

> I am, I need hardly tell you, very personally interested in this novel. I regard it in a way as my particular child, for it was brought to me by Miss Skinner and I at once became deeply interested in it. My enthusiasm is growing all the time, and I am happy to say that this enthusiasm is being communicated to others.

It was a very good Christmas.

Early in January I received the page proof of the book and began work on it. Margaret Conklin wrote, "No definite date has yet been arranged for publication," and Susan Prink, acknowledging receipt of the page proof, said, "When we first discussed the makeup of this book you asked that it be printed on tinted stock. At the time there seemed no reason why we could not grant your request, but it now seems best for us to print the book on ordinary stock paper . . . It is always difficult to get a tinted stock paper from the paper companies at short notice. This delay holds up reprints considerably and we are now taking the precaution to print on ordinary stock books we think will have a large and rapid sale. I hope you will see the reason for our changing this specification and will not be too disappointed."

I looked at Herbert apprehensively.

"Do they think now I've written a best seller?"

"They can't think you wrote it to be a best seller. But if it does sell well — is that bad?"

I could not maintain that any honest way of earning money was bad.

That was the month ex-President Calvin Coolidge died and the mayor of his home city said merchants would draw their shades during the funeral but not close their doors. "I don't think Calvin Coolidge would want that. He knows what they've been through. Every nickel counts."

Farm wages were the lowest they had been for thirty-four years. Forty cents a day and board in South Carolina was only a little below the average. At forced sale by auction of farm property for nonpayment of taxes neighbors and friends, often swinging ropes, grimly prevented bidding, and judges recommended to governors a moratorium on mortgages.

In Russia it was time for the "Five-Year Plan in Four" to end, but there was no celebration. Russians were the hungriest they had been in several years, and sullen Soviet peasants were on strike. The premiere of the most exciting U. S. opera yet written, *Emperor Jones* took place at the Metropolitan Opera House with Lawrence Tibbett in the title role. There was at least a partial retirement of all passenger planes on this nation's transcontinental airways, to be replaced by much faster ones, with a capacity of ten passengers each and a speed ranging from 155 to 187 miles per hour. Two U. S. Nobel Laureates in Physics explained cosmic rays to the members of the American Association for the Advancement of Science meeting in Atlantic City. At the New York Automobile Show Cadillacs, Pierce-Arrows, Packards and Lincolns were shown at a little over two thousand dollars, the Buick 8, Hup, Olds, Pontiac and Hudson at under a thousand, the Plymouth, Chevrolet, Essex 6 and Willys 4 at under five hundred dollars. There were more than ninety bank closings in the U. S. in the first two weeks of 1933, and before the end of January a bank failure wave rather like the rumble and fissure of an earthquake ran down California's Sacramento Valley. Young President Hutchins of the University of Chicago said, "If professors had been listened to more in politics and economics, conditions wouldn't be what they are. But in times of prosperity no one will listen to a professor because he isn't prosperous." Ethel, John, and Lionel Barrymore were appearing together in *Rasputin and the Empress*.

Early in February Margaret Conklin wrote:

"I think I have good news for you this time. If, by any chance, you have not heard that we plan to publish *As the Earth Turns* on March 21st, that is the word now." And she enclosed proof of the material to appear on the back of the jacket. This consisted of one quote from Constance, and another from William Allen White, the nationally famous editor of the Emporia *Gazette* in Emporia, Kansas. Mr. White's comment was at the top.

He said:

As the Earth Turns is an intimate, delightful study of New England. As a story it holds its charm page by page to the end. As a view of American life quite outside of its environment and beyond the story, the book is a contribution to an understanding of the American spirit. Here are courage with humor, purpose without cant, idealism mixed with practical common sense. The characters in this story dramatize the fundamental virtues of America and yet live and shine as human beings. It is — and there is no other word which exactly describes it — a beautiful book.

We liked even more what Constance had written ". . . I *hear* the symphony of the earth as the themes unite in a big, slow, inevitable rhythm of the seasons . . . The speech is laconic, untrimmed, welling out of the core of character, always moving the story on, adding to the portrait being painted . . . But I am still most impressed by the magnitude and beauty of the theme . . . and by the quietly powerful, sure touch with which it has been handled."

Still, Constance had been the friend of this book since before it was begun. Where had William Allen White seen it? How had he happened to? I wrote Margaret Conklin at once, asking these questions, and returned the jacket material saying it was very nice indeed. She did not reply to the questions. But two weeks later Rosa Hutchinson, Macmillan's publicity director, sent me a page from the *Publisher's Weekly*. It was a full page advertisement for *As the Earth Turns:*

Remember *Inheritance*? . . . During the coming month distribution begins of another novel of which we can say with even less hesitancy than of that, "Here is a certain, continued best seller; here is that rare book which the dealer himself will push because he will recognize its positive and exceptional entertainment and literary values." Again we have a virtually unknown author — but again that handicap is more than offset by a completely new viewpoint; again the market is dominated by unusually excellent novels — but there is nothing now before the public which resembles or approaches *As the Earth Turns* . . . ready March 21st . . . to sell at $2.00. The Macmillan Company.

Miss Hutchinson hoped I would be pleased with it "for we consider your book one of the most important on our spring list."

We were pleased enough. But what had suddenly happened? And what was happening now? We could hardly have been more in the dark.

Much was happening everywhere, and most of it little understood.

Bernard Baruch told a senate committee that the country was confronted with a condition worse than war. An attempted assassination of President-elect Roosevelt in Miami resulted in the death of Mayor Cernak of Chicago and the wounding of several bystanders. Into a $500 million bill for direct relief to states, the senate put a $15 million item for transients said to include 165,000 boys and 100,000 girls under twenty-one. Five thousand ragged, hungry men, women, and children crowded into Seattle's ten-story County-City Building demanding food, and stayed there two days. Public utilities were already supplying free light and water to many thousands of homes. A resolution to repeal the Prohibition Amendment passed the house and senate, and for the first time ratification by a majority vote of state conventions in two-thirds of the states was required for actual repeal of an amendment. Adolf Hitler became chancellor of Germany. In Paris waists were lower, lines straighter and looser, shoulders and hats higher, Maggy Rouff showed an evening gown with a front zipper from neck to hem. Publisher Patterson said in his New York *Daily News*, "Whatever President Roosevelt does or doesn't do, we're going to be for him. We're going to withhold hostile criticism for one year at least."

Though not permitted to print appeals for help on my *Household* page, I had offered an exchange service through which girls who had clothing to share and others who needed some could let me know and I would forward letters of request to those who were offering. This was presented as a special opportunity for the making of lifelong friendships, and the response was overwhelming. Some of the most moving appeals which obviously must be quickly met, or which *Household* girl readers were unlikely to be able to meet, I filled myself or gave to my friends or sent on to my mother who packed and mailed what she had and all she could collect in Dover or from our neighbors over home. One of these was a letter from Rhode Island.

> I'm a young married woman eighteen years old and expecting my first baby in March. My husband has been out of work for two months and doesn't know when he will get any, although he tries hard enough. I have no clothes at all for the baby and see no way of getting any myself, so would appreciate it very much if you would send this letter to any girl who may have something I could use. I'm handy at sewing so could make over anything.

She later wrote that she now had everything she really needed and would never forget that her first baby's wardrobe came from Minnesota and Maine.

In January Mr. Moore had accepted a story of mine, "A Twinkle in the Eye," for *Classmate*, saying the next payment for manuscripts would go out about February 15. At the end of February I wrote him that mine still had not come. He replied that checks came more slowly nowadays, but it was "orders from higher up," and mine would come eventually.

Letters were flying between Dover and Minneapolis.

My parents were having a sad, hard winter. In January my cousin Roland's wife, Flora, had died, followed within twenty-four hours by Roland, both of lobar pneumonia, leaving his mother, my father's sister, my Aunt Hattie, alone and very ill. She died three weeks later. My mother wrote, "I think you would have been very proud of all your father has done. It hasn't been easy for him; he thought the world of Hattie and she always depended on him, perhaps more than on anybody else. He can't take it out in crying, as I do." And I replied, "I am proud of Papa always, and especially now . . . I keep wishing you were where Renny could do you as much good as he does me. I find myself depending on him more and more."

Renny had nine words. Renny had fourteen words. He was absolutely no trouble, except that I couldn't keep shoes on him.

> He sits very quietly watching me put them on and tie them up, and the instant I turn away he begins soberly and daintily picking at the knots until they dissolve, pulls out the lacings, throws away the shoes, and begins eating the lacings. What would you advise? Double bowknots don't faze him at all. This minute he sits with both feet stuck out through the rounds of his pen, reaching a hand through, patiently untying — and plop! goes a shoe!

We were continuing to look everywhere for a single family house with a porch and a yard at a rental we could afford. What we wanted was a six-room house with a sunporch — two bedrooms and a study upstairs, a living room, dining room, and real kitchen downstairs, plus a sunporch where Renny could play freely whenever he could not be outside. But there seemed no such thing at a price we could pay, and we were about ready to settle for a five-room house without a sunporch. That would mean that Renny would have the dining room for his playroom, we would entertain at dinner in the living room, and I would continue writing in my bedroom.

Meanwhile we were dreaming of what we would do if the book should really sell well, as the Macmillan people were now at least pretending they thought it would.

> The Minnesota legislature still hasn't settled its budget. One day it talks of a 10% cut for the university staff and the next day

of 50%. People are just beginning to get truly panic-stricken here. It isn't at all inconceivable that Herbert (and many others) simply will get no contract for next year, and if that happened there would be no chance of getting another university position in these times. So what we want most if a small schooner comes in, or even a well-filled lobster boat, is to buy a little farm with a little house on it that we could live in summer times and/or make livable for year round if we need it. It wouldn't be so much fun as building a summer camp but it would be more to depend on. Of course we wish it could be near home. Is the Elijah Boston house still rented? Do you suppose Lafayette would sell it? Will Aunt Hattie's place be sold? If so, what will the price for it probably be? I know it is bigger and nicer than we need, but I love it and hate to think of strangers living there. You keep us in mind and tell us what you think.

Renny had another new word. He and I were sitting in the wing chair and he was touching the flowers in the upholstery with the tip of his finger so I said, "Flower." He looked at me quickly and said, "Ower." I repeated the word several times, he watching me intently, and then he said, "Ower-ff." I repeated my pronunciation and he repeated his. An hour later, when I put him in his kiddie-car in his room I pointed to one of the yellow flowers on the linoleum rug and said the word for the first time since we had been in the chair. "I wish you could have seen the expression on his face. He looked as I have imagined a blind person would if he should suddenly see. And he said softly, "Fower." Since then all he wants to do is go from one flower to another and say its name; as if knowing the name had admitted him to a garden. Remember the snowy day almost a year ago when we put a deposit on that rug to hold it until we needed it? . . . I've been working very late for several nights on my new book and this morning my left eye was swollen almost shut, but it is better tonight and I'm sure will be all right after a good sleep."

I did not tell them the new book was about Old York Road and had my grandfather and Aunt Vinnie in it. I would tell them when I was deeper into it. Next summer I would read to them what I had written. If we got home next summer.

It was twenty degrees below. It was twenty-two degrees below. Renny was walking by holding my hand. He was feeding himself. He was looking at picture books and naming the pictures for a half hour at a time. We saw Will Rogers in *State Fair*. We saw John Barrymore and "the new actress," Katherine Hepburn, in *A Bill of Divorcement*. We saw *The Successful Calamity* but "whenever I see George Arliss I long for *Disraeli*." Somebody gave us a pair of tickets to the symphony and it was wonderful but I nearly froze afterward, waiting on the steps of Northrup Auditorium for Herbert to get around from the parking area in a line of cars that barely moved. Not that our car was any place to warm up, but it did keep out the icy wind.

Renny unaccountably had chicken pox. Renny was quickly over chicken pox. A little girl Renny's age came with her parents for an after-nap call. They stayed two hours during which the two children silently and methodically pushed each other down, hit each other over the head, and struggled fiercely for every toy; all without emitting a sound of any kind. Not until an attempt was made to separate them for her coat to be put on did either have any complaint. Then they threw their arms around each other and began to cry. Their "bye-byes" were heart-rending.

It is very frustrating to have so little time to work on this book. Just as I have everything squared away for a few hours, I have to do something more about *As the Earth Turns*. I'll be so thankful when it's out and I'm finished with it. Right now I have 500 sheets of paper here that I have to sign to be bound into advance copies of the book to be sent to reviewers and booksellers. It seems as if there is no end to those pieces of paper! . . .

P.S. I just got a *telegram* from Macmillan saying publication of the book has for business reasons been *postponed* for about two months! *What* in the world do you suppose that means?

The morning following the receipt of that telegram our telephone began to ring.

I wrote home:

I'm not sure but I guess I had a brief taste of local fame yesterday. First, somebody from Dayton's book department called me to say a Macmillan salesman from Chicago had just been in spreading the news that my novel was "the big thing on the Macmillan spring list" and would be published on March 21 (which, you recall, I had just been told it wouldn't!) and would I give them the refusal of my first personal appearance. All I could think of to say was that I had had word that publication was postponed, so there was no hurry about any arrangements for it and they might call later if they were still interested. I sat right down to write to Macmillan for advice as to how to get out of things like this for *I do not want personal publicity.* I wrote the book. Others are publishing it — I guess — and others can sell it. I'd hardly begun my letter when Donaldson's book department called, asking if I would spend an afternoon autographing copies in their "library room" the week of publication . . . I told them the same thing I'd told Dayton's, and right after that I told Powers' book department the same thing. I don't *know* whether that telegram was intended to be confidential or not, but it was certainly definite, and what else could I say? Getting pretty mad I tore back into my letter and b-ring-g-g — the Minneapolis *Tribune* wanted an interview; I said I'd rather not give one. Then it was the president of the Minnesota Penwomen inviting me to their annual dinner a week from Saturday night. I said unfortunately I had another engagement which fortunately I do . . . The National Education Convention is opening here today, so there are a lot of dinners and teas scheduled for the coming week. Herbert gives a talk on his tests next Wednesday night. We hope to see some old friends from Columbia. I met Marion Engelhardt downtown for lunch today and spent the afternoon at her house. They have such a beautiful one, very close to the river. How I do love that old Mississippi! I rode home with Herbert and when we came in Renny scooted to meet us on his kiddy-car — the warmest welcome you could imagine! We think he is qualifying to replace Jimmy Walker as mayor of New York.

On the first day of March a letter from Constance told me, in great confidence, what she had decided it was high time I knew. She thought Mr. Latham would have told me if he had been in the office but he was still abroad. Anyway, here were the facts, which I must not mention to anyone until I heard them from Macmillan.

As the Earth Turns had had serious consideration at the late January meeting of the Book-of-the-Month Club as its March selection, and two of the five members of the board had voted for it, including William Allen White, but the other three had voted for *South Moon Under* by Marjorie Kinnan Rawlings. However, Mr. White and others had asked that *As the Earth Turns* be reconsidered at their late February meeting and it was their decision then which had necessitated postponement of publication, so I could draw my own conclusions. She would say no more. And I must say nothing.

That night Herbert and I had dinner at a downtown hotel where the convention was holding its meetings and afterward he talked on his prose application tests in the ballroom. We came home late and Donna handed us a paper on which she had written down the contents of a telegram telephoned during the evening. She had asked for a copy of it to be mailed to me. As usual, Donna thought of everything. The message said:

DELIGHTED TO TELL YOU THAT AS THE EARTH TURNS IS BOOK OF THE MONTH FOR MAY STOP PLEASE KEEP CONFIDENTIAL STOP WILL YOU SEND IMMEDIATELY BIOGRAPHICAL MATERIAL WE CAN USE PUTNAM

The next noon another telegram came:

ON MY RETURN FROM ENGLAND AM GREETED BY THE GLORIOUS NEWS OF THE SELECTION BY THE BOOK OF THE MONTH CLUB OF YOUR NOVEL STOP I HASTEN TO PRESENT MY PERSONAL CONGRATULATIONS STOP YOU WILL ALSO BE INTERESTED TO KNOW THAT OUR LONDON HOUSE HAS CONTRACTED WITH US FOR THE PUBLICATION OF YOUR BOOK IN ENGLAND STOP I AM AS HAPPY AS YOU CAN POSSIBLY BE STOP AM WRITING YOU AT LENGTH H S LATHAM

Since Mr. Latham did not stress absolute secrecy — or any secrecy at all — I sent the news home that night:

> Can you imagine it? Constance tried to prepare me for this in a letter which came yesterday. That is, she said it was being considered by Book-of-the-Month and *that* was why publication had been held up. She said if they did choose it they would buy 30,000–40,000 copies for their membership, and she reminded me that my contract gives Macmillan 60% of the price for book club rights and 40% to me. She says of the usual price paid my share will be $4000! So it looks as if the Carrolls really will get to Maine this summer after all! . . . Lots more along that line later. After these two exciting days I should go to bed. Herbert's talk last night was splendid. I wish you could have heard it. As I sat in the audience waiting for it I heard one man tell another that he had come to the convention just to hear more about these prose appreciation tests; that he had read all Herbert's articles on them and was much interested. Afterwards I had a chance to point this man out to Herbert who said he is in the department of education at Northwestern.

I had written Mr. Latham, in response to his telegram, that I was indeed pleased by the news and now wondered at what point book club rights were paid for, as so many interruptions were delaying progress on my new book and I wanted above all to go to Maine for the full summer and rent a cottage on the coast where I could "hole up and get on with it." I asked plaintively, "Why do people seem to want a writer to do everything but write?" I also asked if he felt there was any objection to a novelist continuing to edit a page like mine in the *Household*, saying I liked doing it and did not yet see how we could manage financially without the income from it, though of course I preferred to write novels.

The next day we woke to the news that twenty-two states were now under bank moratoria and severe banking restrictions. At three o'clock that afternoon the Bowery in New York, largest private savings bank in the world, closed with a mob at its doors. Before another morning the governors of New York, Illinois, Iowa, Minnesota, and Missouri had declared moratoria in their states.

It was Saturday, March 4, 1933, the inauguration day of Franklin Delano Roosevelt. We listened to the inaugural ceremonies on the radio. We heard reporters describe the cloudy skies, the chill, President Hoover gravely coming alone to his place on the platform, the President-elect shuffling down a special ramp on the arm of his eldest son. We were told the new President would stand and speak without hat or overcoat. We heard him say:

> The only thing we have to fear is fear itself — nameless, unreasoning, unjustified terror which paralyzes efforts to convert retreat into advance . . . We do not distrust the future of essential democracy. The people of the United States . . . have asked for discipline and direction under leadership. They have made me the present instrument of their wishes. In the spirit of the gift I take it . . . May God guide me in the days to come!

On Sunday President Roosevelt called the congress into special session for Thursday and issued a proclamation closing every bank in the country.

Mr. Latham replied:

> We were quite prepared to make a big success of your book and would have done so, I am sure, without the club adoption,

but even so this is a very gratifying recognition for it . . . Mr. White was a tower of strength. He has stood by the book firmly from the beginning and with grand enthusiasm . . . The Club pays us $10,000 in the month of the book's distribution and according to your contract with us you will receive 40% of that as soon as payment is made to us . . . I see no objection to your continuing as editor of the girls' page if it does not interfere seriously with your time, and you know about that . . .

And now about the personal appearances. When your letter came I already had a memorandum to write you about this. I will show you just how important it is, though no harm whatsoever has been done now that the book has been taken by the Book-of-the-Month Club. But our salesman had been working up enthusiasm for the book with the trade in your area, and one bookstore had ordered 250 copies. When your refusal to appear at his store was given him he cut the order to ten copies. As I say, he will have to order more than 250 copies now so you need have no regrets over your first decision, but this shows rather graphically just how important it is to cooperate with bookstore people . . .

The same is true of newspaper people . . . You are quite right in telling people the book has been postponed, but I should be glad if you would write me, painful as it may be, that you will put yourself in our hands with regard to personal appearances, and let our sales manager work out whatever he may wish to work out with the trade . . . I will promise to make it as easy for you as it can possibly be made . . . We are going after a very big sale and wide publicity and your help is essential . . . Again my hearty congratulations . . . I am sure once we get started you won't mind the personal side so much.

I wrote him on March 6:

I have read and reread your paragraphs on personal appearances and tried to look at the matter from another point of view than my own. It is difficult for me to realize that seeing a writer would make people want to read his book, and so that my sacrifice to do these things would be worth what it would cost me in time away from my family and work, and in effort to choke down my natural inclinations; but I am trying. Your news of the drastically cut order shocks me, the more so as I said the same thing to everyone who called me — that I should prefer to make no agreements until I had been in touch with my publishers, that I had just had a wire telling me publication had been postponed and so there was no hurry about these arrangements; that if they were still interested later they could call me again . . .

As for the future — I can't bring myself to promise to do whatever your sales manager suggests because I take my promises seriously and I don't know anything about sales managers' ideas. But I'll be amenable to his suggestions. Won't it be possible for him to let me know first what, in general, he has in mind, so that I shall be forewarned? My only adverse criticism of the handling of this book so far, Mr. Latham, is that none of you seems to quite realize that as writer of a first novel and rather young wife of a Minnesota professor, I need no end of guideposts. I think somebody should have told me that agents would try to get contact with the book when they knew what you thought of it, and I think your salesman in the Minneapolis territory might have spent a few minutes by telephone explaining to me what he was doing here and what he would like me to do. It is disconcerting, to say the least, to snatch a baby out of his bath and hold him all soapy and dripping while you are told that somebody downtown wants the refusal of your first personal appearance at the time of publication of a book which in the exigencies of the moment you could not swear you ever wrote! I confess to doubts that I shall pick up all my cues properly during the next six months unless you or the sales manager or some other patient person coaches me faithfully. If you will, I'll try to be a docile pupil. Is that a good enough promise? I *do* want to be helpful, for I am not unaware that much of the recognition which has so far come to the book has been largely the result of just such efforts on your part. Unless I had as much hope for my book as you have, I should scarcely be worth publishing for.

But how am I to know, unless you tell me, what arrangements your salespeople have made, and what are the outgrowth of local interest? For instance, the Penwomen. They want me to attend a dinner, and join, and give and receive "inspiration." Must I, or is this a matter in which I may follow my inclinations? Interviews — must I give them to all who ask? I am sorry to know so little, but trained up in the way I should go, I'll be less trouble next time . . .

Could you possibly advance me half my share of what the club is to pay in May as soon as checks can be cashed again? We *must* move into a house at once. A growing family in a small apartment doesn't leave much room for two careers. Also we should turn in our old roadster at the first opportunity for a car in which a baby can be taken to Maine where I've asked my parents to look for a shore cottage in which we can live and I can write during three months which I trust will be complete peace and quiet. I think I need that now. It is beginning to be obvious I'll need it much more by then.

On March eighth I received two checks from *Classmate.* Mr. Moore wrote:

I am sure you will be interested in the enclosed comment from a fellow editor in the Presbyterian Church, South, who uses your material simultaneously with us and likes it too. Please, a Thanksgiving story, and may I have it in April at latest? How's the littlest Carroll?

I replied the same day:

Your checks are here and though I can do nothing but admire them at present I have faith to believe that they will be negotiable eventually . . . I am delighted to know that Jen is holding her old friends. She is making new ones too. The book from which your "Love Story" serial was excerpted has been chosen by the Book-of-the-Month Club for distribution to its members. I am surprised to find that this development is going to tie me up through April and somewhat beyond, so I am obliged to refuse the opportunity to do your Thanksgiving story. If by any chance I can, I will, but you mustn't depend on me . . . The littlest Carroll is prospering mightily. Banking moratoria disturb him not one whit.

The next day I wrote Mr. Latham:

I had lunch yesterday with the book buyer for Donaldson's and a reporter for the Minneapolis *Tribune*. Mrs. Woods, the Donaldson buyer, is anxious for me to go there first to sign books and I should like to — but Dayton's and Powers' first asked me the same day she did. (That near-fatal day!) I have not heard from Dayton's or Powers' since. I am told Mr. Wells of Powers' is furious with us all — with your salespeople because he has not yet received any kind of copy of the book and because he is not kept informed as to the progress of it; with me because I did not go to the Penwomen's dinner. Marching orders, please?

Family letters came and went nearly every day filled mainly with questions and answers as to what everyone was doing about money for daily necessities. Herbert's parents fortunately had quite a bit of cash on hand. My parents happened to have been nearly out of it, and had never had a checking account, but Harold was writing checks which were being accepted to cover the exact cost of his and their necessities. In Minneapolis we were able to do as Harold was doing.

The March 11 issue of *Publishers Weekly* had a full page advertisement saying:

"NOTICE . . . Because of its selection by the BOOK-OF-THE-MONTH CLUB for a later month AS THE EARTH TURNS by GLADYS HASTY CARROLL necessarily has been postponed from March 21 . . . MAKE YOUR PLANS AHEAD FOR CASHING IN ON THIS GREAT NOVEL."

I shuddered. Herbert clipped out the page and put it in a drawer. He said the first thing he was going to buy, when he could buy anything but groceries, was a scrapbook.

On March 12 I wrote home:

I have such a peaceful house this afternoon that I cannot be grateful enough for it. Herbert is at a special committee meeting, Renny playing *so* happily in his pen, my rolled roast baking in the oven with potatoes browning around it, and sunshine streaming through open windows. I can think of nothing to wish for but that this be Maine and you two within running-in-and-out distance. But I have so much of all I want that it almost frightens me . . . I'm enclosing a clipping from this morning's *Tribune*. You will notice that the book club choice isn't mentioned. I asked the reporter not to mention it since, as far as I know, neither the club nor Macmillan has yet officially announced the date.

The *Tribune* report began:

She's shy, quiet, and a bit bewildered by all this stir she is creating in hardened old New York literary circles, this Minneapolis author we promised not long ago to introduce to you readers of novels of merit. Gladys Hasty Carroll is her name, and . . . who wouldn't be bewildered with one's first novel accepted by one of the oldest and most dignified of publishers, Macmillan? She came into our office looking about as unauthorish as any young matron a-shopping bent, with a quick, frank smile and a somewhat inquiring glance from her schoolgirl eyes. She had never been interviewed before, she admitted, and the prospect looked anything but bright. However, she went to lunch with us . . . Her novel *As the Earth Turns* was completed just a few days before her son was born eleven months ago. So there's a new idea for the expectant mother — write a book; the creative fires should burn bright at such a time.

On March 17, Mr. Moore wrote me:

The Cincinnati banks opened three days ago on the basis of unlimited withdrawals, so your *Classmate* checks ought to be good now. I am much pleased by the Book-of-the-Month selection. They have made no mistake for "The Love Story of Jen Shaw" is making real friends among our colleagues in the story paper game . . . I am not giving up on the Thanksgiving story. If it doesn't arrive here before June it will still be in time.

Mr. Latham on March 20:

I have delayed replying to your letter of March 8 until I could enclose with it the check for $2000 which you requested. There was, of course, a temporary difficulty on account of the national bank holiday. Things have now cleared up sufficiently to make it possible for us to forward the payment, which I have great pleasure in doing . . . in order that you may make the plans you are desirous of making at this time . . . *As the Earth Turns* will be published by us on May 2nd . . . I could not ask for anything more than your promise to "try to be a docile pupil." (Had I really promised that? Docile? What a word to choose!) I have asked Mr. Blanton, our sales manager, to let me know exactly what he would like for you to do about the bookstores and he in turn has written to the manager of our Chicago office . . . In general he hopes you will be willing to appear at specified places (we will specify them) at specified times to autograph books and meet people informally . . . I think it would be very nice for you to attend the Penwomen's dinner; also it is distinctly desirable that you give as many interviews as you are requested to give. As a matter of fact, you ought to resign yourself to devoting two or three weeks before and after publication to personal appearances . . . The Macmillan Company of London has bought from us 1000 copies of sheets of the book, which they will bind . . . Few American books do much of anything in England. The English have a prejudice against American novels. It is only one out of fifty that gets any attention. If we can succeed with these 1000 copies . . . in building you up into a valuable property in England (as you are of course in this country!) the returns on future sales . . . will be far more acceptable.

Me? Anyone's "property," valuable or not?
On March 22:

I hope you will not be disturbed when I tell you that we are proposing to change the entire format of *As the Earth Turns*. The Book Club feels that this must be a $2.50 book . . . What the book club proposes to do, therefore, is to take off our hands those copies we had printed before the book club adopted the book, using these for subscribers in Canada or some other foreign part, and we would then make our edition uniform in every respect with theirs, as they insist . . . I hope you will not be disappointed by the change in style . . . I am writing you about it at once as I do not want the news . . . to reach you from some other source.

I replied at once that I was disappointed if I was to lose my ploughman and his shadow on his furrows, but what must be must be. I reminded Mr. Latham that he had promised me a dozen author's copies of his edition; now I must receive an equal number of each of the two first editions. I added that I hoped *somebody* in England would like the book, and "Mr. Wells of Powers' here is warming toward us. He telephoned me that he was giving a radio talk on books this afternoon, and I heard him. He spoke very kindly of *As the Earth Turns*."

Meantime Herbert and I were on a whirlwind of revisiting houses for rent which we had already seen and liked but had crossed off our list because we could not afford them. Like most others, we still had no access to our savings account, but checks were being honored and we were elated by the present size of our checking account.

I had written home on March 15:

I *know* what you would like best is to have us spend the summer at home. And so would we (you know *that*!) IF I didn't have to write and could do my share of the housekeeping. But there is no doubt I *must* get on with this book. It goes slower and slower now, which I wouldn't have thought possible if it moved at all, and my frustration is awful! So do keep looking for a big beach cottage for us. It has to have at least four rooms downstairs and four bedrooms upstairs, AND, hopefully, an attic where I can get on top of everything and write. The reason for the four bedrooms is that we need one for ourselves, one for Renny, one for my household help (both Donna and her sister Marion would love to come with us and we'll bring them if we possibly can — that is, if you find us a big enough cottage and we can get a big enough car), and one for you two whenever you can be there. DO you suppose you can find one with a bathroom, or at least an inside toilet? We want a cottage right on the beach (not across a road) so Renny can safely run in and out — how he will love to do that! It doesn't have to be at Wells, but I thought that would be nearest to home, safest for Renny, and quietest. We'll take anything you think meets our needs . . . I *believe* we have settled on the house we are going to take here. I *believe* Herbert will sign the lease tonight. If he does, more about it very soon.

And in the morning of March 16:

We have our house at last! Herbert did sign the lease last night, for a year, so our address by the first of May and we hope by the middle of April will be 2724 West River Road. We have driven along that road so many times just to watch the river and see the trees and now we'll be where we can do both from our own windows. There is a street and a sort of park between us and the river, but we can see the palisades from every front room and from upstairs windows can see the water. The house is English colonial, brick and stucco, with four big trees on a small, formal front lawn and a dozen or more in a 250-foot back yard which is closed in all around with a high wire fence painted green. Flower beds along the fence, and a rock garden in one corner. The inside needs paper and paint throughout, and the owner has agreed to do it, *us* to choose papers and colors. We'll have a living room, dining room (at last!), kitchen with breakfast nook, and a sunroom downstairs, two bedrooms, bath, and a study upstairs. And according to the present tenants, our running costs, including rent, heat, water and all, will be almost exactly the same as for this apartment. I'm sure the rent has been reduced since we saw it first. But of course we'll have to get some more furniture (everything for the dining room) and will have the responsibility for the grounds. Yes, there is a garage, too;

unheated. Our rugs will fit . . . Donna has left us for the rest of this week to make a tour of Minnesota and Wisconsin with the cast of a play she is in, so the Carrolls are managing by themselves, and very comfortably, too! Actually, Marion studied here last night to listen for Renny while we went for the lease-signing and then saw *Cavalcade* . . .

That night I wrote again:

Can't you even get to your security box in the bank over home yet? You do have cash there, don't you? Surely everything will be settled in a few days now . . . Our banks are all open and everyone talks as if we are starting a new era of prosperity. The only painful part of the prophecies is that prices will double within six months. That, if it happens, will be hard on people living on fixed incomes, also on teachers' salaries which go down easily and come up hard. But it should be good for books and educational tests — and pine woodlots!

I can't imagine why letters travel so slowly and erratically these days. All I get have been at least twice as long as usual on the way. I've certainly written to you as *often* as ever. I am sure I did write you about Herbert's talk at the national convention. He speaks with such simplicity and directness, yet all he says is clearly important . . . Here's one thing his experiments have established — girls as a group make a higher score on any test of artistic appreciation than boys and the highest single scores are almost invariably made by girls! And D. C. Heath & Co., Publishers, have contracted with Herbert and Al Eurich for their textbook in educational psychology which they are to have ready next April . . . Is that enough about my illustrious husband?

My illustrious son will indicate his hair, ears, mouth, toes, and hands on request, and glad to oblige. He frequently announces "Dada bye-bye," meaning either that his father is going or has gone away. He has seventeen words now. I have been busy all day. Finished an article I started a long time ago on rural New England as it is today; proofread and signed some fifty *Household* letters; started my July page; cooked macaroni and cheese and made a tossed salad for supper; and had fun with the baby whenever he wanted to have fun with me . . . We are all fine tonight and about to listen to Rosa Ponselle on the General Electric Hour. Remember when we heard her together in New York in *La Traviata*?

On Warren Hasty Carroll's first birthday, I received from my parents a deed to the home place to become effective on the death of the survivor of my mother and father.

I cannot tell you what you have done for me. As it happened, a check from Macmillan came in the same mail for half the amount of the book club payment, and all I could think of was how little many times that amount of money would have seemed to me compared with what you had sent. You have given me the greatest security I could have. You have given me my first property. You have given me what is dearer to me than anything or anyone in the world except my family. When I began to read the deed I was frightened because I thought you had made the place mine already and I shouldn't like that a bit. As it is, we just know for a certainty that some of us will be taking care of it as long as any of us live. Herbert is *very* happy about it, too. He said, "Well, then that's where I'll have my sheep flock some day, isn't it?" I told him a sheep pen door was all ready for them to run in and out of. As soon as he can get there, he wants to go right out to the barn and see that pen and door! . . . I am so glad Harold approved of your plan and that you have been able to give him what he wanted more. Nothing else could mean anything comparable to me . . . On this the twenty-fourth of March — his First Birthday — Renny weighs exactly twenty-four pounds and is thirty and a half inches tall. He has a big blue and gold celluloid duck named by him — prepare yourself — Ducky, and a new picture book from you and ever so many cards . . . Macmillan has asked for a photograph — *fast.* I hurried downtown to get a dress fit to "sit" in. It is black with silver-gray figures and wide white silk organdy collar and cuffs . . . It must sound ridiculous but I can no longer go inside a bookstore without being spotted and welcomed and even strangers on the street smile and speak and use my name. I know it is friendly of them, but still it seems queer and always surprises me and I don't like it. I'll be so glad when, if that still happens, I can tell myself they're thinking about my book, not me . . . I haven't said nearly all I want to about what you have done for me, and I never will because I never can. I just hope you know how I feel about it . . . I didn't realize until you told me that you would like copies you could keep of printed things I send you, but now I'll try to get an extra copy for you whenever I can. Herbert seems set on making a scrapbook with his.

In the *Retail Bookseller* for April first Macmillan had a two-page spread advertising *As the Earth Turns* — "We shall publish Tuesday, May 2, a great novel . . ."

On April 5 Mr. Latham wrote that he could "arrange to send you six (6) copies of the original edition and twelve (12) copies of the new edition without charge . . . The book is under consideration for the Prix Femina. Mrs. Dwight Morrow, who is on the committee, is very enthusiastic about it . . ."

Mrs. Dwight Morrow was the widowed mother of Mrs. Charles Lindbergh. The Lindberghs were now living with her in Englewood, New Jersey, having given their house near Hopewell "to provide for the welfare of children without regard to race or creed," and they now had another little boy of their own.

I wrote Mr. Latham on April 10:

My six copies of the original edition and the first one in the new format reached me Saturday and I am delighted with both. The original is striking and unusual . . . but I cannot regret the change when I look at the finer paper, wider margins, and more generous spacing in the new version. I feel extraordinarily fortunate in having such an attractive dress for a first novel . . . I also received on Saturday a copy of the Book-of-the-Month Club bulletin for April. A note from Miss Skinner today suggests that she is sympathizing with me a bit because of the headline adjective "pleasant" and some of the reservations in Dorothy Canfield Fisher's review. Do I need sympathy, do you think? It seems to me a very generous review . . . and I am rather proud to be said to have written a good, "pleasant" novel.

I do regret the "biographical notes" the bulletin says I wrote for you. You and I know I only forwarded to you a "birdseye biography" written two years ago for a church story paper where I think they fitted. To prepare anything like this to help launch an adult novel would be unlike me and I writhe under it. Do, *please*, if that story paper is still about, *destroy* it! *Don't* let it travel any farther! *Don't* let *anybody* know I once admitted to having begun a novel at the age of six.

I was writing home about the redecoration of the West River Road house. We had decided to have more done to it than the owner wanted to do, and now must pay half of the cost; our share would be $100, and all old wallpaper was being steamed off (I sent samples of the new), the kitchen was being painted "antique ivory" with Chinese red inside the cupboards and drawers, and the wall lights had been removed; we would have only lamps and in some rooms ceiling lights. "The workmen are so nice, and so glad to have the work." We were beginning to realize I must have some household help for at least a month after we moved in, so I had telephoned eight women who "advertised for 'any kind of housework' in this morning's paper," explaining I needed someone to come at eight in the morning to clean, do Renny's laundry, get lunch and clear up after it. Four said they had to find full-time jobs; the other four would come to the apartment to talk it over with me.

Finally I found my new helper. Her name was Anna Johnson, she was only a little older than I, and she said, "I just love to cook and clean." She looked and sounded to me like a Scandinavian Jen Shaw. She promised to be at the house the day we moved in.

My parents had returned home. I could again address their letters to South Berwick, Maine. We moved and I wrote:

I like this house so much I am all in a whirl. How I wish

you could see it! Last night we said we felt as if we had "come back" to it from a long trip. No use talking — the best apartment in the world isn't home. [I enclosed a room plan with all the furnishings drawn in.] The playpen is discarded. Renny walks everywhere, chuckling with delight in everything, absolutely no trouble and hasn't been through all the moving process, seems to assume the change has been made entirely for his entertainment. Anna is marvelous. So is Donna. It would be impossible to do the things I seem to have to do now if I couldn't depend on them as I do.

The telephone had been ringing whenever it was not in use since it was installed. Twin City newspaper people — interviewers, reviewers, photographers — came to the house by appointment. The mail was voluminous, most of it requiring prompt reply, and included not only letters from publishers, agents, booksellers, old friends, and warm, friendly handwritten ones from novelists and poets I had deeply admired for many years, but as many as ever from my *Household* girls, and clippings from all over the country.

Mr. Latham forwarded a copy of a letter from Richard F. Fuller of The Old Corner Book Store in Boston who said, "For a quarter of a century, which covers my connection with the book trade, I have looked for a novel which completely satisfied my every requirement for a perfect book. My search has at last been rewarded in *As the Earth Turns* by Gladys Hasty Carroll. Not only is this *a* great American, it is, in my opinion, *the* Great American Novel for the particular phase of American life which it portrays." He added that he had made two bets that day; one, "that the public sale will exceed 30,000 copies by January 1, 1934," and, two, "that it will be the choice of the Pulitzer Prize Committee as the 'best novel of 1933.'" Mr. Latham enclosed also a check for the balance of my share paid for book club rights to the book.

We were having dinner guests and Anna was happy to stay all day to prepare and serve dinner whenever we needed her. "She wanted serving dishes which she could bring in and carry from one guest to another, so now we have a meat platter, two covered vegetable dishes, a gravy boat and tray, all in pewter. Very special. I'm practicing acting like some grand lady, just sitting there talking while she does it all, but hanging onto the edges of my chair to keep from hopping up out of habit. She does it beautifully . . . Now what have I and what haven't I told you? Oh, we have the new car. It is a Pontiac, a two-door sedan. Everyone who has children advised the two-door because it can be opened only from the front seat. We got black with black wire wheels but there is red striping . . . Whenever I'm with Renny and call to Herbert, if he doesn't answer or come in an instant, Renny throws back his head and *roars*, 'DADA!' This afternoon I took his high chair out on the back porch for his 'tea,' and we sat there together for a long time in the sun. He loved it, and so did I."

I sent home bundles of clippings, mystified as much from the number coming in so early as by what was being said. Twin City clips were headlined PROFESSOR'S WIFE HONORED FOR NOVEL, and A FIRST NOVEL BY MINNEAPOLIS WOMAN WRITER, and even OUR GENIUSES.

I wrote home, "I'm dizzy. If I didn't have my family and this house I don't know what would become of me."

I sent home a Minneapolis *Tribune* photo of Renny and me sitting in the wing chair by our fireplace, looking at a scrapbook in which we had pasted magazine pictures he liked. The headline was NEW BABY COUNTS MOST TO MINNEAPOLIS YOUNG AUTHOR OF BOOK-OF-THE-MONTH NOVEL. In the write-up below I was quoted as saying, "Sometime I shall get this book to the point where I shall say, 'I can do nothing more for you; as far as I am concerned you are done.' I am sure that time never comes with a child. He is forever yours and always has further possibilities, new fascinations, more claims on you." The interviewer added, "So with a tenderness bigger than emotion and sentiment free of sentimentality, both seen in her eyes as they rest on her child, Mrs. Carroll regards Renny as her wonder of the year . . ."

I wrote home:

> How I wish I could see the Newichewannock overflowing its banks. Two or three days ago Herbert, Renny, and I all watched a riverboat and two barges go by our place. It was just sunset and they were starting downriver, a big old white boat with the big wheel churning up the water in the back, pushing two red barges ahead of it . . .
>
> Herbert and I drove by Donaldson's and one of the windows had nothing in it but a globe and stacks of *As the Earth Turns*. Do you suppose I'll have to sign *all* of them Tuesday?
>
> We were out so late last night Donna stayed over and slept in the study. She said why didn't she get Renny up this morning and give him his breakfast while I slept. Herbert thought maybe I should so I tried. It was the first morning I haven't given him his breakfast since he was born. But do you think I *could* sleep? No, I was downstairs visiting with him before he had fairly started to eat, and already I had missed part of the fun. I shan't try that again . . .
>
> Our flowering almond bushes are budded. Are yours?

That same day I wrote to Mr. Latham thanking him for the book club check and for the copy of Mr. Fuller's letter. I said, ". . . I feel overappreciated and go about as quietly as possible not to attract any more attention. Not that I am not grateful; I am incredulous and bewildered. I didn't know such things were ever really said, only daydreamed by adolescents . . . One store window here has a placard reading, 'The first first novel ever selected as Book of the Month.' Will advertisers stop at nothing? I feel that when I go there I should be a sandwich-man with boards fore and aft reading, 'Mine is NOT the first first novel ever selected, etc.' . . . Miss Skinner has certainly performed as satisfactorily as any agent could have in placing my book with you. Will you tell me what is the usual financial arrangement between an author and his agent? . . . I have just had a charming letter from Dorothy Canfield Fisher saying that in her review of the Book-of-the-Month News she 'didn't begin to say how much I like your book nor how much I hope from you.' My mother will be enchanted with this letter for Dorothy Canfield has long been her favorite writer. I *liked* her review. I especially liked her reference to 'Yankee cussedness' for I know exactly what she means — and I suspect you are finding out, with Mary Ellen Chase, Robert P. Tristram Coffin, and now me on your list!"

Mr. Wells of Powers, the Minneapolis Grand Old Man of books, had mellowed and relented and sent the manager of the Macmillan branch in Chicago a glowing tribute to *As the Earth Turns* ("I believe it is of New England what Rolvaag's *Giants of the Earth* was of the Northwest"), adding enthusiastic quotes from all five highly literate members of his staff. And so, as arranged between Mr. Wells and a Mr. Trenkle of Chicago, I spent the morning of May second in Powers' book department.

That noon I came home to the delicious lunch Anna had prepared, and so did Herbert. Anna, who had insisted on serving us as if we had guests, made a low but clearly irritated sound when the telephone rang as she was bringing in a soufflé.

Herbert answered, wrote down the message, asked Western Union to mail a copy of it, and as he returned to the head of the table, left by my plate the notepad on which he had written:

CONGRATULATIONS ON THE PUBLICATION TODAY OF AS THE EARTH TURNS. ADVANCE SALES APPROXIMATELY TWENTY THOUSAND WITH FOURTH PRINTING ORDERED. FRONT PAGE FAVORABLE REVIEW HERALD TRIBUNE SUNDAY AND OTHER FAVORABLE REVIEWS NEW YORK TIMES SUNDAY AND VARIOUS OTHER NEW YORK PAPERS TODAY. BOOK OFF TO EXCELLENT BEGINNING. ENTIRE MACMILLAN ORGANIZATION JOINS ME IN THESE FELICITATIONS. H. S. LATHAM.

I read it, glanced at him, and we began to laugh. There was some nervousness in our laughter but it came more from incredulity combined with exuberance and real amusement. We were so *far* from New York publishers, New York newspapers, and entire organizations inside marble buildings on lower Fifth Avenue. The metallic voice of Western Union had programmed these words through prairie air into our little English Colonial house on the west bank of the Mississippi River and Herbert had put them down in his characteristic, all but illegible scribble. We were young, we were hungry, and there was Anna uncovering the soufflé, looking at it doubtfully, and then glancing from one to the other of us as if to ask, "What in the world is there to laugh about? It was perfect when I left the kitchen, but now —"

I said, "Oh, Anna, it smells heavenly. *Please* give us some. We hated to keep you waiting. Luckily, it was an important message."

Presumably it was important. As far as we could judge, the soufflé was still perfect. So was the tossed salad. So were the ginger muffins, and later the butterscotch pie with Herbert's coffee. I had not yet learned to like coffee.

He had picked me up at Powers'. After lunch, and after we brought Renny in from the backyard to have his in the kitchen, I was dropped off at Dayton's and Herbert returned to the university. Robertine Howe Rice, Bates '24, met me at Dayton's, stood by me staunchly all afternoon as she had promised she would, and her husband, Bob, called for us at Donaldson's about five o'clock.

I wrote home that night:

I liked it best at Donaldson's as I had expected to. Do you remember their book department? Over between the magazines and the lending library they had placed a carved oak desk and chair on an Oriental rug, and on the desk there was a blotter in a tooled leather frame, an onyx inkwell and pen, a half dozen copies of my book between brass bookends, and two dozen huge red roses in a crystal bowl. That was where I sat to do the signing. A little farther over there was a big round table covered with a white linen cloth with a mound of sweet peas and a silver tea service. Everyone who came was given tea and introduced to me, and I signed *and* signed. Robertine opened each copy to the page I like best to sign on and then someone from Donaldson's took it away (I suppose to make out a slip on!) before it went to its owner. If I haven't seen bushels of As-the-Earth-Turnses today! It was good to get back here and find there *are* books in other bindings with other titles. But it truly wasn't bad, as I had dreaded it might be. Mother Carroll always worries about my wrist, but it is still going strong, as you can see. I guess I've done too much with it to give out in one day's work. And everyone was so nice! I loved it when they said, "I had a course with your husband last year; it was my favorite course," or "I saw a picture of you and your baby. He's beautiful," or "Remember me? I pinned up that dress you're wearing the day you bought it" . . . I wish I could tell you every interesting detail — about the elderly twin sisters who were born in Bangor, Maine, and came in together; the woman who was getting the book as a birthday present for her mother; the man who went by three times before he made up his mind to buy one and I was afraid he couldn't afford it and wished I could give him one. If I have thought well of the human race before, I am in love with it tonight . . . But I suppose I should go to bed to be ready for St. Paul in the morning and the campus bookstore tomorrow afternoon. I suppose my arm *could* get unruly and then who knows how many perfectly good books I'd spoil? . . . I am so pleased to see the flood pictures. May I keep the one of Newt Russell's house? I remember we used to hear that the people who lived there were often marooned in the bedchambers in flood time.

Our section of the Mississippi knew its place and stayed there . . . What 2724 West River Road was flooded with was clippings and letters.

On May 8 I mailed a bundle of them home, including a long and most thoughtful column by James Gray in the St. Paul *Dispatch*. ". . . I do not seriously believe that Mrs. Carroll . . . is deliberately trying to overthrow a trend and start a new one. But it really seems to be true that literature unconsciously seeks to maintain emotional balance . . ."

In my letter enclosed in the bundle I wrote:

> Of them all we think you will like Elizabeth Shepley Sergeant's review in the *Herald Tribune* "Books" best, as we do. Not because it is the whole front page (which pleases Macmillan so much) and not only because of the lovely, understanding things she wrote, but because of the headline. [THE REAL FLAVOR OF YANKEE PROVINCIAL LIFE; A MAINE GIRL'S FIRST NOVEL; RICH, SATISFYING, AND NATIVE] It seems to say I have done exactly what I tried to do, and at last given some proof of how much I love my State . . .

An all but miraculous event of that week was a letter from the editorial rooms of *Redbook* magazine, 230 Park Avenue, New York, dated May 3, and forwarded to me by Macmillan:

> A very long time has gone by since I saw anyone drop orange or lemon or anise-flavored sugar lumps into a cup of tea, and the voice which now addresses you is so dim and distant that you may barely remember it.
>
> But I do want to say that the night before last I finished reading *As the Earth Turns* and that, if people don't soon stop calling it *The Good Earth* of New England and refer to Mrs. Buck's book instead as the *As the Earth Turns* of China, I shall be tempted to take steps. I am not going to add any clumsy phrases of my own to the encomiums that I have already seen,

but I would like to go on record as saying that I think that you have written a perfect book.

As I read it, I was attended on either side by a great pride and a great fear. The pride lay in the fact that in 1928 or 1929, I must have been one of the earlier readers of the manuscript, itself in an earlier form. The fear springs from the idea that there may, somewhere in somebody's back files, be a letter to you in which I said something which will get me into a footnote on some future history of English literature in a very derogatory light — a sort of an editorial "man who dropped the punt." But if it isn't merely that the wish is father to the thought, I am persuading myself that I remember having said something then which I am merely reaffirming now. I do hope so.

The reason for this letter is to express the hope that you are in New York for the launching of your book, and that in the midst of these duties there might be some opportunity in which I could call on you. It so happens that a few days ago I reverted to my original type and am once again in a position which gives me the luxury of reading other people's manuscripts. And whose would I like again to read better than your own, particularly now that I am no longer saddled by an audience that merely wants sheriff to capture villain and brave Jack Dauntless to marry the lovely Gwendolyn? Yours sincerely, Eric Hodgins, Associate Editor.

I replied quickly:

Be reassured. You not only did not drop the punt but carried the ball at least thirty yards. A letter from the editor of *The Youth's Companion*, dated January 21, 1929, says, among other things, "It is a fine story and reminds me of a canvas by Meissonier in the extent to which it covers every square inch of surface with true, well observed and carefully recorded detail. The characterization is simply superb . . . It is practicality that rules it out of the *Companion*. The only way of using it would be to eliminate everything which makes the story really fine."

By "eliminating everything which made the story fine" I managed to get that manuscript accepted as a juvenile book.

Taking what was left over, and a year and a half of time, I made *As the Earth Turns*, and though I can't quite agree with you that it is a perfect book, I am most awfully pleased that you think so.

As you see, I am not in New York. To have you to call I could wish I were. But for all the other reasons I am glad I am not. It is bad enough having to sign copies in Minneapolis stores, sitting at carved oak desks and using onyx inkstands, also having Penwomen giving teas in my honor, willy-nilly. What I am really interested in is our house, only lately achieved — on the west bank of the Mississippi, twenty-four trees on our premises, and a big garden. And I don't suppose you know that I have a son? A few weeks over a year old, and utterly charming.

I am sending to you the only short story I have by me at present. I haven't written many short things lately, and two of the few I have done are with Helen Everitt of Curtis, Brown — a Christmas story in a setting similar to that of my book, and called "No More Make-Believe," and an article entitled "Mist on the Mirror" which defends the assertion that rural New England still exists. Mrs. Everitt thought she could place these at once, but I have not heard from her in a couple of weeks about them, so if you are interested you might telephone to find out whether they are still available. Those two and the one I am enclosing are my all just now.

Forget Eric Hodgins? That is very funny.

A blizzard of clippings . . . Lewis Gannett in New York: ". . . the smells of New England spring and the rhythm of the season finds a deeply satisfactory expression . . ." Harry Hansen in New York: "It seems odd that the first thing worthy of remark about *As the Earth Turns* should be its normality. Here is a novel of farm life in New England which has in it nobody you would be ashamed to know. And that's news . . ." William Soskin in New York: ". . . a lyric celebration of the glorious simplicities of farm life in Maine . . . She refused to give us descriptive rhapsodies or literary stylizations . . . She talks, that is, in terms of her own characters. She sees with their eyes, feels with their solid, healthy simplicity." Donald Davidson in the *Saturday Review of Literature*: "In these Maine folk, so unaffectedly depicted, appear again the indubitable Yankees . . . It is good to see their ruddy features emerge through the socialistic pallor of our times. They were said to be lost; now by amazing grace they are found . . . Country people looked like yokels only so long as city people behaved like cockneys . . . This balance comes necessarily from an intimate understanding of what a Maine farm is like . . . Thus the novel becomes a genuine pastoral which neither idealizes nor protests, but gives its version of 'the mean and sure estate' . . ." The *New Yorker*: ". . . this quality of meticulous understanding, mixed with a kind of capaciousness of imagination, gives the book its greatest charm . . ." And "*As the Earth Turns* ranks AAA in the American News Company's hard-boiled bulletin to the book trade." In the first week after publication the book topped the New York fiction best seller list.

The blizzard became a protracted nor'easter. The *Christian Science Monitor*: ". . . about clearly realized people who pass through universal experiences with dignity and zest . . ." Ted Robinson in the Cleveland *Plain Dealer*: "They live, they are real people, and the setting in which they moved is so true as to bring a nostalgic thrill even to the reader who never saw a New England farm . . . I think *As the Earth Turns* is the best American novel I have read in ten years." Washington *Star*: "James Thomson, eighteenth-century English poet, wrote in the years 1726–1730 his four-part long poem, 'The Seasons' . . . Gladys Carroll has taken the same basic, earthy theme for her novel . . . The style is simple, almost epic. Ladislas Reymont, Polish novelist, did something similar, more powerfully, less pleasantly, in his four-volume novel, *The Peasants*." The *Boston Transcript*: ". . . a completely truthful portrayal of her own people." *Harper's* magazine: ". . . the amalgamation of foreign and native elements goes on . . . Many readers, surfeited with the harsh and cynical fiction of recent years, will be glad to see courage, idealism, and joy appearing in an American novel of the soil." Fanny Butcher in the *Chicago Tribune*; ". . . this first novel by a young woman who is daringly original in writing, today, in a world where frustration is our watchword, a happy book . . ." *Kansas City Star*: "A symphony of the soil . . ." Erskine Caldwell in *Scribner's*: ". . . none of the so-called quaintness of rural New England that is usually mistaken for a people's character. But there is, in its place, a knowing interpretation of a stalwart breed . . ." Paul Jordan-Smith in the *Los Angeles Times*; ". . . here is verihood without viciousness . . . sentiment divorced from sentimentality. Here, oh eager intellectuals, is Greek simplicity without incest; tragedy without vileness; comedy without burlesque . . . Joseph Henry Jackson in the *San Francisco Chronicle*; ". . . a strong, slow-moving piece of fiction beating with the irresistible pulse of the earth's own seasons. Without appearing to aim at poetry, the author has achieved it . . ." *Salt Lake Tribune*: "Life moves in this book with its Maine background, moves slowly, steadily on . . . It is a small life, flowing in narrow boundaries . . . but it is not that barren and bitter life so many urban writers have pictured as the existence of farmers . . . These are homely folk, descended from pioneer stock. Mrs. Carroll, who clearly has intimate knowledge of the life she describes, belongs in the tradition of Sarah Orne Jewett; there is integral truth in her picture of the Shaw family . . ." Edward Weeks in the *Atlantic Monthly*: "Down East a new writer has come to light . . . a homely story whose strength lies in its people, whose humor is Yankee to the core, and whose feeling is like a deep spring which only occasionally bubbles to the surface."

This was the literary climate in America, three long years

and a half after the Wall Street Panic of November 1929, a few weeks after every bank in the country had been closed by Presidential edict, and while many banks were still locked and many others had opened only to inform their depositors that a large percentage of their savings was not payable at present and might never be. At home most of our neighbors as well as my parents passed the village bank with incredulous glances and tucked their bankbooks into bottom bureau drawers.

By mid-May, First Pasturing Day had come and gone in Maine, and *As the Earth Turns* led the best seller list in every major city in the country.

Now the clippings were from smaller papers, from Canada, and from the British Isles. The London *Times*: "The earth and its fruits are drawn as faithfully as the men and women who depend on them for their existence. The relationship between the farmer and his land is expressed with a fine sense . . . In all these activities Miss Carroll makes us feel the close unity of man and nature . . . the family portraits . . . are well conceived and set in a noble landscape." Dublin *Evening News*: ". . . more a picture of life on a farm than a novel . . . evidently written with inside knowledge, and well deserves the tribute it has received in America . . ." The Toronto Saturday Night: ". . . a sober novel of New England farm life . . . the dialogue laconic and real . . . If you find humor a little wanting, remember farming is no joke . . . It doesn't move fast enough to make a movie . . ."

But that was exactly what it was about to do!

I had sent my parents a Mother's Day card reading, "Your children may grow taller; they may grow older, too; but they will never grow away from the love of Home—and You," and gone conscientiously about being (somewhat shamefacedly) the Penwomen's guest of honor at a tea at the St. Paul City Club, giving interviews to *The Amateur Golfer*, opening our door hospitably to photographers, becoming an honorary member of Delta Phi Lambda, speaking at a Symphony benefit in Minnetonka, responding to many other invitations to speak, including one from the New Jersey state association of English teachers meeting in Atlantic City the following November. (I wrote home, "I don't see how I could possibly bring myself to leave Renny to go to Atlantic City in the fall, but Herbert wants me to, and I know I do have things to say to English teachers.") I was writing *Household* pages ahead, dictating more *Household* letters than ever, trying to keep up with all personal correspondence. ("I had a sweet note from Mrs. Belisle, wife of the superintendent of schools in Fall River. She says Margaret Bogle just gave a talk at the Fall River College Club on 'your charming old home in Maine. How lovely that you have been able to spread its spirit so far!' ") Robertine Howe Rice, Bates '24, had given a tea for me in her home, inviting some fifty of her neighbors and church friends. ("I thoroughly enjoyed it, which is more than I can say for most teas. The Rices have a sweet little house overgrown with vines and Bobbie had the rooms filled with flowers — sweet peas on the tea table and masses of huge pink peonies. Bobbie loves entertaining and does it beautifully. One woman there said the most moving part of the book for her was when Mark Shaw picked up stones in the field where Ralph always set down his plane when he flew home. Another said it was the only book dealing with pregnancy and childbirth she had ever seen that she was eager for her young daughters to read. A clipping the other day said it was recommended at a state meeting of Girl Reserves, so apparently other women feel somewhat the same . . . I'm so glad you told me Henry wants a copy of my book. I'm sending him one today . . .") Henry Warren was the son of my father's Uncle Josephus and lived alone in a camp he had built on the cellar hole of his father's pre-Revolutionary house which Henry had torn down in search for pirates' gold said to have been hidden between the partitions or floors or in the foundation. I had not known he liked books but I did know that on his almost daily walks across the field to talk with my father he always picked flowers if flowers were blooming along his way, put one in his hatband, and gave the rest to whatever woman or women were in the Hasty House.

We were writing often and at length about beach cottages.

Three hundred and fifty dollars is more than we expected to have to pay. Herbert had thought we could get something for two hundred and fifty dollars since we'll need it only from the first of July to the middle of September. We do want rooms enough, a way to keep warm, and no traffic between us and the water. I don't care how the building *looks* and a fireplace isn't necessary; in fact, I'd rather have a living room stove. We want Renny to be warm enough on cold mornings and evenings and on foggy or rainy days, and I don't believe anything but a stove would do it. If we have to pay $300, we will, but we couldn't go over that. We do appreciate all your hunting! . . . I am to get 37½ cents on each copy of the book sold, but not until November 1934. Statements are issued to Macmillan authors each July, covering what has been sold up to the first of May, and this amount is paid in November; but mine won't get into this year's statement because it wasn't published until May 2. The Book-of-the-Month payment has cleared up every bill we owned, bought our car, made this house what it is, covered expenses for clothes for all these doings and for the extra help I've needed, and will take care of the summer. What luck! I can hardly believe it yet.

We celebrated Herbert's birthday by going to Northrup Auditorium to hear Lawrence Tibbett in recital. ". . . He was marvelous! I liked best his "Standin' in de Need of Prayer" from his role in *Emperor Jones* . . ."

Then came a tornado week of which I wrote home nothing

until it was over, when I telephoned my parents to tell them that Warner Brothers had bought motion picture rights to *As the Earth Turns.*

The next day I wrote:

I *needed* to talk with you last night. Really, this thing is almost getting away from me. I'm in over my head. But don't think I've let New York agents or Hollywood producers know it. I'm as hardheaded a businessman as you ever saw, with Herbert right at my shoulder all the way. You should have heard the wires buzzing all the past week. I've had about as many telegrams as letters and that is not a few, not to mention long distance telephone calls. This is the gist of it:

"Western Union calling G.H.C. Message signed Annie Laurie Williams. Message reads — Universal offers 5000 movie rights. Also 4% royalty. Royalty always hard if not impossible to get. Must decide at once. Shall I close?"

"Message to Annie Laurie Williams, New York City. — Hold out. If will pay that will pay more. Try for 25,000. G.H.C."

"Western Union calling G.H.C. Message signed A.L.W. Message reads — Warner's wants to produce ATET on stage, you and Constance to write play. Will pay you each 500 and royalty. Picture rights can then be sold only after play has been produced."

"Message to A.L.W. — See no stage play in book. No time to work on play. Fighting for chance to get on with another book. Besides, who would then own picture rights? G.H.C."

"Western Union calling. Message signed A.L.W. Message reads — Warner's would own half of picture rights to play-combined-with-book. Remainder between you and Constance. Successful play production might raise bid for movie rights to 50,000."

"Message to A.L.W. — Of that 50,000 about 12,500 would be mine. Too little. See no chance for success of stage play. Want to write a book. Hold out for 25,000 straight movie rights. G.H.C."

"New York calling G.H.C." This is Annie Laurie to say

Constance does see a play in the book and wants to collaborate on it. G.H.C. stands firm. You see, there is just one thing she is sure she knows, and that is what is and what isn't in that book. If anybody is going to stuff it with what isn't there, she will have no part in the process. Annie Laurie contributes many arguments in favor of letting Warner's have it. "They want to make a really big and beautiful thing of it; not just another play or movie." G.H.C. is tired. She snaps, "Let them pay for it then" — and after that can't sleep all night, but don't tell anybody.

Yesterday morning. "Western Union calling G.H.C. Message signed A.L.W. Message reads — Metro-Goldwyn offers 25,000 picture rights. Open for today. Shall I close?"

Message to A.L.W. — "See if Warner's will match it if you think they will make a better production. G.H.C."

Yesterday afternoon. "Postal Telegraph calling G.H.C. Message signed H.L. Latham. Message reads — Congratulations on successful termination of campaign with Warner's. Just heard from Miss Williams. Very wise of you."

Within an hour. "Western Union calling G.H.C. Message signed A.L.W. Message reads — Closed with Warner's for 25,000. Contract will be mailed to you tomorrow."

The only hard part is about Constance. She is hurt and disappointed and feels I have acted ungratefully; and I'm sorry. But I can't think I owed it to her to try to do what I am sure cannot be done, certainly not by us. I am no dramatist and I don't believe she is. I'm trying to get back to work on a book and I think that is what she should be doing. She gave me her friendship and advice and took my manuscript to Macmillan. I gave her my friendship and appreciation, and am sending her 10% of what I get from Macmillan, the usual agent's fee, the same percentage Annie Laurie asks for placing picture rights. In my one-track mind I am convinced I have done right by all concerned . . . If you wonder where I came by that magic figure of $25,000, I'll tell you that we are sure our share of it is just what we need to either buy a good old house in southern York County, Maine, and restore it, or build a good house as near to you as we can buy a good site. Somehow, some way, *we are coming home*! I don't know yet when we'll get this money, but it is coming and we can wait.

Meantime, Eric Hodgins has bought two of my short stories for *Redbook* magazine, one for $400 and one for $600. The second was my beloved "Columby Maples." So if The Greylock at Wells is still available, with that nice little cottage right in its backyard for you, we *can* pay $500 for the two for the season, so grab it! That will mean you can use either one you want to through June, and invite anybody you want to to use the other. Then when we get there we'll all be for two whole months and a half just as I wish we could always be — within calling distance (and I don't mean by telephone); if I have my way, some day we *will* always be . . . If you get The Greylock, we'll drive straight there after our trip, leave the girls, and be home in time to help you get supper. You know I *have* to come home before I can go anywhere else. You don't know how I long to get there . . . Isn't it wonderful our own "Columby Maples" will be published at last?

Your tired goose-that-laid-the-golden-egg.

Tired, yes; but I was having fun. I had never ceased to miss my correspondence with Eric Hodgins, and now it had begun again.

He:

It was charming to hear from you after all this water has flowed under all these bridges. And for the first time since 1905 I was frankly delighted with myself that it hadn't taken a promotional campaign to make me recognize a fine thing when I saw it . . . The rest of the office agrees with me that your "He Who Had Been Blind" is delightful . . . But I am going to suggest that you change your ending . . . Let him, in other words, go back to his store and regard Marcia Drew in exactly the same unseeing way he has before . . . One of my main interests in the story is that it is so completely unmagazinelike . . . I do think that in one story a month we can afford to get off the beaten track. So don't spend too much time sitting at carved oak desks and using onyx inkwells, for I would love to see some other stories. I called Helen Everitt and asked her to send over "No More Make-Believe." I want to read it because I know it will give me another shock of surprise to realize that there are a few places where the old handicrafts still flourish and not every story is turned out by a great die-casting machine . . . Are you *ever* coming East?

I:

I shall be East this summer, but probably not in New York. You don't by any chance do much cruising along the Maine Coast? Because our cottage will be one of the dots between the Nubble Light and Kennebunkport and I should be more than willing to put out in a dory to rescue you if you were going to pieces on any handy reef.

Do you perhaps know A.W. Smith who reads for Atlantic-Little Brown and who is a friend of Ted Weeks who turned down my book when it was entered in the *Atlantic* contest? (A.W. *told* him he shouldn't of!) The Smiths live in Portsmouth and we plan on getting together and being very literary in August, after I get in a July stretch of work on my new book. Could you be wrecked in August as conveniently as any other time? . . . Here is your story with the new ending, as specified. Personally, I don't find the change an improvement, and return the original version in case you now concur with me in this opinion . . . What is the significance of the year 1905? Don't tell me you were born *that* recently!

The next day I received from Macmillan a contract for my "next novel (title to be specified)." After consultation with Herbert I sent it air mail to Eric with the following appeal:

S.O.S. . . . My personal relations with Macmillan have been happy. I appreciate the enthusiasm with which my first novel has been handled. I want them to have my second, and hope to be able to continue to deal with them without an agent; agents can be disturbing factors. But I am conscious of surprise that this contract is identical with that for *As the Earth Turns.* Is that fair? I am also disturbed that the accompanying letter promises me an advance on ATET royalties IF I will sign this contract and return it at once. Am I being bribed? I can wait for the royalties when due . . . You understand that this is confidential . . . I apologize for the trouble I cause you, but there is no one else to whom I can turn for advice. I am most grateful for the consideration I know you are by this time giving this appeal, and I await your orders . . . Incidentally, it seems I must stop over in New York en route to Maine. Somebody wants an interview and I have now learned (kicking and screaming at every lesson) that when somebody wants an interview, you get yourself interviewed, by golly!

My "orders" were swift, detailed, unequivocal; and I returned the contract to Macmillan with a letter requesting exactly the changes Eric recommended.

In another letter from him, written at the same time but sent under separate cover, he said:

Redbook is now the owner of 66⅔% of the world's visible supply of Carrolls. . . . The only reason why we have not a corner on the market is that Mrs. Everitt of Curtiss Brown told me she was sending me your Christmas story and then sent it to the *American* instead. When you come to New York remember that this is a very wicked city . . . Please do let me know the exact dates of that visit. I am tremendously anxious to whisk you out from under the stamping heels of book publishers and the slavering jaws of magazine editors long enough to have a leisurely conversation about our previous conversations, and other things . . . I should like to hear more about what your contract calls Her Next Novel (title to be specified).

I agree with you that the revision of "He Who Had Been Blind" does not add to the original and so . . . the story will run as you wrote it and will appear on newsstands on September 1. Now will you please continue? The art editor of the magazine, a hard-boiled lad who has never been west of Hoboken or north of 125th Street in his highly urban life, has been going around with a dreamy look for the last six days, ever since he first read "He Who Had Been Blind"; I think he has been down to the market district to inquire the price of straw cuffs . . . There may be other magazines which, as time goes on, will be in a position to offer you more munificent sums of money . . . Look these lads long and steadily in the eye. Don't go on a quantity production basis.

I replied:

Other sensations than that of gratitude assailed me upon reading your letter-with-contract (the advice in which I have followed precisely). One was admiration of the rare ability you have for expressing yourself with absolute clarity. Even I could see at a glance exactly what you meant — and if you could know how I have racked my brain over the indulgently, condescendingly explanatory letters I have had from various agents and business executives, telling me what I already knew but little that I didn't and wanted to. You make even royalties and copyrights sound like part of the English language . . .

I am and have been urging Helen to let you see whatever she has of mine. It is not of vast importance to me that there are editors paying more than you do. I should like best to be a more or less regular contributor to one magazine, whose editor could be depended on to look for value rather than pattern in a story, did not mind my peculiar way of getting at things, and was a friend of mine. Naturally, since I am not a New Yorker, you can depend upon my honesty.

The "exact dates" of my first call on New York should be put in the singular. I shall be there only through the daytime of June 23, and anything leisurely will be impossible then. So suppose we postpone our meeting until a more tranquil occasion. I may have to go back for a few days later in the summer, by the first of September at the latest. Or won't you still be in town?

One more reference to "He Who Had Been Blind" — you understand, don't you, that all sections which have been crossed out in the original version were so treated during my attempt at renovation? They *should* be left in.

Eric:

I shall be keen to know how Macmillan reacts, although it's obvious they'll do anything short of giving you a half interest in the business to keep you . . . I am sorry to hear you are going to be in New York only for one day and that I shan't have the opportunity of seeing you. I shall unquestionably be in town through September 1, but it seems dreadfully remote. Please let me know if there is any change in your plans which might make it possible for me to catch a glimpse of you . . . I am enclosing copy of a box which I am dropping into the September issue to herald the coming of "He Who" the following month (that is, the October issue which I told you — and don't let me confuse you — reaches the newsstands on September 1). You are not permitted to make any corrections out of modesty but if there is anything factually wrong with it, let me know.

I was also having fun with Minneapolis friends. They had taken up reading clippings and following best seller lists as a brand-new game. Someone was always calling us up to invite us to dinner, provided Herbert would bring his scrapbook plus all loose clippings he had not yet had time to mount. I soon began responding that we couldn't afford that many hours of baby-sitting for another year and a half. When they asked if we would meet them downtown for dinner and then take them home with us to help us listen for Renny while they read clippings, I sometimes said yes, but oftener said I'd rather they came to dinner with us so that we would be there to give him his supper and put him to bed; or, if this was impossible, I said, "Come after dinner and read to your heart's content." They came, and came again — the Engelhardts, the Eurichs, the Jacobsens, the Benjamins — and we were all enthralled by how many different things could be said in so many different ways about one book, also by the similarities in reaction in widely separated areas. Everyone pounced on sentences he had to read aloud. The combinations were often hilarious. It made no difference who had written the book. This was a book we had all read, and had our own opinions about, and for the first time in our lives we were finding out what critics, more or less professional, were saying about it in big cities and small towns, here and abroad; also what publishers and book-sellers do in advertising.

Two successive evenings we did go out.

I wrote home:

> I know this letter is late, but we have been on a spree! Thursday afternoon about four o'clock the Jacobsens and Carrolls set off on a picnic — drove to Afton which has a lovely brook known as Valley Crick running through it among those strange, conical hills you can see from the train. I liked it much the best of any country I've seen here this side of the North Shore. We explored until almost dark, and climbed trees — then built a fire and broiled steak. We had taken rolls, dill pickles, cookies, apples, raisins, chocolate, and coffee in a thermos jug, so had a feast. Afterward we lay on the grass and talked a long time. It was so late when we got home and we were so sleepy from all that exercise, good food, and prairie air that I couldn't stay up to tell you about it . . . Yesterday was filled with Renny and mail until we left to spring a surprise on the Eurichs.
>
> You see, Johnny had told us on the picnic that Al Eurich was to give the graduation address last night at the high school at Belle Plains, about forty miles from here. Johnny said he had told Al he and Marion would go up to hear him if they had a car, and that Al said he'd take them with him and Alice if he had more than one seat! So Herbert said, "Why don't we all go — but not let them know we're going to?" It was all spur-of-the-minute, like the most fun things. So we did. And guess what! Al mentioned my book — as an indication that people's minds were turning toward more enduring things than money! In the schoolyard afterward I accused him of having put that in after he spotted us in the audience. Al said no, he didn't see us until *after* he had said that, and when he did see us was the point where his

talk "began to go downhill fast." It all sounded fine to us. As we were feeling young and crazy, we decided to stop for supper in Shakopee, which is about halfway back to Minneapolis, and that Alice and Marion would ride there in Herbert's front seat and Johnny and I with Al. As we rolled off in the coupe Al was still insisting that we had given him a real shock but Johnny and I didn't believe it until, about two miles down the road, he ran out of gas! For *that* to happen to a methodical man like Al did seem to mean *something*! So he had to hop a ride into Belle Plains, and hop another ride back with his can of gasoline. By the time we got to Shakopee we had a lot of explaining to do to one husband and two wives. I felt for a little while as if we were back in college, which doesn't happen often enough these days.

Parts of other correspondences than Eric's were also fun.

Mr. Moore of *The Classmate* wrote, "I can't tell you with how much satisfaction I am reminding many of my superior friends (who say I'm wasting my time on church school publications) that the place to look for the Book of the Month before it comes out is in a Sunday school story paper."

My mother had asked me for several extra copies of the current *Household* which had an editorial headed "Honor for Our Mrs. Carroll." ("No member of *The Household* staff is more closely in touch with readers or better beloved of them than the editor of The Crossroads, our page for girls. So I know thousands of reader friends of hers will rejoice. . . . We who realize that she writes the best page for girls in the United States will not be surprised at the sympathy and power of her fiction.")

When I sent them I wrote her:

How friendly of Mr. Crawford to say that! But it makes it all the more difficult to tell him that I can't keep on with the page — and I know I can't. I wouldn't want to do the page if I didn't answer the letters and they are what take the time. I've just finished dictating for two whole afternoons and at the moment am all caught up — but tomorrow it will snow again, despite our present heat wave (which has Renny all broken out with prickly heat rash, though he has four baths a day; you just don't know how hot it gets here, and *stays*). So I am resolved to write him that having now done the pages ahead for several months, I hope he will get someone to replace me as soon as possible. The replacement I'd like is Rebecca Caudill Ayars because I know she would do for the girls at least as much as I have done; and I'll tell him so. But of course I don't know what her situation is now . . .

Practically *everybody* has been so friendly toward this book that it is almost overwhelming. The other day after Robertine had told me some kind things her church friends had said to her about it, she said they were as gratifying to her as if she had written it. I told her that, being the generous person she is, they might be more so; because if she had written it she would be embarrassed by so much appreciation for what surely could have been much better . . . I am touched by the *Household* claiming me, and by Minnesota seeming to want to claim me, but I can tell *you* that what means most to me personally is what my own family thinks, then our neighbors, then the areas close to home, then the rest of New England. I loved what you wrote me about the man talking with Papa at the Navy Yard, after a while asking his name, and then inquiring, "Are you any relation to the woman from South Berwick that wrote that book?" I can *hear* Papa answering, "Well, yes — distant . . . She's my daughter." Wasn't Mr. Tebbetts' review in the Portland *Telegram* wonderful?" ("After reading *As the Earth Turns* one feels sure Mrs. Carroll has written a great book, a very authentic book, a book which a thousand years hence could be read as an accurate description of New England life of the early 20th century. It is far more vital than history because it is a record of the daily lives of a remarkable people . . .") "What I want to say to everybody — and all I want to say to anybody — is that it was these "remarkable people" who gave me this book; they, and what some English review called "a noble landscape," and the creator of our solar system.

My mother had sent me an editorial from the Dover

Foster's Daily Democrat, printed in large type and saying:

New England has its prose poem at last. Whittier gave us . . . *Snowbound* . . . forever the great snow poetry of New England . . . Gladys Hasty Carroll has given us a prose picture of New England life as lived in Maine. It is not a winter scene only. The four seasons come and go with slow, stately rhythm . . . You actually see the people and live with them . . . Mrs. Carroll has none of the ennui which some popular writers affect. She is neither preaching at you nor making fun of all you hold worthwhile. She tells a story that is wholesome, gripping, and very real . . . She is the daughter of Mr. and Mrs. Warren V. Hasty of South Berwick, Maine, who spend their winters in our city. She is a graduate of Berwick Academy and Bates College. During her college course she helped pay her own expenses by waiting on tables, holding the position of head table girl. She was a house senior and for three years an assistant in the English department . . . Her husband, Herbert A. Carroll, also a Bates graduate, now teaches psychology at the University of Minnesota. Mrs. Carroll, who will be twenty-nine years old this June, has always studied people and loved them . . . Her success is an inspiration to every girl who seeks to make something out of her own life.

I wrote back:

I could have shed tears over the editorial in *Foster's*. What am I saying? I *did* shed tears . . . No reservations whatever. A second Whittier, and done with it . . . This noon I had lunch at Young Quinlan's with Laura Volstead Lomen of St. Paul. Her father is the Volstead Act man, and she has spent most of her life in Washington. Now lives in Nome, Alaska. Her husband has big reindeer ranches. Very interesting woman . . . Oh, that beach house sounds so good! Right now I'd like to tumble onto that couch hammock and not move for twenty-four hours. Only I won't until we've been up home for overnight and gone to the beach all together. Just think, this very week we start east! These are the places we expect to be nights:

Sat. — Stoddard Hotel, LaCrosse, Wis.
Sun. — Faust Hotel, Rockford, Ill.
Mon. — Hoffman Hotel, So. Bend, Ind.
Tues. — Rieger Hotel, Sandusky, O.
Wed. — White Inn, Fredonia, N. Y.
Thurs. — Syracuse Hotel, Syracuse, N. Y.
Fri. — Wellington Hotel, Albany, N. Y.
Sat. and Sun. — with Herbert's family in Rowe; we'll leave Donna and Marion at the Charlemont Inn.

This makes a reasonable amount of riding for Renny each day. We may not always make these destinations but we expect to, so call or wire me if you should need to get a message to me while we are on the way. I'll either call or wire you at least twice en route. Renny has just had a Schick test and is still immune to diphtheria. I've been to the dentist and am discharged for six months. Herbert is fine but tired and can hardly wait to get started on his long vacation. I have told you, haven't I, that I find I have to be in New York City all day Friday? What I'll do is, I'll put Renny to bed in Syracuse Thursday night and then, if he is all right, get on a train for N.Y.C. and go to the McAlpin. It is the only hotel downtown that I have ever been in . . . except the Vanderbilt where the church editors had their convention. Remember the McAlpin was where the bus tour started when we were there on our way to Washington? . . . Then Monday morning, bright, and early, June 26, my twenty-ninth birthday, we leave Rowe for home! ! ! You don't mind not being at the cottage when we see it first, do you? We'll stop in Wells *only* to pick up the key at the store and then drop off the girls. I won't even go inside! I know it's lovely, and you and Papa can show it to us Tuesday. I want to come home first. We want to eat supper with you in the kitchen, put Renny to sleep in the alcove he loved so last summer, talk until we can't hold our eyes open, and sleep in our own bed. Tuesday we'll have a leisurely morning and then can't we go to Wells by way of York so we can take you and Papa to lunch at the Wayside? I keep thinking about their clam chowder! . . . You don't really mean you think I must have changed since you last saw me? That's silly. I'm a year older — well, nine months — and that's ALL.

On our way through Cleveland we stopped at a park for Renny to play while I called at the editorial offices of the *Plain Dealer* to ask if Ted Robinson was in. He wasn't. A week later, in Wells, Maine, I found the following among the new clippings:

She approached my desk the other morning; a beautifully gowned, youthful, and very charming person. She asked for Ted Robinson and when I explained that the Philosopher of Folly was spending the summer on Cape Cod, she asked if he had an assistant she might speak to. I reported that Mr. Wadovick would be in soon if she cared to wait. She did, so she sat down and we chatted about everyday affairs. Suddenly she glanced at her watch, said she couldn't wait any longer, and asked if she might leave a note. A bit later, when Mr. Wadovick arrived and read the note I had stuck under his door, he came steaming in to tell the office force that the caller had been Gladys Hasty Carroll, author of *As the Earth Turns* which . . . stands a very good chance of winning next year's Pulitzer award. It may be of some interest to the extremely modest Mrs. Carroll to know that had she told us her name, our little group would have risen and cheered her as the author of the season's finest book.

Beautifully gowned? Which, I wondered, of my morning cottons could I have been wearing? And surely it must have been somewhat wrinkled across the front from the activities of a fifteen-month-old boy. But the office staff had chosen not to notice imperfections, and for this and for Ted Robinson I would always love the Cleveland *Plain Dealer*.

Only mothers about to leave a first-born child overnight for the first time in his life know how I felt the night I left Syracuse. Renny was sleeping placidly in his crib in the corner of Donna's and Marion's room. They were sitting in the connecting room with the door ajar when Herbert drove me to the railroad station. Renny was as much at home as he had been throughout the trip. I was the one who was leaving, alone — for what, I had no idea. The night seemed dark. The station seemed poorly lighted. The train had few passengers.

The lobby of the McAlpin, when I reached it between one and two o'clock in the morning, was completely deserted. As I stood irresolute at the desk a clerk emerged sleepily from the back. I told him I had a reservation and gave him my name.

He said, "Oh, yes. I think we have some messages for you . . . And some flowers."

He gave me three envelopes, tapped for the night porter, and went out back for the flowers. The porter came, took my bag, two long boxes and two large vases, and operated the elevator himself to take me to my room where he said goodnight and left me. The first thing I did was to open the boxes, fill the vases with water, and arrange the flowers. There were a dozen red roses from Macmillan and a huge mixed bouquet from the Everitts of Curtiss Brown; these comforted me.

Next I shook out and hung up the dress I had brought to wear in New York, and got ready for bed. I nearly fell asleep in the tub.

Finally I read the messages. One was from Mr. Latham welcoming me, and saying Elizabeth Shepley Sergeant would call me from the lobby at 8:00 A.M. and would like to take me to breakfast and get the material for a front page feature story in *Herald-Tribune* "Books." This was very important and would take some time, so would I be ready when she called, as he had allowed her only until 10:30 when he would call for me and take me downtown to meet Mr. Brett, Sr., after which he was having a luncheon for me at the Brevoort, and we would go from there directly to Curtiss Brown, after which we had an appointment with Ben Pinchot to have a photograph made for *Town and Country*, and then until my train time we would be visiting bookstores of which we could reach all too few. Was I sure I could not stay over a second day? I was sure.

The second message was from Constance who said she and Annie Laurie would see me at the luncheon, and the third from Helen Everitt who said she and Raymond had been invited to the luncheon but had pleaded a previous engagement in order to be in a position to insist that I be brought to their office where they could talk to me privately.

It was after three o'clock when I turned out my light. I had not been up that late since the night of Herbert's Commencement ball at Bates ten years before. From my own Commencement ball Herbert had taken me back to the dormitory early because the next evening we were to be married and ride a hundred miles or so into the Maine wilderness.

A week later, in Wells, I wrote Eric:

> Your letter which trailed me halfway across the country and back has just reached me. There is practically everything factually wrong about your box; but let it go, let it go.
>
> My one day in New York came and went — one long gasp. I truly hadn't a minute to call you, as I *wanted* to and was resolved to. I did a lot of things I hate without fully realizing it; like under an anesthetic. Some things I liked. I liked meeting the wily, charming little Mr. Brett in his sanctum sanctorum with big, kind Mr. Latham looming encouragingly behind me. I liked Ben Pinchot who took pictures; he said, "I'm a very mild man. Nobody pays any attention to me." And how bright and beautiful the Everitts are! Like the leads in a Viennese operetta! Even the way they walk and talk — you expect them to burst into song at any moment.
>
> About the new contract. I wrote a polite first paragraph and then listed your points exactly as you had, very neatly, 1, 2, 3,

and so on, omitting nothing. The contract you saw was enclosed, and the whole dispatched. I shall never be done feeling grateful to you. When you have a magazine all your own, I'll do you a lovely story gratis. A wire, sent promptly on receipt of said letter, told me my (your) terms were being accepted in toto. I didn't even need the "acid smile" you had armed me with. So you can figure what your advice meant to me, over and above my appreciation of your friendly interest. I should certainly not have signed the first contract even without you to reinforce me, but quite as certainly my terms would have been easier.

Sorry you didn't like the Christmas story when you finally got a look at it. I would offer to try to revise it but you know my heart would not be in it; so always remember that if you don't like what I do you would like even less whatever I did to change it. Besides, the *Delineator* has now taken the Christmas story. But just before I left Minneapolis Helen asked me to dig into trunks, tear off wallpaper, *somehow* come up with more short stories. The result of that was that I took her two of my old favorites which have already been everywhere, including to *Redbook* (before you got there) and nobody has wanted them yet. Has she shown them to you?

She had, and he had taken both. One of them was "So Clyde Was Born," the story of which I had written to an unnamed *Redbook* editor, a year before, "A few summers ago I came upon a rather young old maid who laughed a great deal and scalloped the hems of her skirts. So I wrote a story about her and about a kind of girl who never does become an old maid . . ." It had indeed been everywhere, had been returned to me by twenty-five magazines, some of them two or three times. But now it was at last to emerge from oblivion and be selected by Martha Foley to represent Maine in her anthology of U. S. stories.

Eric wrote:

I do tremendously like these two "new" ones . . . Now what about this novel you are working on this summer? Helen talked with me about it this afternoon, following which there was an editorial huddle out of which came the obvious conclusion that we are very much interested in it. Probably, however, it would not be wise for us to indulge in the luxury of an option payment. On the other hand, my scouts who are everywhere tell me that another magazine is suggesting just that to you. Will this rule us out? I hope not, because I would tremendously like to have the first look at the new work whenever it begins to develop. I would even like to hear about it before much of it gets down on paper. Can I, do you suppose?

I replied:

Before I left Minneapolis the Everitts wrote me that this other magazine was offering a $500 option on serial rights to whatever I did next. When I was in New York the Everitts talked to me about it and were eager for me to sign the agreement then and there, but I suggested they let you know first that this arrangement was pending. They did not think you would be at all interested but I felt you would be the best judge of that . . . Now, knowing the associate editor of *Redbook*, I can't believe that a similar offer would not be forthcoming from him *if* he really thought this might be something he could use. It isn't as if *Redbook* didn't have $500! If it didn't I'd be all sympathy because I well know how it feels. But obviously it does, and obviously you don't, and I agree with you. I don't have nearly enough done on this book to let anybody see it and I absolutely could not talk about it at this stage with anyone; but I strongly doubt that it is or ever will be a magazine serial, any more than *As the Earth Turns*. So isn't it best all around to let it go as it is?

He:

Alas, we are misunderstanding each other! If there were no such things as deputy comptrollers and the like, I would be delighted to back up my very genuine interest in the new novel with actual coin of the realm . . . But I can't do it, and I don't quite understand why you give a rap whether anybody does or not . . . Have you cast the die? If you haven't, Mr. Balmer and I would like very much to voyage into Maine and talk to you about plans and possibilities.

I:

Are we misunderstanding each other? If so, it is because others stand between us, scrambling the airwaves.

Here is the true story. I am not writing a serial. I am writing a book. I should much prefer to write it *before* it is "marketed" but apparently agents move far more rapidly than that . . . Soon after I got here I was told that "in conference" you had been very frank and honest, saying I almost certainly was not writing a serial, and that, though "like any good editor" you would like to have first look, you would not consider offering an option, and you agreed that it was best nothing be done to annoy a magazine that thought it wanted what it probably wouldn't. I thought I understood you perfectly, the more so because I thought you were right. So when your first letter about it came I assumed, frankly, that your Mr. Balmer might be more or less taking advantage of both of us — making it necessary for you to ask for what you did not want and for me to go along with it because of our friendship. I was truly under the impression that you hoped I would refuse. Was I wrong?

However, now that you say you wonder I give a rap about an option payment, I will tell you that I don't — except as a symbol. It indicates to me that the magazine offering it does think it is a good gamble. If none had been offered I certainly should not have expected it. But now it has been offered and has been just lying around for weeks *because* I keep postponing signing the agreement. You know the reason why I don't sign it, and so do the Everitts (but they are losing patience with me); the other magazine doesn't. Because of your deputy comptrollers and other things which I freely admit are a complete enigma to me, do you *want* me to tell the Everitts that despite their efforts and urgent advice, they are now to return this agreement unsigned, take the consequences (whatever they may be I wouldn't know), and give *Redbook* first look at this book when it is done for the reason that I like *Redbook*'s associate editor very much and he has long been very good to me? If so, so state above your own handsome signature in a letter addressed to ME. Meanwhile, the die has not been cast. The agreement with the other magazine is still on my desk. Having lain here this long, it can lie a week longer. This does not mean Messrs. Hodgins and Balmer have to trek into Maine within a week, happy as we should be to see the former any time. The mail will do. We also have a telephone (Wells, 8917). I didn't want one, but it was here, and it works. I'd *like* to talk with you. I am not used to our misunderstanding each other and I wish you would tell me we don't.

Two mornings later Eric telephoned. In his characteristic, quizzical, Yankee drawl he told me all was crystal clear between us, and all obstacles to our current negotiations had been removed, as I would now hear from Mr. Balmer if I would be so good as to hold on while being connected with *Redbook*'s editor-in-chief. I held on and heard for the first time Edwin Balmer's warm, rapid, midwestern speech. He said he would have taken serial rights to *As the Earth Turns* if he had seen it in manuscript; he was in the process of shifting the whole emphasis in his magazine, already was lining up such authors as Somerset Maugham and Sinclair Lewis; he fully intended to publish my new novel, whatever it was; he was about to break all precedent (farm out his deputy comptrollers?) and call my agents to offer the same option the other magazine had, offering at the same time a better price than its for serial rights if — when — he picked them up. I said that should make everyone happy.

I never knew whether this was exactly what Eric had intended and expected all along, but I suspected so.

I telephoned my agents that *Redbook* had just called and was about to make them an offer which I counted on them to accept . . . The reaction was understandably cool. I was asked, "Do you really feel this is ethical?" I said, "From my point of view, yes. For many reasons, I feel my first commitment is to *Redbook*." I was told, "After this the other magazine will never publish a word you write." I said I was sorry about that but if that was the decision I would live with it; *Redbook* had taken several of my short stories, Eric was my friend, and I liked what Mr. Balmer said he was now undertaking with his magazine; if my book could make a serial, I trusted *Redbook* to present it well.

Then I went across the yard to recount this astonishing episode to my parents before climbing the stairs to their quiet attic to write for two hours before Herbert came back from Portsmouth to hear the news. In the afternoon we were all going up home to get our supper and watch the sunset over the marshes.

This was what our beach "retreat" had become — a scenic and comfortable spot, filled with the sound and smell of the Atlantic; where Renny could splash in and out, build sand forts and castles and grow brown; where Marion and Donna answered the telephone and took care of whoever was in the Greylock, so all our friends were welcome to drop in at any time and stay as long as they could; but from which Herbert and I were often absent for hours, he because he was conferring with real estate agents and inspecting every old house in the area which was or might soon be for sale, I because I was writing in the attic of the little house across the backyard. Often no Carrolls or Hastys were at the beach because we had all gone home for the mail and were staying for the day or for overnight.

There, as always, everything seemed in proportion, slipped silently and painlessly into place. We were entirely ourselves, no longer confused by what anyone thought of us.

There it was just a pleasant incident to read that Miss Joanna Sprague, Salt Lake City librarian, had stated in her monthly report, "While western novels are still in great demand, demands for 'weighty' volumes are steadily increasing.

The most popular book all summer has been *As the Earth Turns*, a fiction of farm life" . . . Even pleasanter to be reminded in mid-August that early in July "The Bookworm" had said in the San Francisco *Call-Bulletin*, "The Worm is inquisitive about Gladys Hasty Carroll . . . he'd like to know more about her . . . How old is she? Is she married? Did she live on a farm? When did she leave it? How did she happen to become a writer? And who told her just what details to put into a book or did she come by that naturally? . . . You see why the Worm is so enthusiastic about *As the Earth Turns* . . . Because it's a homely and true and a good book to be handing around and telling people to read."

Under the towering maples our father had set out as saplings I persuaded my brother to accept the money he had contributed to my college expenses to be placed now in a fund for his little boy's education. And I had the joy of repaying my scholarship from Berwick Academy so that it could be awarded to some other student who would need it as I had.

One Sunday afternoon we were surprised by the arrival of a feature writer from the Boston *Transcript* who later wrote:

> Although she is spoken of everywhere, in literary circles and out, as the logical winner of this year's Pulitzer Prize, I saw and talked with her and nothing will make me believe that the Pulitzer or even the Nobel prize will in any way affect Gladys Hasty Carroll . . . I had decided to make something of a game of finding her, for in reading *Land Spell*, that book for girls which is so definitely the seed from which *As the Earth Turns* blossomed, I wondered if the title page inscription plus the frontispiece drawing would not combine to make both the Shaw farm and the home of the author. Actually they did. However, I finally had to make an inquiry of a country woman surrounded by a brood of children. Instead of saying, "Oh, that woman who writes," she said with noticeable friendliness, "Oh, Gladys Hasty? She must be up at her father's."

There it was, set up and back from the dusty road, unmistakably the home of Jen, that inarticulate, capable member of the Shaw family . . . And there on the porch sat Gladys Carroll. She is young, but old enough to have dignity. She is neither tall nor short, but well-developed and poised — the type which can lend charm to a low neckline and flamboyance to being stockingless.

My mother said, "For heaven's sake, what did you have on — or didn't you have on — that day?"

Her voice is soft, and she is careful but not studied in what she says. She accepted with gratitude the sincere tribute we paid her books, but with that same steady quietness. She is a comfortable, gracious person as unaffected and real as her books. It was Sunday, a day when no writing is ever done, and she was quite willing to talk to us . . . Her thinking is clear, honest, and often not a little stubborn. She is interested in the reviews because of what they reveal of the book and because of what they tell her of those who write them . . . She has no idea what Warner Brothers will do with her book and is not worried about it. "The motion picture rights are now theirs. I am not experienced in their medium. I have promised to go out to help with details, but I will not superintend. The production will be theirs, not mine." . . . Yes, she is at work on a second novel. No, it will not be a sequel to *As the Earth Turns.* There will never be a sequel to *As the Earth Turns.* No, she has no final statement for our readers. "I am not a woman with a Burning Message."

But mostly we just glanced through the mail to see if anything needed immediate attention, and packed up the rest to be taken back to the beach when we had to go.

While we were at home we just wanted to be at home. Nobody else knew when we were going to be there. Few if anyone knew when we were there. For those hours it was our whole world.

And every time we went Herbert and I were more sure that we could never be completely at home in any other place. We loved old houses but we loved this land more, and we would build an "old" house. We were negotiating with George Albert Earle, who had been my grandfather's oldest friend and who lived at the dead end of the lane, for the Columby Warren field which he had bought of Henry as soon as Henry fell heir to it. It was directly across the lane from home, and if we built a house there we would put it either on Uncle Columby's cellar hole or on the site of the Warren Garrison. George Albert did not want to sell more than the hilltop and a right of way to it, because he still kept cows and needed the hay. We said we would like to have the whole hill, including the big hickory tree at the western rim of it and the pine grove on its western slope; we pointed out that little hay grew there as it was mostly bare ledges. George Albert said he would have to keep the hickory tree as that was what he hitched his horses to when he was haying. We said we would put in hitching posts at the boundary line but he said horses liked shade. So we were still talking, but Herbert and I knew that sooner or later we would buy whatever George Albert would sell us, and build a house on it; we were already buying bricks from old cellar holes in the neighborhood for our fireplaces, and door rocks where there were no longer doors. In the meantime, we would have a one-room camp built on the home place, with an alcove for Renny, and a little woodshed. That could be done this coming fall, with my father supervising it, and next summer we would be there, on a hill close to the marshes, all running back and forth between The House and the camp. Maybe by then our house would be going up. Maybe by then we would be expecting another baby. Maybe by the time we had the house and another baby a way would open up so that we should not have to go away again.

That was what we wanted. We wanted to stay at home. We wanted not to have to go away.

This year we would return to Minneapolis. Eric would meet us in Albany for a long evening of talk; he was about to leave *Redbook* to go on the staff of *Time* and then of *Fortune.* This fall Herbert would complete the first draft of the sections he was writing for the textbook on which he was collaborating with Al Eurich. Before Thanksgiving I must be in Hollywood for the filming of *As the Earth Turns*, taking Renny and Donna with me.

But one day . . .

Somewhere some man on some street was whistling:

"The music goes down and around — and it comes out *here.*"

A Current Note from the Younger Generation

Our parents built on the site of the Warren Garrison in 1935. They lost their second child at birth in Minneapolis in 1936. The next fall Dad took leave of absence from the University of Minnesota and they went to Europe for several months with their four-year-old, after which Dad joined the faculty of the University of New Hampshire in Durham, a pleasant driving distance from the Cape-style house across The Lane from our grandparents. They had a daughter, and we lived for nearly twenty years with old pine-paneled walls, four fireplaces, exposed beams, open chambers, corner cupboards, kitchen garden, sheep, chickens, dogs and cats.

Mother, who had already published three novels, wrote six books there, including *Dunnybrook*, a social history of the neighborhood from the time of its first settlement through the Second World War. She also directed an outdoor folk play based on *As the Earth Turns* in which all parts were played by our neighbors for a series of performances each summer, the action taking place in our grandfather's meadow with audiences seated on hillside benches overlooking meadow, pasture, and marsh. The proceeds of these productions restored the neighborhood church and parsonage, bought the deserted district schoolhouse and made it into a community center, brought in electric power, and provided educational, musical, and social advantages as well as such utilities as fire extinguishers for every home.

Dad became chairman of the Department of Psychology at the University of New Hampshire, head of the student counseling service, and first president of the New Hampshire Psychological Association. His college text in the field of mental hygiene continues to be widely used throughout this country and abroad and he updates it for a new edition every few years.

Our grandparents died within a year of each other, and in 1954 our parents moved Down Home where they have been most content ever since. Dad retired from the university in 1962 but until recently continued to teach his favorite graduate courses in summer sessions there. Now he is busy with research and textbook revisions, enjoys sports broadcasts, and keeps a close eye on his pine trees. Mother has written eight more books; one of them is *Only Fifty Years Ago*, the story of a year of life on the George Hasty farm about 1912; another, *To Remember Forever*, is based on journals and letters written during her sophomore year at Bates College. Apparently she is still writing new ones, though it is not easy to find out when she does this. As far as we can tell she is always making applesauce for which she has earned renown, or trying out other health food recipes; she is an ardent advocate of organically grown vegetables and fruits, stone-ground whole grains, wheat germ, honey, and brewer's yeast. Or she is walking in the woods, sitting on some riverbank, visiting friends, working on community projects, or driving her Beetle along the coast. If none of these things, she is writing letters. Her correspondence is unbelievable. She writes to old friends, new friends, friends she has never seen, broadcasting companies, newspaper editors and legislators. She thinks we should all have views and make them known. If devotional exercises are ever again permitted in our public schools, those who disapprove of the practice should know whom to blame. Mother believes in prayer, in sound and thorough education, in the power of love, but also in self-defense for both the individual and the nation. She opposes the neglect or abuse of any living thing or any natural resource.

Our parents rarely find time to visit us, but always seem glad to see us come home. As we, too, are busy people, the grandchildren get there oftener and stay longer than we do. Caroline, aged eight, Kent eleven, Ricky eight, and James six, are given the clear impression that they are more welcome than the flowers in spring and that theirs is a welcome which will never wear out.

Traditionally we are reunited at Christmas, though sometimes one or more of us is too far from Maine to make it. We try to get to Japan or Mexico or Australia or Europe and back betweentimes. Last Christmas we were all there, and four stockings awaited Santa Claus at the fireplace though we could not be certain who expected him literally to come down the chimney and who didn't. We were ten at table — well, two tables — in the kitchen. The House still has no dining room. The girls usually prepare and baste the turkey, Mother being preoccupied with steaming things like unpeeled vegetables and figgy pudding. Very good it all is, too, as Wanda Gag's Funny Thing said of dolls and jumjills and is still saying in Mother's voice to our children exactly as we first heard it from the same dog-eared books.

Dad has imaginary games he plays, a different one for each grandchild. Every little while we see one of them collecting mysterious props and then disappearing with him behind a closed door. The others like to peek through the keyhole and listen at a panel in an effort to find out what is going on, but they don't learn much. We assume the games are the same ones he used to play with us, but there is no way of knowing more than that he remains a Pied Piper.

WARREN HASTY CARROLL
Washington, D.C.

SARAH CARROLL WATSON
Provo, Utah

June 15, 1972